GOOD WRITING IS GOOD BUSINESS

Your go-to guide to stylish and successful business writing

MARGARET CHANDLER

Green Fuse

Published by Green Fuse Inc.
www.greenfuse.ca
www.goodbusinesswriter.com

Design and layout: Dean Pickup
Cover design: Patrick Brooks
Indexer: John Barkwell
Book editors: Jo Hildebrand, Kelley Kissner

Includes bibliographical references and index.
Issued in print and electronic formats.
ISBN 978-0-9959769-0-0 (paperback) ISBN 978-0-9959769-2-4 (pdf)
ISBN 978-0-9959769-1-7 (epub) ISBN 978-0-9959769-3-1 (mobi)

To Steven, without whom this book wouldn't exist

And to my parents, without whom I wouldn't exist

Contents

Note to Instructors

Thank you for adopting this book (or considering its adoption). *Good Writing Is Good Business* is ideal for courses, workshops, and presentations with a focus on business or technical writing, grammar, or style. Drawing on my experience teaching thousands of people over the years, I have emphasized what I consider to be the modern business writer's key challenges. I have found that people from all walks of life and educational levels have similar issues. Business and technical writing is largely ignored within traditional academia. But for many people, it's the kind of writing they do all day long, every day.

I've used the materials in this book to teach three-hour workshops, one- or two-day workshops, and four-month undergraduate courses. Even if you're teaching a short workshop on writing effective emails, I'm confident that your students will benefit from this book. As you know, the participants will have questions not only about emails but also about style, grammar, and revising. And they often won't know where to turn for answers to their many questions. This book will help you deliver a successful workshop and leave students with a resource that they can continue to use. *Good Writing Is Good Business* is not the only writing book people should own, but it does provide some excellent reference materials and a comprehensive list of other useful print and online resources.

When teaching, I usually start with grammar (Part Three) because we need a common vocabulary to discuss other issues. Then I move on to either process (Part One) or style (Part Four) depending on the audience. Because this is a business writing book with a general reader also in mind, I've shifted the order, and the book leads off with process. But for your purposes, you might consider a different order.

The book includes some exercises and an answer key to complement your own exercises. You'll find plenty of material within these pages to spark and guide productive discussions as you help people work through their writing challenges.

Foreword

"Writing a book is a horrible, exhausting struggle," George Orwell remarked, "like a long bout of some painful illness." For a writer, the task of writing anything, even a simple message or letter, may induce the same malady. Margaret Chandler has prepared a wonderful elixir to cure writing sickness for the business professional. Whether you have the writing sniffles or a full-blown case of writing influenza, this book will make you feel better. Drawing from many years of experience, Margaret has written a useful, entertaining, and serious book for business writers.

People want answers quickly and this book delivers. It can be read in its entirety or selectively to address specific writing challenges. Whether you want to plan a writing project, learn how to write more efficiently, improve your writing to advance your career, get a handle on grammar and punctuation, deepen your understanding of style, learn about the strategies that professional editors use, or work through a healthy collection of exercises to apply what you have read, it's all here in a simple and concise format. The structure of this book encourages rather than overwhelms, making the book an ideal choice for anyone who writes to get a job done and understands the importance of effective business writing.

To write a book like this you need to have "walked the talk," and Margaret, a language enthusiast, editor, writer, business owner, and educator, certainly has. For almost two decades, our paths have crossed in areas such as curriculum development, guest lectures, student internships, and editing. The depth of her experience and her understanding of the challenges that many writers encounter are reflected throughout this book because she delivers answers to real-world writing concerns. This is a book written for the business community by someone with a strong understanding of how business works.

Margaret reminds us that "a well-crafted and articulate document reflects something deeply meaningful." Through examples, anecdotes, and exercises, she illustrates how to write reader-centred documents that make the writer proud and the reader happy. This engaging and instructive book will help the contemporary business writer in countless ways and is a worthy addition to his or her writing toolbox.

Glenn Ruhl, PhD
Professor, Information Design
Mount Royal University

Acknowledgments

I would like to express my gratitude to all the people who have helped this book see the light of day.

Thank you to my parents, who awakened my love of language at an early age and always encouraged me to be both a reader and a writer. And many thanks to my sister and brother, Siobhan and Simon, for their support and advice.

I was fortunate to have the benefit of two superb editors: Jo Hildebrand, who provided many thoughtful comments on early drafts, and Kelley Kissner, whose meticulous edits of later drafts and commitment to helping me went far beyond the call of editorial duty. Any errors that insist on remaining are mine alone.

Thank you, Patrick Brooks, for designing the book cover and being such a dependable friend, and Dean Pickup, for making the words look so good.

Special thanks to the friends who offered encouragement and advice, in particular Connie Boyce, Sarah Kerr, Maria MacMinn, Glenn Ruhl, Kim Sanderson, Marian White, and Sheri-D Wilson.

I'd like to express my gratitude to the many students whose efforts to make sense of the language have inspired me so much over the years. When my spirits flagged, I thought back on our rich and often humorous discussions and your enthusiasm for this book. And I kept going.

Finally, heartfelt thanks to my husband and best friend, Steven, for his steady love and cheerful willingness to help out in so many ways. Because we met online, we had to rely on words alone for our initial flirtations. I can think of no finer example of how writing well is worth the effort.

Introduction

Over the years, frustrated business writers have shared many poignant and heartfelt stories with me. I've heard these stories with minor variations so many times that I know these experiences are not unique. Legions of business writers have similar tales of woe. I have written this book with these writers in mind—the ones who take classes to improve their writing and who read books like this—because these stories can end well. These common exasperations and challenges can be resolved.

Here are some anecdotes from the trenches. Do you recognize yourself in any of them?

- From a senior engineer recently promoted into management: "Why do I spend 60 percent of my time writing, but I had only one technical writing class in eight years of university? And I was 19 years old, and all I could think about was beer, calculus, and girls! Now I'm struggling with major writing projects while also helping my subordinates figure it out."

- From an administrative assistant to a CEO: "The emails flood in by the bucketload every day—I can barely keep up. I need to find ways to manage all the emails and write quickly and concisely without sounding too brusque."

- From a non-native speaker of English who has worked hard to perfect his English: "The usage rules are so different in this company from what I learned. Whose authority should I trust? And should I correct my boss when I know she's wrong?"

- From a manager: "I'm tired of editing other people's work. But I can't ignore the quality of the writing because it reflects badly on our company. Can't my staff clean up their work before they hit send? What's the best way to tell them that mediocre writing is not acceptable?"

- From an accountant: "I used to work primarily with numbers, but in my new role, I'm writing financial summaries. I worry about the quality of my work because I never enjoyed English at school, and I've forgotten most of what I did know. I need to get my business writing up to speed, and pronto."

- From a duo with different ideas about usage and style: "We never agree on whether it's *color* or *colour*, whether it's *5%* or *5 percent*, whether it's *9 am* or *9 a.m.* We waste a lot of time arguing about the details."

This snapshot of the life and times of the modern business writer is revealing. It tells us that we need to refine not only our writing but also our interactions, whether we're the most junior person in the organization or the most senior. To be successful writers, we need to attend closely to our writing and to our relationships with our readers and our colleagues. And we can help others do the same.

Mastering the art of successful writing is like mastering the art of cooking or the art of driving. In fact, most of us do all three: write, cook, drive. Just because we can do something, however, doesn't mean we do it well. Not everyone's cooking is worth sharing, and not everyone's driving is roadworthy. And not everyone's writing makes for an easy and pleasant read. But with persistence and patience, we can improve.

The beauty of writing well goes beyond the satisfaction of producing a reader-centred, smartly written business report or receiving a promotion because you're the team's strongest writer. It brightens the overall quality of your life because it strengthens your rapport with others. Good writers know how to connect with people: they are respected and valued because they respect and value the needs of their readers. Such writers prioritize getting read, being understood, and eliciting the desired response. They value two-way communication and connection rather than a one-way information dump and run.

For many people, writing is an everyday business, technical, or academic function—must finish the report by Friday, have to write a compelling executive summary, need to edit those instructions, should email my boss with the bad news, must get an A on this science report or else, need to persuade the funder that our organization merits the $50,000 grant. You name it—it's being written right now by someone somewhere.

But writing is more than just a mechanical, get-it-done task: it's also a creative expression. Our writing speaks volumes about us—our clarity of thought and word, our engagement with readers, our ability to use language efficiently and elegantly, our approach to style and substance.

And unlike other creative expressions—that abstract painting you thoughtfully consigned to the basement or that lovesick letter you tore into shreds at 4:30 a.m.—our business writing is very much in the public eye. Sometimes our writing is shared with hundreds, even thousands, of people, yet few of us have the training to carry off such a public performance with confidence and professionalism. No wonder this business of writing can cause such angst!

When you're writing, words are all you have. Use them wisely. And remember that readers read for their reasons, not yours.

■ ■ ■

If you answer yes to any of these questions, then consider this book your friend in need:

- Do you find yourself gazing wistfully at a mostly blank screen hoping for inspiration and immaculate prose to flow forth? (This is what I call an Oscar Wilde moment: when asked what he had done all day, Wilde replied that he had spent the morning putting a comma in a poem and the afternoon removing it.)

- Does the mention of a dangling modifier fill you with the dread of the unknown?

- Does your boss return your reports with so many changes that you can barely read the original text? And you thought you'd done a good job!

- Do you know whether it's *north-west, northwest,* or *North West?* Do you need that final comma in *bees, wasps, and bugs* or not? Do you know where to find the right answers quickly when you're uncertain?

- Do your sentences cry out for more vitality, more precision, and more warmth, while remedies elude you?

- Do you find commas and semicolons so challenging to use that you resort to the long dash—because it seems more flexible—at every possible opportunity?

- Do you find mastering some of the imprecise rules difficult because English is not your first language and you can't find the answers to your specific writing questions?

- Do you know how to edit under pressure? If you had two hours to edit a 15-page document, would you know what to focus on?

- Do you look at your organization's reports and see inconsistencies everywhere? Would you like to know how to create an easy-to-use style sheet that would ensure consistency and answer common in-house questions?

CHANDLER'S LAWS ON WRITING MISHAPS

Anything that can go wrong, will go wrong. ~ Murphy's Law

As a teacher, writer, and editor, I've witnessed everything: minor irritations that almost no one noticed and even fewer cared about through to major disasters that led to cost overruns and people losing their jobs. Inspired by Air Force engineer Ed Murphy, I've come up with a few of my own laws to help the bitter pill of experience go down a little more smoothly.

1. If the writing is unclear or incorrect and leads to two—or even worse, more than two—potential interpretations, the unintended meaning is the one the reader will infer. For example, what does *you love grammar more than Cleo* mean? Does it mean that you love grammar more than you love Cleo? Or does it mean that you love grammar more than Cleo does? Two radically different meanings!

   In the words of playwright George Bernard Shaw, "The single biggest problem in communication is the illusion that it has taken place." This quote is so apropos that I've put it on my business card.

2. The chance of missing something when proofreading your own work is astronomically high. Your brain will persist in tricking you, which is why I ended up with tickets to the Red Hot Chilli Pipers when I thought I had purchased tickets to the Red Hot Chili Peppers.

   Part two of this rule: The first person to glance casually at your writing once it is in print or online will immediately see the mistake.

3. All writing and editing is ultimately a process of abandonment: you run out of time, energy, or money. This is not necessarily a bad thing because a piece of writing can be overworked. But sometimes

another hour or day could have made the reader's life a lot more pleasant. We know this—so why so much resistance to organizing ourselves and our expectations accordingly?

As Napoleon said, "Disorder is always in a hurry." And we all know what disordered writing looks like.

4. Business writers who write like students miss the mark. It's amazing how many business writers forget that (a) a student's work is read, no matter how weak it is, because it is someone's job to read it and mark it; as a business writer, you easily risk losing the reader to more enticing words; (b) students are often writing to show a subject-matter expert that they, too, know a little; as a business writer, you are often the subject-matter expert; and (c) students are usually assigned a certain number of pages; as a business writer, you decide when to stop.

MYTH BUSTING

Now that you're equipped with Chandler's Laws, let's turn our attention to some myths—actually, more like complaints—that I hear constantly. Let's bust up these barriers to good writing, once and for all!

Myth No. 1 I have to memorize all the rules.

Response No, you don't. A chef doesn't have all the recipes in her head, but she knows where to find them. Even a professional editor doesn't know all the rules; that would be impossible unless he were some kind of encyclopedic monstrosity. What's important is that you know how to frame the question, and you know where to find a reputable answer. This means that you haven't just googled the question, muttered abracadabra, and hoped for the best. You can stand out from the crowd by resting on the shoulders of authorities and not on the flimsy props of amateurs.

Myth No. 2 Standard rules exist that all teachers, grammarians, and other language nerds use. I just don't know them. (This rule is a variation of Myth No. 1.)

Response Truth is, disagreement and discord abound. English is a language in flux, spoken by people all over the world, with no academy as a guiding—or some would say limiting—force. Even language scholars often disagree about correct usage, which is why writers need to make their own informed choices based on good resources.

Myth No. 3 I can't write. I'm not a natural-born writer. I'm hopelessly inefficient. My work comes back covered with so much red ink that it looks like the Red Sea. I'll never improve!

Response How much time do you dedicate to your writing practice? If you practised piano randomly a few times a year for an hour or two, would you expect to be a good player? If you don't practise, don't have good resources, and don't know what you don't know, then, yes, you'll probably continue to flounder. You may never win a prize for business writing—and take comfort in knowing that there isn't a Pulitzer Prize in this category anyway. But if your expectations are in line with your commitment, you will progress.

The story goes that one day violinist Mischa Elman was leaving Carnegie Hall in New York by the backstage entrance when he was approached by two tourists looking for the main entrance. Seeing his violin case, they asked, "How do we get to Carnegie Hall?" Without looking up, Elman replied, "Practice."

Whether you're hoping to play at Carnegie Hall or to perfect the art of the written word, it all comes down to one thing: practice.

Myth No. 4 You can't teach an old dog new tricks. I've been writing this way for a long time, and I don't plan on changing now!

Response Don't let yourself fall into this trap. For starters, you're not a dog. Let's say you've just found out—perhaps while reading this book—that there is one space after the period at the end of a sentence and not two. Despair not! Just accept the truth, and before you send out your documents, do a find and replace. Eventually, one space between sentences will become natural.

Not believing in yourself and your potential to adapt is an instant door slammer. Open the door and step through!

RESOURCES AND AUTHORITIES

The value of good resources cannot be overstated. Would you trust a carpenter who arrived at your house to build a deck with no tools—and immediately needed to borrow yours? And as soon as she had a logistical detail she couldn't figure out, she pulled out her netbook (the only tool she seemed to have) and randomly googled her problem until she came up with a solution she thought *might* work? Wouldn't you quickly lose confidence in her ability to do the job?

In the same way, it's impossible to be a proficient writer without the right resources. At the very least, you need a grammar and punctuation guide and a dictionary. Online resources can be helpful, but you must be careful because the Internet does not discriminate between the good and the bad. Fortunately for you, this book does. Chapter 18 provides an annotated list of suggested print and online resources for writers. This book relies on these authorities:

- *A Canadian Writers Reference*, 6th edition. The usage rules in Part Three of this book are based on this handbook, which is widely used in postsecondary institutions across Canada.

- *Editing Canadian English: A Guide for Editors, Writers, and Everyone Who Works with Words*, 3rd edition. This book provides guidance on spelling, punctuation, and other relevant topics from a Canadian perspective.

- *The Canadian Press Stylebook*, 17th edition, and *The Canadian Press Caps and Spelling*, 21st edition. Together, these are useful tools for Canadian writers given the extremely wonky way the English language works—or doesn't. These reference books are the Canadian equivalent of *The Associated Press Stylebook*, used in the United States.

- *The Chicago Manual of Style*, 16th edition. In its own words, this is "the definitive guide for anyone who works with words."

Note: If you're an American reading this book, you might find that the spelling occasionally looks a little odd because we Canadians love our colours and our metres. But otherwise, everything here applies to you. British readers will be more comfortable with the spelling choices, but not with some of the punctuation choices that follow American usage. But these are minor details. Good writing is good writing; the principles are the same whether you're in Hastings, Austin, or Calgary.

STRUCTURE AND TERMS

This book contains five parts, eighteen chapters, and three appendices. Part One leads off with a discussion of the writing process, followed by a review in Part Two of some of the main forms of business correspondence, including social media. Part Three provides a contemporary tour of grammar, punctuation, and mechanics. Part Four shines the spotlight on the heartbeat of all good writing:

clarity, energy, concision, and flow. And Part Five concludes with an exploration of the writer and editor toolbox, which contains tools and techniques that will prove invaluable throughout your career.

Concepts are accompanied by examples and follow-up exercises that afford plenty of opportunity to practise. Some of the examples used to explain grammar and style are based on British history, not because I think we should all learn more British history but because the language we speak today is grounded in that history. If it hadn't been for the Roman, Viking, Germanic, and French invasions of the British Isles, we wouldn't be speaking such an extraordinarily rich and decidedly eccentric language—and we wouldn't have to grapple with innumerable spelling irregularities.

I would like to clarify a few terms because you will encounter them throughout the book.

Business writing Although this term is used throughout the book, it doesn't mean the kind of writing done only in a business setting. *Good Writing Is Good Business* focuses more broadly on any writing done in the line of duty—in commerce, education, science, health, law, government, and so on. In other words, this book is about prose that has a job to do.

Document This term is used throughout the book to define anything that you write as a business writer, be it a memo, a five-volume procedures manual, or a web page.

Editor Don't be intimidated by this fancy word. Of course, *editor* is used to define a person who fulfills a specific role, from document project management to book editing to major structural rewrites. However, every time you rewrite and revise, you are editing. And as author E. B. White reminds us, "The best writing is rewriting."

See yourself as both an editor and a writer, and take pride in your profession by upholding the standards.

Grammar grump Unfortunately, the writing world abounds with these nuisances. Instead of accepting that we are imperfect people (the grammar grump, of course, is an exception), living in an imperfect world wrestling with a language in flux, they inflict their archaic rules on the rest of us. These grumps often have a weak grasp of current language usage, and they do their worst damage when they "edit" the work of others. It's easy for someone to be a know-it-all when he or she doesn't know all that much.

Ignore these grumps! The exuberant English language, democratic and anarchic, belongs to all of us.

Language ladder How do you determine the level of formality required for your writing tasks? Linguists define levels of formality in terms of "language register." *Good Writing Is Good Business* uses the metaphor of a ladder and its rungs to discuss degrees of formality. First, ask yourself this: what ladder am I on—the speaking ladder or the writing ladder? Speaking is more informal and often wordier; when we're speaking, we don't have the luxury of time to refine our words. Since this is a book about writing, the discussion will take place from the perspective of the writing ladder.

Visualize the bottom rung of the language ladder as, for example, a text to your colleague reminding him to bring donuts to the meeting and the top rung on the ladder as a cover letter for your dream job. Different writing scenarios call for different rungs. One rung isn't better than another; it's just different. No matter what rung you're on, in business writing scenarios, always use Standard English and correct punctuation and grammar. And no matter where you are on the ladder, the message should be clear and concise.

Organization This term is used in the book to encompass every possible work scenario from a one-person home office to a non-profit society to a major corporation. If you write nonfiction as part of your livelihood, consider yourself included!

Standard English *The Merriam-Webster Dictionary* defines Standard English as "the English that with respect to spelling, grammar, pronunciation, and vocabulary is substantially uniform though not devoid of regional differences, that is well established by usage in the formal and informal speech and writing of the educated, and that is widely recognized as acceptable wherever English is spoken and understood."

Standard English is only one dialect of English. It is not the only correct version of English, but it is the form used in business, government, academia, and other formal contexts. Therefore, the rules and principles suggested in this book are based on Standard English because it is the English that business writers use.

Style This word has two important—but different—meanings. Usually when we talk about style, we are referring to qualities of style, such as clarity and brevity. This version of style is the focus of Part Four. But style also refers to rules and conventions laid down either by published or in-house style guides. These guides provide direction on matters such as capitalization, numbers, dates, and many aspects of grammar and punctuation, some of which are decidedly baffling. In Parts Three and Five, this version of style makes its appearance.

■ ■ ■

Good Writing Is Good Business is not an exhaustive—or exhausting—reference book. You won't find 10 pages of rules on comma usage. What you will find are the basic rules of business writing, illustrated by plenty of examples and reinforced with exercises. Some of these exercises encourage you to think critically and evaluate your own work; others require you to fix common usage and style mistakes.

Whether you've picked up this book to find ways to write more efficiently or more eloquently, to freshen up on grammar and punctuation rules, to resolve some of the issues highlighted in the anecdotes above (and there are more anecdotes scattered throughout the book), or to acquire some editorial tools that will make revising easier, you will find the help you need to hone your writing craft. Business writing is only one medium of communication, but it's an important one, and for many of us, it's our primary one. It's a medium that demands commitment to quality.

The way you write is one of the fundamental ways you establish your identity, especially in the electronic age when many people know you only through your writing. If you write well, you identify yourself as thoughtful, smart, and coherent: you value your readers' needs and try to meet them. If you write poorly, you identify yourself in less flattering terms, and their respect for you will certainly diminish.

Peel away some of the mystery from writing and learn how to achieve your desired results. Maybe it's about showing empathy in your email for someone who just lost her job. Maybe it's about writing an elegant executive summary or a successful proposal. Maybe it's about realizing your ambition to move into management. Whatever your reasons, I hope this book will become a trusted companion.

PART ONE

Process: Right from the Start

Good writing is a core business process—communication performed efficiently. When you write well, you mean the most in the fewest words; you get the most out of the fewest inputs; you waste no one's time or money; you spend that most precious resource, language, wisely, and with it you manufacture sense.

~ MARK TREDINNICK AND GEOFF WHYTE

All writing is ultimately a question of solving a problem. It may be a problem of where to obtain the facts or how to organize the material. It may be a problem of approach or attitude, tone or style. Whatever it is, it has to be confronted and solved.

~ WILLIAM ZINSSER

Design informs even the simplest structure, whether of brick and steel or prose.

~ E. B. WHITE

Good writing begins with attention to process. Understanding the process and applying this understanding consistently throughout the writing stages will improve the efficiency and quality of your work. Whether you are writing content for a website or minutes from a board meeting, your writing will evolve naturally and logically once process has set the wheels in motion. Whatever the task, you want to take pride in the results and be confident that you did the best possible job in the time available. For this, you need to be faithful to process.

Process begins with an analysis of purpose, audience, context, and tone; this analysis is especially important for any substantial projects, such as proposals, reports, and manuals. Once you have clearly defined these key elements—the who, why, what, where, when, and how—you can turn your attention to the stages of writing. These stages, from initial brainstorming to final critiquing, provide a structure that will help you generate your best work.

When thinking about process, also remember the importance of good design. Although document design is usually carried out after the writing has been completed and sometimes done by a professional designer, the astute writer thinks about it early on. Document design is not mere window dressing. Design is fundamental to a well-structured and reader-centred document. In harmony with words, design helps the writer achieve the key objectives of satisfying purpose and audience.

CHAPTER ONE

Plan First: Purpose, Audience, Context, and Tone

Before anything else, preparation is the key to success.

~ Alexander Graham Bell

In the literary community, writers like to debate the merits of plotting versus the merits of pantsing. Plotting means planning the plot, creating detailed outlines, and building structure before the writing begins. Pantsing means flying by the seat of your pants.

Fortunately, business writers don't need to wade into this debate because pantsing is not an option if you want to write quickly and efficiently. Plotting is liberating—you know why you're writing; you consider your audience; you minimize writer's block; you write efficiently; and with your goal clearly in mind, you write directly toward it. Yet many business writers spend too much time writing aimlessly—or worrying about writing—and not enough time planning the details. These details, however, make the process easier and often distinguish great writing from mediocre writing.

Before you begin to write, think carefully about the purpose, audience, context, and tone (the PACT), and for major writing projects, complete a PACT evaluation provided at the end of this chapter.

PURPOSE

First things first: know why you are writing and what you want to accomplish. Do you want to persuade the funder to grant you $35,000? Or cancel a board meeting without too much upset? Or write a complaint letter to a service provider and receive a 25 percent discount on the next six months of service?

If you write with your purpose firmly in mind, your writing will have direction. And your readers will clearly understand your intent. Focus first on purpose, and ask yourself the following questions:

- What events or previous documents led to my need to write?

- Do I write to inform, to persuade, to critique, to instruct, or to negotiate?

- What do I want my audience to know, believe, or do after reading my writing?

Even for a short document, write a purpose statement before you begin, such as *My purpose is to update Masoud on the new price structure effective on March 1 so that he can inform the marketing department.* Make sure that the focus of your purpose statement is not too broad. The more precise it is, the more successful your writing will be. As language scholar and author Bryan Garner reminds us, "So much depends on your *purpose* in writing that you must fix it firmly in your mind."

AUDIENCE

Not everyone will read a document from beginning to end. Some people will browse for information, especially if reading online. Others simply want to use the document—an instruction manual, for example. Knowing whether you are writing for users, readers, or browsers will help you determine structure, tone, and design.

Good writers attend to the needs and expectations of their readers and engage in a graceful and easy conversation with them. But first they get to know them a little. Ask yourself these questions:

- Am I writing for readers, users, or browsers?

- What questions will my audience want answered?

- What level of language will my audience understand?

- Do I have more than one audience—non-technical and technical, for example?

- What will motivate my audience?

Having established some key things about your audience, now go further, and ask yourself the following:

- What are my audience's expectations? A three-page memo? A 20-page report?

- What are my audience's feelings about the subject—neutral? hostile? sympathetic? Will my audience consider my message to be good news or bad news?

- Under what conditions will my audience be reading? As volunteers gathered around a board table or at a construction site? On a cell phone or a large screen?

- What is my professional relationship with my audience, and how does this relationship influence the message? What cultural differences might affect my audience's expectations or interpretations?

- What specific factors or values—e.g., competition, safety, regulatory issues—are important to my audience?

- What will my audience do after reading the document? Discard? Distribute to others? File?

One simple way to find out what your audience wants is to ask them. For example, you're writing a feasibility study to see if your organization should open a branch office in the Maritimes. You're not sure what the chief financial officer will want to see in the study. Could you arrange a 15-minute phone call to discuss what he wants covered and how technical the language should be?

It's also a smart idea to visualize your audience. Business tycoon Warren Buffet has this suggestion: "Write with a specific person in mind. When writing Berkshire Hathaway's annual report, I pretend that I'm talking to my sisters. I have no trouble picturing them: Though highly intelligent, they are not experts in accounting or finance. They will understand plain English, but jargon may puzzle them."

After completing your PACT evaluation, you may find that you have several audiences. To make one document work for all of them, satisfy your primary audience first and your secondary audience(s) when possible. Your primary audience is most likely the one who requested the document and will use it to make decisions or take action. Your secondary audience(s) might read part of the document

— Ask Maggie —

I graduated with a master's in public policy a year ago and was thrilled to land a job nine months ago. But my boss returns my draft policy papers with umpteen revisions. He's told me that my writing is not geared to a public lay audience. I'm afraid he's going to fire me. Any advice?

Signed,

Worried Wendall

Dear Wendall,

How clearly have you envisioned your reader picking up your policy paper and reading it? Could you describe her background, education, profession, motivation? Create an imaginary reader, as a novelist would, and keep that reader close to you as you write. A friend of mine uses her mom and stepdad because they represent the audience that she and her team write for. Identify your reader and befriend her. And ask your boss to share a policy paper that he likes with you to give you a better idea of his preferred style.

because they want to keep up to date with developments. These two audiences might not have the same level of subject-matter understanding. If your primary audience is a manager and your secondary audience is a technical specialist, don't include a lot of technical detail that would distract the manager. Instead, include an appendix that meets the needs of the technical specialist.

Focus the content of various elements and sections of the document according to the audience(s). The following table illustrates how you might achieve this while writing a report on a proposed development. A senior government bureaucrat, who requested the report, and two deputy ministers are the primary audience and the decision makers. Concerned citizens (primarily lay people) and some technical experts who work for the government are the secondary audience.

Audience-Specific Considerations

Document Section	Audience
Cover	Everyone
Abstract	Decision makers
Table of contents	Everyone
List of abbreviations	Lay audience
Executive summary	Everyone, but primarily the decision makers
Body	Primary audience
Conclusions and recommendations	Everyone, but primarily the decision makers
Sidebars	Lay audience
Headings	Experts (to scan); lay audience (for overview)
Summarizing lists	Experts (to review); lay audience (to help capture important information)
References	Experts; other researchers
Appendices	Secondary expert audience; lay audience (background information)
Glossary	Lay audience

CONTEXT

Context refers to the situation, setting, or circumstances in which the writing takes place. The document is the picture that sits inside this frame. The context could be internal (e.g., you're writing a report with a colleague) or external (you're responding to a public relations crisis). Consider these questions about the context of the project:

■ Have I selected the right medium—email, brochure, website— for my subject and audience? This is an important question because you don't want to waste time composing a brochure when you need a website overhaul instead.

- Does this medium reinforce audience understanding?

- What is my word count? It's useful to think in terms of word count because page count is arbitrary. Is it 250 words a page or 400?

- Am I writing alone or as part of a team?

- Are there other people who will need to be involved, e.g., an external editor or a designer?

- Is there an informal or formal review process? How will this affect the schedule?

- How much time do I have? Abundant? Modest but manageable? Ridiculous?

- Do I have the necessary resources to get the job done?

- What is the anticipated lifespan of this document?

TONE

Tone is the way you choose to express yourself—through your choice of words, the level of formality, and your attitude: humorous or serious; detached or familiar; objective or subjective. The tone you select can make the difference between your message being well received or not. The French have a proverb that sums this up nicely: "It's the tone that makes the song." Ask yourself the following about your tone:

- Have I selected the appropriate style—formal or informal—for my audience?

- Is the tone friendly, respectful, and professional?

- Does the tone foster a cooperative working relationship?

- Did I use positive words such as *please, can, will, help, appreci-ate, give,* and *happy?*

- Did I avoid negative words such as *blame, cannot, neglect, care-less, fail, error,* and *disagree?*

Choosing the correct tone is essential to conveying your message professionally and effectively. Your tone depends on the purpose of the message, your audience, and your relationship to this audience. Use the right tone to achieve the desired results.

Tone in harmony with audience

Matching tone to audience will help frame the content of the message and the words you use. These examples illustrate how audience considerations can shape the tone of the message.

External client

When writing to an external client, you are representing both your-self and your organization. Your tone embodies your personality and values—and your organization's. Put the needs of your client first, and make sure your message meets his needs and expectations. Generally, external communications tend to be more formal because they are written for presentation to the "outside world."

Example: *Thank you for your email of January 15. Please note that we have improved the functionality of our website, and you can now place your order online. Alternatively, you may complete the attached order form and send it back to me. I will process your or-der as soon as I receive it. Please contact me if I can be of any further assistance. We appreciate your business.*

Supervisor or manager

Put yourself in your manager's shoes for a minute, and think about what pressures and ambitions she may have. What will motivate her to respond favourably to your message? And what are her expectations? Managers don't want to be correcting your work; that's not usually part of their job description. As Scott Martens, a senior manager of a large team of engineers, puts it, "Write it as if no one else is going to check it." That's excellent managerial advice!

Note that in the following example the writer understands why his boss is unhappy. He doesn't make excuses, and he offers a solution. His writing is courteous and solution-oriented.

Example: *I followed up with Jerry this morning, and you're right. He didn't submit the first draft of the feasibility study to the external reviewer last Friday. I understand that this delay has created problems with the production schedule and the timing for the final report. I've made some adjustments to the production schedule (see attached) to get us back on target. And I've also built better feedback mechanisms into the schedule so that the team can deliver on time. I'm confident that there won't be any more delays from this point forward.*

Also think about your manager's writing style. Does she usually want detail or just facts? Does she have a sense of humour? Look at the way she writes, and see what strengths you could model in your own writing. There's some truth in the proverb "Imitation is the sincerest form of flattery." Of course, as a writer you need to be versatile because you won't always have the same boss.

Sometimes writers are not comfortable assigning a supervisor a due date. Providing more details can be helpful.

Not this: *I need your decision by Friday.*

But this: *If you let me know your decision by Friday, I can inform the rest of the team at our Monday meeting.*

Not this: *We need to meet with the sales manager by June 15.*

But this: *Could you please let me know when we could meet with the sales manager. We need to meet with him by June 15 so that we can proceed with the marketing plan.*

Co-worker

When writing to your peers, focus on a message that demonstrates a collaborative and friendly team spirit.

Example: *Did you have a chance yet to review the latest round of changes to the LTE-Advanced System report? I think Olivia and I did a good job of incorporating all the changes that management wanted, but I'd like to get your feedback. You often catch the things that we miss. We need the final version printed by the end of August, so if you could get back to me by July 15, I'd appreciate it.*

Subordinate

This is your opportunity to model the kind of writing you want to receive. It's also the opportunity to show support, define corrective action, praise an employee for a job well done, and inspire the writer or the team. The correct approach can generate support for your leadership and motivate people throughout the organization.

Example: *You did an outstanding job on the draft business plan for our new start-up. You captured the key elements the finance team was looking for, including some they hadn't considered. The board will appreciate your recommendations and the inclusion of the marketing plan. Thanks for an excellent draft, especially given the tight timeline!*

Kinds of tone

You have many different kinds of tone at your disposal. Select the one that best suits your intent and your audience.

Conversational

Write with a smile in your voice and a warm and natural tone for readers receptive to your message.

Example: *I'm glad we had a chance to meet and select the keynote speakers. It's going to be a great conference. We just need to let the rest of the team know. Let's discuss when we meet on August 4. In the meantime, enjoy the long weekend.*

Persuasive

Use a confident tone when you want to persuade readers to do something. Make the benefits clear.

Example: *As a follow-up to our conversation on Friday afternoon, I'd like to advise human resources to hire a program assistant. We can shift some of Simon's work to the new hire allowing Simon to work on the backlog of applications. An extra pair of hands will definitely improve the team's productivity and morale. I hope you agree. Please let me know if I can proceed with the hire.*

Conciliatory

Use a conciliatory tone for a hostile audience. Try to find the common ground, and show that you understand the reasons your reader is upset. Set the context first, and do your best to identify a solution.

Example: *I am writing on behalf of the IT manager to follow up on your email, which she received yesterday. She is out of town until September 10 and asked me to contact you.*

We were concerned to read about the problems you experienced while unsuccessfully attempting to log in to your account and retrieve your files. We apologize for the inconvenience, and we are working to resolve this problem and should have it fixed by tomorrow afternoon.

I will contact you as soon as I have an update. In the meantime, please let me know if there is anything else I can help you with. Thank you for your patience.

Assertive

This can be a challenging tone to manage because you don't want to be read as brusque. Begin with a friendly greeting and finish by expressing your appreciation. Use *please*, even if you're the boss, but you don't need to repeat *please* throughout the email. For example, if you are assigning a list of tasks, use *please* once in the introductory sentence.

Make sure you provide sufficient information for your readers to understand your motives and your message. This is especially important in sensitive messages.

Not this: *Your suggestions are not that helpful.*

But this: *Could we discuss your suggestions at next week's meeting because I do have some concerns. Thanks.*

Not this: *I'm not able to help you this week.*

But this: *I wish I could help you this week, but I will be out of town for the rest of the week. Could we schedule another time?*

Regretful

When relating bad news, you probably can't change the situation, but you can try to make the news a little more palatable. Use language that communicates empathy, such as *I understand that this is not what you had hoped for.* Be careful not to patronize the reader because that will only add to his annoyance. Do not use language that suggests the reader is a complainer, and do not blame him, even if the situation is his fault.

Not this: *You should have told me sooner that you wanted to bring a guest to the open house.*

But this: *I am sorry, but we do not have room to accommodate additional guests.*

Start the message with positive language such as *Thank you for writing to us about the incident on June 17.* If appropriate, explain or provide a reason(s) why the decision was made or the event has occurred. See if you can find a way to end on a positive note, and try to offer another solution or information that will help the reader.

Example: *Thank you for your application for funds to attend the IABC conference later this year in Santa Fe. The professional development committee has reviewed your request for $2,500 to cover travel and hotel costs.*

Our company has increased its professional development and travel fund by $18,000 this year. However, we have received many requests for funding, and because the end of the fiscal year is approaching, we have already delegated our funds for this year. Although we would like to approve your application, we do not have the funds.

I encourage you to reapply for conference funding next year. Because your request was turned down this year, your application will receive priority next year. Please contact me if you would like to discuss further.

Informal versus formal tone

As discussed in the introduction, consider what rung of the language ladder you're perched on. If you're on the top rung and writing, for example, an executive summary, you're going to use the most formal tone you can muster. If you're on a rung halfway up the ladder and writing an email to a colleague, you're going to use a more informal tone. The formal tone isn't better than the informal tone; the tones simply serve different purposes and audiences.

Informal Tone	Formal Tone
Similar to a conversation, but language and grammar tidied up.	More reserved than a conversation.
Speaks directly to the reader using a first-person pronoun (*I* and *we*) and a second-person pronoun (*you*).	Speaks indirectly to the reader using a third-person pronoun (*he, she, it,* and *they*), except for business letters, which use a first-person pronoun (*I*).
Short sentences are acceptable.	A mix of sentence lengths is desirable.
Contractions and abbreviations are acceptable.	No contractions. Abbreviations must be spelled out when first used, the only exceptions being well-known acronyms (e.g., NATO).
Used for emails, texts, and business correspondence between close associates.	Used for all other business correspondence (e.g., cover letters, reports, proposals).

Be consistent with the tone you have chosen. If you shift from a formal to an informal tone halfway through a letter, you will confuse the reader. Err on the side of formality if you're not sure how formal your writing should be.

A PACT EVALUATION

Before beginning a report, proposal, or other complex writing project, dedicate some time either alone or with any co-authors to complete a PACT evaluation. Modify it as necessary to suit your specific project, but do spend time on this preparatory work. It's time well spent.

Purpose

What led to this document? A request from a manager? My idea? A routine report? Other?

What is the main purpose of this document? To persuade? To critique? To inform? To instruct? To negotiate?

What do I want to accomplish with this document?

My purpose is to . . . so that my audience will . . .

Audience

Readers, users, or browsers?

Do I have more than one audience?

If so, who is the primary audience?

And the secondary audience(s)?

What is my relationship to the audience(s): e.g., client, employer, regulatory body?

What is their attitude toward the subject? Neutral? Skeptical? Excited? Other?

How will they use the document? To perform a task? Solve a problem? Present a business case?

What does my audience(s) already know about this subject? Nothing? A little? A lot?

What information is important to the audience(s)? The basics? My interpretations? Costs? Recommendations? Other?

What additional information will they need? Executive summary? References? Glossary?

What questions or objections are they likely to have? Questions about cost? Safety? Deliverables? Others?

Under what conditions will my audience(s) be interacting with this document? Online? At a job site? At a board meeting? Other?

Context

What level of coverage does my subject require? Comprehensive? Concise? Other?

What is the most useful arrangement of the material? Problem–cause–solution? Chronological? Priorities? Other?

What is the projected word count?

What other people are involved in the document project? Other team members? Reviewers? Editor? Designer?

What other resources are necessary?

What is the due date?

Tone

What is the desired tone? Formal? Regretful? Persuasive? Assertive? Other?

What is the desired effect that the tone will help achieve? Promote understanding? Win support? Change behaviour? Other?

EXERCISES

A. Rewrite these sentences with a focus on the reader, not the writer.

1. To enable us to update our funder records, we request that the enclosed card be returned by May 31, 2018.

2. Our warranty becomes effective once we receive your registration.

3. We are issuing a refund, which we will send by registered mail early next week.

4. It is imperative that we receive the information by June 30 if we are to activate your account by September 15.

5. Our company wants to finalize the agreement with you as soon as possible; therefore, we require your audited financial statements by December 1.

B. Rewrite this email removing the hostile tone and improving the chance of a good outcome.

Mike,

As a fellow GAC board member, I'm really annoyed that you never get the minutes and the agenda out on time. Once again, the meeting starts in 20 minutes, and you just sent out the minutes from the last meeting and an agenda for the upcoming one!! Nothing new, actually. You do this all the time, and I'm not the only one who notices this.

I don't know why you agreed to take on the position of secretary, when it's obviously not something you're good at. Your careless attitude makes it hard for the board to function properly.

Tazmin

C. Look around.

Collect some recent emails, memos, and short reports that you are confident were well written. Evaluate the samples from a PACT perspective. What do these samples tell you about how well these writers understood their purpose and audience? Do you think these samples achieved their desired effects? If these samples were from your organization, what do they tell you about the culture of your organization?

— CHAPTER TWO —

Hold Fast to the
Four Writing Stages

*Whatever joy there is in the writing process can come
only when the energies are flowing freely.*

~ Dr. Betty S. Flowers

Experienced writers break down the process of writing—from start to send—into distinct stages. They use different names to refer to these stages. But in essence, the process is some variation of three to five stages: prewriting, drafting, revising, editing, and publishing. These stages provide a framework for writing quickly and efficiently.

— Anecdotal Evidence —

Over the years, I've discovered that many writers judge themselves very harshly. But the problem isn't their writing skills; it's their process skills.

Too often they begin writing (the carpenter stage) without having done any planning (the architect stage). Soon they're judging themselves and their abilities to write (*I'm a hopeless writer; I have nothing to say; I don't have time to do a good job*) before they've even written 100 words.

Don't let the judge step in too quickly. Let the madman, architect, and carpenter have their time on the stage first.

In 1979, Dr. Betty Flowers, a poet and professor, wrote a short essay titled "Madman, Architect, Carpenter, Judge: Roles and the Writing Process" that describes four stages of writing. Her description of the stages is both light-hearted and easy to remember. Most importantly, however, her model illustrates the need to do the right work at the right time. A writer who follows the stages envisioned by Dr. Flowers will soon appreciate her wisdom. These stages are described in detail in the following pages but can be summarized as follows:

Madman The madman writes with abandon. His emphasis is on brainstorming, clustering, and free writing—whatever it takes to stimulate the flow of ideas. His mantra is **generate**.

Architect The architect creates the outline. Her job is to organize the madman's ideas, and she will probably eliminate many of them. The architect directs her energy toward structure and order. Her mantra is **organize**.

Carpenter The carpenter follows the architect and nails the ideas together logically and cohesively. He provides the details and crafts the sentences, according to the architect's specifications. His mantra is **write**.

Judge The judge critiques the writing. She looks for ways to improve the style by checking for clarity, eliminating wordiness, ensuring smooth transitions, and so on. She also corrects any grammar, punctuation, and consistency problems. Her mantra is **refine**.

These stages are not rigid steps in a straightforward journey from A to Z. Consider them instead to be overlapping parts of an activity that can be repeated throughout the writing process. For example, while revising a section of a report, you might decide to tweak the outline. And you might continue to generate ideas while you're writing. Stages can and will blur at times.

THE MADMAN: GENERATING IDEAS

Sometimes it's difficult to begin writing because the creative thinking that should come first is deemed unimportant. By taking the time to generate ideas as a first step in a major writing project, you'll avoid finding your best ideas too late. And this can happen. As Mark Twain said, "The time to begin writing an article is when you have finished it to your satisfaction. By that time you begin to clearly and logically perceive what it is you really want to say." Obviously, this is not the best approach!

Writers have different strategies for this creative, and hopefully engaging, first step. Here are some suggested ways to get started, especially if you tend to have writer's block:

- **The imaginary conversation** Have an imaginary conversation with someone about your writing project. How would you describe your project? What are the key points? Can you express your key ideas in a couple of sentences? As you are talking to yourself, write down the points. Do this for a few minutes, and then see if you can start writing.

- **Free writing** Jot down all your ideas on the topic. Don't worry about grammar, style, or format. Give yourself a specific amount of time or a specific word count, and write down everything that comes to mind. Use the strategy of journalists when they write stories: What happened? Why did it happen? When did it happen? How did it happen? Who was involved? Not all these questions may be relevant, but some of them will be.

- **Brainstorming** This is best done if you are writing as part of a team. In collaboration with others, you can explore topics, develop themes, and decide how best to proceed with the project. When brainstorming, withhold criticism and encourage the random exploration of ideas.

- **Listing** Make a list of single words or phrases. Note arguments, facts, questions, sections, and key messages. Listing is different from free writing and brainstorming in that you generate only words and phrases. Don't start outlining; just enjoy the process of listing all the points that come to mind.

- **Clustering (or mind mapping)** Begin with a circle in the middle that contains your main idea, and then draw lines to smaller circles that contain ideas related to the main idea. Try to group similar ideas together to help organize your thoughts. Clustering is an easy way to add new information and make connections between ideas. There are software programs you can use for this process, but you can do something as simple as this example—a cluster of ideas about writer's block.

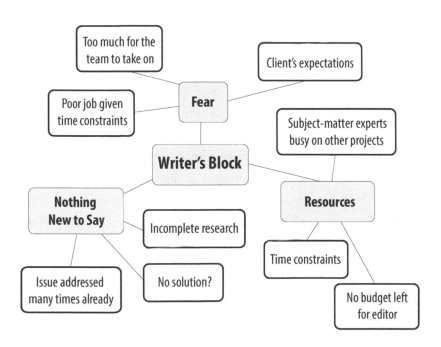

THE ARCHITECT: CREATING ORDER

Now it's time to get organized before you instruct the carpenter to start writing. The logical first step is to create an outline.

Three types of outlines can be used to write reports efficiently: 1) a planning outline (a guide for research and initial planning); 2) a working outline (a blueprint for the first draft); and 3) an informal paragraph outline (a tool to write coherent and unified paragraphs). The working outline is the one most business writers use.

The working outline determines the overall structure of the document and the relationships among the pieces. Don't see it as a straitjacket; see it as a framework to help you progress. And for a lengthy document, the outline will be the basis for the table of contents.

Of course, your organization might have templates that you can use in lieu of creating your own outline. Or you may have to follow specific instructions when completing routine reports. Before you begin your outline, determine whether there is an in-house process that you can apply.

An outline will allow you to map your thoughts in a coherent and logical fashion and to observe where you have missed important information or added extraneous information. An outline will clarify whether you even have sufficient information to proceed or need to do more research. Regard it as a living and flexible entity and not something written in stone. As you progress through your document, keep your outline handy, and modify it whenever necessary. See your outline as your roadmap to your destination—a well-written and successful document.

Begin an outline by writing your purpose statement at the top of the page. Then determine what is the best organizational structure for presenting your content. Certain familiar patterns make it easy for you to work efficiently and for your audience to understand and re-tain the information. Take advantage of these logical and consistent patterns! Patterns of organization include the following:

- advantages–disadvantages
- cause–effect
- chronological
- comparison–contrast
- deduction (general to specific) and induction (specific to general)
- priorities
- problem–solution
- sequential

The same information can be organized in different ways—depending on your purpose and audience—and two or more patterns can be combined to create the final outline. For example, if you were writing a report on your team's priorities for 2019, you might decide to apply a chronological pattern: your first-level headings (section headings) would be First Quarter, Second Quarter, Third Quarter, and Fourth Quarter. Your second-level headings (subsection headings) could then be priorities for each quarter. The outline for the first section might look something like this:

First Quarter 2019

1. Preparation for June 2019 move
2. Follow-up to the 2018 audit
3. Staffing and contractor needs for 2019
4. Workback schedule for annual report

Bring related materials together under general headings, and arrange sections that relate logically to each other. For larger reports, some writers use an index card system by creating an index card for each separate item of the report and then sorting them as necessary. The more detailed the outline, the more useful it will be.

Each section and subsection should have sufficient detail to trigger your thoughts when you write the corresponding sentences and paragraphs. And remember that if a section has a subsection, there must be at least two subsections. You cannot split something (the whole) into one piece.

As you work on your outline, if you think of a strong sentence or transitional phrase, include it in your outline.

Needs assessment table

A needs assessment table is another strategy for organizing a report and has these advantages:

- You can add new columns as you identify new groups of readers.

- You can add new rows as you identify the needs of these new groups.

- Each of the needs in the left-hand column can become a heading (with some modification, if necessary).

The following is an example of a needs assessment table for a report to a city manager on a proposed overpass.

Sample Needs Assessment Table

	Planning Department	Finance Department	Engineering Department	Residents
Background Site, traffic history, and rationale	✓	✓	✓	✓
Project Costs Equipment, labour, excavation, construction, etc.	✓	✓		
Project Timeline	✓	✓	✓	✓
Planning Issues Traffic diversion, relocation of water lines, landscaping, etc.	✓	✓	✓	✓
Conclusion Summary and next steps	✓	✓	✓	✓

By crafting a well-organized outline, you establish coherence and a shapely structure. A coherent document exhibits a clear and close relationship among the ideas being presented. When your writing is coherent, your ideas flow smoothly. Coherence is established by writing cohesive, well-structured paragraphs, where all the ideas are arranged in a logical order, and the reader can follow your reasoning. Coherence begins with a great outline. For more information on flow, see Chapter 14.

When writing an outline, consider getting feedback on the draft from a potential reader or a colleague. Other people might see things you have missed or things you don't need. The architect stage is the best stage of the process to incorporate suggestions. After this stage, it gets much harder.

You may want to revisit the organizational structure later in the writing process by using a technique known as reverse outlining. In reverse outlining, you remove all the supporting writing and review the document's main points—which can be represented by headings and subheadings or by topic sentences. (Microsoft Word also provides a range of outlining features that allow you to look at the overall structure: e.g., the navigation pane and the outline view.) The beauty of the reverse outline is that it provides you with a bird's eye view of the document structure. Reverse outlining allows you to test your drafts for the logical sequence of points and to see where there are gaps in information or unnecessary information.

THE CARPENTER: WRITING CONTENT

The carpenter can now get to work. Your task is clear because the architect's specifications were set out. You might have already started filling in parts of the outline, and along with the madman work you've done, you should have plenty of content.

The important thing now is to write quickly and not slow down to critique your work. Allocate a block of quiet and uninterrupted time to focus on writing. Don't think about word count, grammar, or style. You might even go off-topic while writing a first draft; that's fine. If you get stuck in a certain section, just move to another section. You can always return later to the section where you felt blocked; sometimes the right words fall into place once you've had a break.

The important thing to remember is that you may have to write several drafts at this stage before you are satisfied with the content.

This does not mean that you are a weak writer; strong writers revise in earnest and often. In the words of author Rachel Carson, "Writing is largely a matter of application and hard work, of writing and rewriting endlessly until you are satisfied that you have said what you want to say as clearly and simply as possible. For me that usually means many, many revisions." The amount of time you spend writing and revising depends on the amount of time you have and the importance of the document. And just as a carpenter on a jobsite might revise a few architectural details, so might you revise some of the structural details at this stage.

When revising at this stage, you are carrying out a macro-edit, meaning your primary focus is on revising for content, structure, and organization. And no matter how many revisions you make, the document should remain faithful to its original purpose and the needs of its audience. The carpenter stage is also the best time for reviewers to provide feedback and for you to incorporate any suggested changes, additions, or deletions. Details about the macro-edit are provided in Chapter 15.

Once you're satisfied with your final draft—and only then—it's time to bring in the judge.

THE JUDGE: ENSURING QUALITY

If the madman, architect, and carpenter have done their jobs well, the work of the judge, a.k.a. the quality-control inspector, should be straightforward. The judge looks for consistency in tone and style, adds or deletes text as necessary, reads for cohesion and coherence, and checks for clarity and brevity. The judge also ensures there are no misplaced modifiers, commas in the wrong places, missing words, inaccurate citations, vague pronoun references, run-on sentences, and so on. The one thing that the judge should not be doing is major restructuring of the document. If she is, then the architect and carpenter have failed in their jobs.

The work of a judge is contemplative and reasoned. Dedicate enough time to this stage because the judge does not carry out her best work in haste. Just as the carpenter may have to write many drafts before he has done his best job, the judge may have to carry out several rounds of editing. These rounds of editing can be separated so that you are only checking for one thing at a time (e.g., one review that checks solely for grammar and punctuation mistakes). In this book, this level of editing is referred to as a micro-edit, that is, stylistic editing and copyediting.

The judge's role—and the conventions and principles she applies—is explored more in Parts Three, Four, and Five of this book. Chapter 15 also provides more detail about micro-editing and includes editing and proofreading checklists.

CONCLUSION

Depending on the actual piece of writing you're contemplating, currently working on, or editing, you can modify the strategies explored in these first two chapters to suit your purposes. But the more you apply the techniques of professional writers—that is, generating ideas through brainstorming, organizing these ideas in an outline, writing a draft of the content, and then revising the draft until you're satisfied with it—the more comfortable you will become with these techniques. As they become second nature, you will find that your writing becomes more efficient and purposeful. And hopefully more enjoyable!

EXERCISES

A. After several years of working as a dog walker for PawsPooch Inc., you've been promoted into management. A new hire is taking over your job. Identify a specific issue that could be challenging for your replacement, and then complete these two steps:

First, write a quick list as a prewriting strategy. Then, write a short email (between 200 and 250 words) to the new employee that outlines your specific instructions for dealing with this challenge.

B. The most commonly used patterns of organization are listed below. Match the situation to the organizational pattern most suitable. In some cases, you can suggest more than one method.

a. Advantages–Disadvantages

b. Cause–Effect

c. Chronological

d. Comparison–Contrast

e. Deduction (general to specific) and induction (specific to general)

f. Priorities (most to least important)

g. Problem–Solution

h. Sequential (step-by-step)

1. ___ To examine the way three organizations solve the problem of staff recruitment and retention

2. ___ To write a daily report of your tasks

3. ___ To find out why your policy manuals are not being read and recommend changes

4.___ To compare two trucks and decide which will cost less to operate

5.___ To brief your manager after attending a meeting for her

6.___ To describe the procedure for tracking work-related expenses

7.___ To write a memo to your boss about problems your team is having with the workload

C. Try this.

Take a few minutes to analyze how you currently tackle your writing projects. Do you usually generate ideas before you start writing? Do you spend sufficient time organizing and outlining when working on major projects? Are you too critical about your writing too early on? How can you take these suggested four stages of writing (Madman, Architect, Carpenter, and Judge) and tailor them to your own style and writing tasks?

— CHAPTER THREE —

Look Good Too: Visual Smarts

Design is intelligence made visible.

~ ALINA WHEELER

Readers judge the professionalism and quality of writing not only by its content but also by its appearance. Even an email can be improved by introducing subheadings or bolding an important concept. A poorly designed document that is difficult to read conveys a lack of professionalism.

When referring to document layout, we mean the arrangement of predetermined items on a page. Design is a much broader concept: it refers to the art of combining text, images, and other items into a visually harmonious relationship.

As the writer, you may not be responsible for the document's final design, but you should, at least, have some basic understanding of design.

DESIGN PRINCIPLES

Visual design is functional, not only aesthetic. It helps readers find information and interpret it. Page design and headings help with comprehension because they visually reveal the structure of the document.

Visual clutter is a distraction. Use different fonts, boldface, italics, and other highlights sparingly, usually no more than three per page.

The principles of design for graphic designers are alignment, repetition, contrast, proximity, and balance. The discussion in this chapter focuses more on document design fundamentals, including the text treatments that writers can use to highlight important information.

Font For print materials, designers generally recommend a serif font for body copy and a sans-serif font for headings. For websites, designers historically recommended a sans-serif font for body and headings; this is changing, however, as high-definition screens and more font options become available. Many web designers are starting to appreciate that great web typography does not have to be sans serif.

Serifs are semi-structural details or small decorative flourishes on the beginnings and ends of the strokes that make up letters and symbols. Typical serif fonts are Times New Roman and Georgia. Sans-serif fonts do not have these structural details or flourishes. Typical sans-serif fonts are Arial and Calibri.

Choose a point size that meets the needs of your readers. In print, the optimal size is 10 to 12 points for most readers and 14 to 16 points for seniors and people with visual impairments.

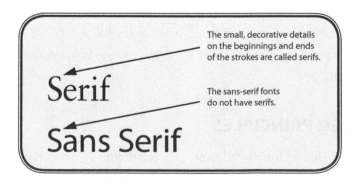

On the web, the optimal size is 15 to 25 pixels. But you need to fine-tune these guidelines based on the specific font you are using. Let your eye be the judge.

Decorative fonts tend to distract readers. Also avoid low-contrast formatting: a black font on a white background provides the highest contrast possible and looks clean and sharp.

Variation in type style Shifting from regular type (roman) to italic type, from regular type to bold, and from lowercase to uppercase letters will attract attention. Writing in uppercase will be interpreted by your readers as yelling. Too many shifts create an untidy look and slow readers down, so use these variations sparingly.

Underlining Underlining emphasizes the material but it reduces legibility. And underlined text can be confused with hypertext links. Boldface, italics, and variations in point size are better choices than underlining.

Prose versus visual representation Paragraphs are best for narratives or explanations. When the subject is complex or you know that the audience is probably scanning rather than reading, a visual may be a better choice. Use tables, charts, and graphs to present data that would make for tedious reading in your main text.

Paragraph length Simplify complex or unfamiliar material by keeping paragraphs short and using white space. Sometimes, however, long paragraphs are necessary to develop complex thoughts. If you do have a series of long paragraphs, try to break them up with the occasional short paragraph. Dense, lengthy paragraphs can intimidate readers already struggling with new ideas or challenging information.

Navigation Think of the document as a map that guides the reader through the ideas being presented. The organization of the writing should be visually clear. For example, use headings or different fonts to distinguish major ideas from supporting details. Help the reader identify and locate important information. Page numbers should be easy to find; the table of contents should identify all major sections and, depending on the nature of the material, the subsections; and visuals should be labelled and located close to their mention in the text.

Layout When reading English, we read from left to right and top to bottom in print documents. To maintain that linear flow when laying out your documents, place main headings at the top left of the page, and use subheadings, vertical lists, and bullets. Make sure that visuals do not disrupt the text. The reader's eyes should move smoothly across and down the page.

This reading pattern of left to right and top to bottom does not apply as readily to web pages because the pages often contain multimedia elements, such as photos, animations, and interactive components, that change the reading patterns.

White space Any part of a page that is unmarked is referred to as white space or negative space. White space helps the reader break the information down into manageable chunks. On most pages, white space appears in the margins, in spaces between paragraphs and sections, and around visuals. A well-designed document always has a balanced amount of white space.

LISTS: KEY POINTERS

Lists can be run into the text or set vertically. Short, simple lists are often better run into the text, especially if the introduction and the items form a complete grammatical sentence. Example: *When you are at the warehouse, can you please pick up three computers, two desks, and one filing cabinet.*

Lists that are best set vertically are those that require prominence, have more than four or five items, contain items of several levels, or are each a complete sentence or several sentences. When used too frequently, however, lists lose their impact. Here are some general guidelines on how to construct lists in your documents:

- Use a lead-in sentence (not a sentence fragment) to introduce the list that indicates the meaning or purpose of this list, and punctuate the end of the lead-in sentence with a colon. Although many writers do not follow the convention to use a complete sentence as a lead-in, it is still best practice to do so.

  Not this: *We recommend that you include:*

  But this: *We recommend that you include the following:*

  For more information on the use of the colon, see Chapter 9.

- Ensure that each item in the list makes sense with the lead-in sentence.

- Do not use a heading as a lead-in for a list.

- Make sure all items in a list have parallel grammatical structure, whether they are phrases, clauses, or full sentences. Do not mix actions and explanations in the same list.

- Use bullets instead of numerals or letters unless there is a good reason to do so: e.g., to suggest relative importance or a sequence of steps.

- Watch out for unnecessary punctuation. Not all items require a semicolon at the end. See below for specific examples.

- Do not use more than nine bullets in one list. If you have too many items, then subdivide or consolidate the items.

Here are some examples of lists. Your organization might have its own conventions, but if not, use these examples as models.

1. If the items are numbered, a period follows the numeral, and each item begins with a capital letter.

   Complete these steps:

   1. Turn off the computer.

   2. Unplug the printer.

   3. Install the cartridge.

2. Items made up of sentences begin with a capital letter and end with a period or question mark.

   Several differences exist between the three reports:

   - The "State of Our City" report provides data and analysis.

   - The "Measuring Up" report presents raw data only.

   - The "Toronto's Place in the Region" report focuses on the regional perspective.

3. When items are not complete sentences, they begin with a lowercase word and have no closing punctuation.

   During the meeting, we discussed the following:

   - the purpose of the program

   - the timeline for completion

   - the budget

4. Use a semicolon after each item (and a period at the end of the list) if one or more items contain internal punctuation or after each item of a list ending in *and* or *or*, even if the items contain no internal punctuation.

Please complete these tasks before you leave for Charlottetown:

- finish the project by Friday, December 4;

- place everything you've completed, including this report, on a USB drive; and

- label all the files with your designated code.

HEADINGS: STRUCTURE REVEALED

Headings—that is, the titles and subtitles inserted into the running text of a document—help create structure and order. They keep you, the writer, focused and organized (just as the outline does), and they help the reader to navigate the text with ease. Use them wisely to increase the readability, scannability, and professionalism of your documents.

Headings allow a reader to scan a document and decide if it will be useful. They also divide long documents into sections that the reader can select from and read separately. When writing headings, keep the following in mind:

- Be consistent with your heading design.

- Make the headings parallel in phrasing. A first-level heading might use *how/when/where/what* phrasing, and a second-level heading might use gerund phrasing (*–ing* words).

- Make the phrasing of headings sufficiently descriptive. Readers use headings to get a quick thumbnail idea of the content in a section.

Not this: *Technical Information*

But this: *Physics of Fibre Optics*

- Make sure your headings are the right length. If they're too short, they don't provide enough description; if they're too long, they make the text underneath them unnecessary.

- Omit articles (*the*, *a*, and *an*) from the beginning of headings, when possible.

  Not this: *The Latest Advances in Pain Management*

  But this: *Latest Advances in Pain Management*

- Avoid orphaned headings—a heading at the bottom of a page with the text that it introduces at the top of the next page. Keep at least two lines of body text with the heading, or force the heading to the next page.

Watch out for the following common heading mistakes:

- lone headings—a heading by itself within a section without another at the same level in that same section

- stacked headings—two consecutive headings without intervening text

- pronoun references to headings. For example, if you have the heading *Torque*, don't begin the sentence following it with something like this: *This is a physics principle . . .*

- headings as lead-ins to lists or figures

VISUAL REPRESENTATION OF CONTENT

As you are writing, you may decide that some of your content would be more credible and understandable if you represented it visually. Perhaps there is some narrative that could be presented more effectively as a table or an illustration. This visual should complement rather than conflict with the writing. Never expect the visual to speak for itself. Advantages of representing content visually include the following:

- Information can be summarized quickly.

- A substantial amount of information can be conveyed in a small space.

- An argument or a list of recommendations can be reinforced.

- The document is more visually appealing.

Disadvantages include the following:

- If not done properly, visuals can distract the reader.

- The wrong type of visual can lead to misinterpretation.

Make sure the visual representation of the content matches the content of the document. Here are some examples:

Content	Visual Representation
People and objects	Photos and illustrations
Processes	Flow charts
Geographic data	Maps
Numeric information	Tables and charts

Some visuals are better than others at relaying information. Pie charts, for example, are used frequently, but often a table or bar chart would be better. Edward Tufte, a pioneer in the field of data visualization, has written extensively about the failure of the pie chart to convey information accurately. In a 2013 tweet, he wrote: "Pie chart users deserve same suspicion+skepticism as those who mix up its/it's, there/their."

CAPTIONS FOR VISUALS

Include a descriptive caption for each visual. Conventions about caption length and content vary according to the discipline. In the sciences, a lengthy explanation may be acceptable. But for most writers, the caption should be descriptive and short. Think of the caption as a topic sentence that tells the reader what the visual is about and how it is organized. Conventions will also depend on the preferred citation style, but here are some common practices:

- When labelling and referencing visuals, refer to graphs, charts, and diagrams as *figures* and refer to tables as *tables*. If your document has more than five visuals, list your figures, tables, and photos separately on your table of contents page(s), under the headings *Figures*, and so on.

- A table caption appears above a table, and a figure caption appears below a figure. Typically, the word *Figure* or *Table* and its associated number in the caption is boldfaced. The caption should be written in plain text with sentence case capitalization (only the initial letter of the caption and any proper names in the caption are capitalized). Example: **Figure 6** Area of the Milk River watershed in Alberta, Saskatchewan, and Montana.

- Focus on completeness and concreteness. For example, **Table 4** Programs to reduce light pollution would be more descriptive as **Table 4** National organizations in Europe with programs in 2017 to reduce light pollution.

- If your figure or table is essentially the same as or based on another author's, but you adapted it, include the words *Adapted from* followed by the author's name and a citation at the end of the caption.

- If the data used in a figure or table came from another source(s), make sure you cite the source(s) in the caption.

EXERCISES

A. **List the design problems you see with this short promotional piece. Are there any questions the reader might have that are left unanswered?**

> **Join us in Support of Mental Illness Awareness Day, October 16**
>
> <u>What</u>:
>
> *A presentation by Joe E. Edwards on the ethical responsibility of journalists to educate the public about sensitive issues. Mr. Edwards is a science writer and journalist from Rochester, New York, and a long-time advocate for providing better services for those who live with mental illness.*
>
> **<u>When</u>**: Monday, October 16, 10:30 a.m. – 11:30 a.m.
>
> <u>Where</u>: Room 1509, Health Sciences Building, U of C
>
> **Register by contacting Jamie Thwibble by phone at (403) 123-4567 or by email at jthwibble@xyz.com**

B. **This rambling email is an unpleasant chore to read. Rewrite this email using subheadings to organize the material and help readers get the message faster. Remove any information you consider unnecessary.**

Hi Luis,

If we're going to go ahead with the plan to get an in-house style guide in place, let's start by asking Nawara in marketing to help us out. She's really particular when it comes to language. And of course, we'll have to get Charlie in finance onboard because he's going to have to approve the funding for it. He's not going to like spending the $1,500 that I estimate it's going to cost (I need to draft a budget too), but I'll have to make the case for the way it's going to improve our external image. And it really shouldn't just cover language issues; we'd probably get more senior buy-in if we covered off on design issues too like basic rules for logo use and colours. So better get Yuri, that new designer we just hired, involved too. I'm sure he'll want some rules in there about whether people should be creating their own visuals (that illustration that Jessie did in that feasibility study was an embarrassment!).

And we have to convince senior management that a style guide will pay for itself quickly in time saved editing and debating a lot of random things, so maybe the CEO's EA, Ruth, would join our little style guide committee. Another good thing about it is that employees will have to spend less time correcting their work. That is, of course, if we can get everyone to use the style guide. Well, we should because it's the only way our reports are going to start looking more consistent.

I know it's going to be a daunting project. There's no point thinking it's going to happen overnight. But maybe we could start working in July, and we should be able to get it done in a couple of months. Maybe by September 1, we could roll it out?

Please let me know what you think so we can get going.

Sylvia

C. Review the information below regarding a hotel's media budget. Does the pie chart or the bar chart present the information better? Provide a rationale.

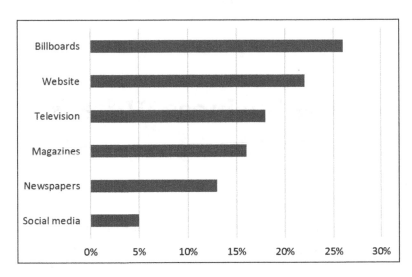

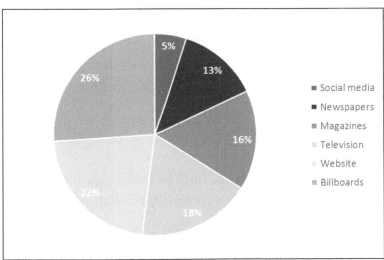

PART TWO

The Business Writer's Showcase

*How well we communicate is determined not by how
well we say things but how well we are understood.*

~ ANDREW GROVE

*A writer always tries, I think, to be part of the solution,
to understand a little about life and pass this on.*

~ ANNE LAMOTT

*Writing is hard, but the more you write,
and enjoy what you write, the better it gets.*

~ ALICE MUNRO

You may not regard yourself as a writer: you neither set out to be one nor trained as one, even though you may have several certificates, diplomas, or degrees. But if you spend 30 to 50 percent of your workday writing—and many of us do—then a writer you are. You are in the business of writing. And this business deserves the same degree of professionalism as any other occupation.

Professionals work hard to hone their craft: for business writers, part of the craft is becoming adept in streamlining daily writing tasks. Writing efficiently saves time, a precious commodity worth saving and spending somewhere else. This part of the book isn't a prescriptive or comprehensive guide to all the documents you might write, but it does provide strategies, advice, and specific writing examples.

The focus here is on the common forms of business writing from the humble email to the elegantly written proposal to the chatty blog post to the career-defining cover letter. No matter the form, the length, the complexity, or medium of delivery, they are all written, we hope, with clear intent for a specific audience.

CHAPTER FOUR

Write Reader-Centred Emails and Letters Quickly and Efficiently

Write letters more like emails and emails more like letters.
From the email, a letter writer could learn to relax;
from the letter, the emailer could learn to take care.

~ MARK TREDINNICK AND GEOFF WHYTE

What business writer—or any writer for that matter—can escape the constant round of reading and responding to email? Add to that the time spent writing more formal correspondence, such as cover letters and acceptance letters. After all, the letter did not fade away quietly upon the arrival of email. Little wonder our fingers have become so attached to their keyboards!

The principles outlined in this chapter can help you elevate your everyday writing from ho-hum to well done. Take pride in even a standard business letter to a client, and know that every time you write well, you show that you care about language and you care about your reader.

EMAILS

Rose-Marie: *Nice to meet you! What do you do you for a living?*

Jeremy: *I email.*

Emails—curse or convenience? The jury is still out. Email is a drastically different beast than the business letter once was. Emails are what we do—for some of us, all day long. According to the Radicati Group, a technology market research organization, writers on Planet Earth now send over 260 *billion* emails a day. And most of these emails are no works of art: they are often long-winded, seemingly pointless, or hastily written.

Many people now find themselves clocking in several extra hours a day just to manage their inboxes. But dedicating all this time to answering email is seldom part of a busy person's job description. Yes, some of the dozens of emails many of us receive daily do require an immediate response. Other emails, however, create a sense of urgency, but it's an artificially inflated urgency.

We need to do all we can to email less often and more efficiently. There isn't a person alive who wishes to receive an unceasing barrage of email, so remember this: the more you send, the more you receive.

In other words, just because you *can* send emails at any time for any occasion doesn't mean you *should*. Before deciding to write an email, take a minute to consider if the email is truly necessary, and if it is the best medium. Ask yourself these questions:

- Is it appropriate to be emailing this person? Is he the right person? Is this a trivial request?

- Have I checked carefully to see if I could answer this question myself before overloading someone else's inbox?

- Has this person indicated that email is not her preferred method of communication?

- Instead of thinking what's best for me, should I respect this person's holiday time and wait until he returns to send this email?

- Is this a delicate matter best discussed first in person and then followed up with a written note to confirm the details of the conversation?

- Would a phone call or a quick walk down the hall be a better choice?

— Ask Maggie —

My colleague recently told me she never reads her emails because she's too busy. No wonder she wasn't getting back to me! I assumed people read their emails, but I guess that's not true. How am I supposed to know if people actually read their emails? And how many of them read the entire email?

Signed,

Ticked-off Tess

Dear Tess,

It would have been nice if your colleague had told you earlier that she didn't read her emails. Then you could have stopped writing them! Some people seem to have a peculiar idea about how emails work. The solution, when possible, is to ask what people's preferred communication style is, especially if you're not hearing back from them.

And yes, people often don't read the entire email. That's why it's imperative to get the most important information up front in the lead paragraph and even in the subject line. And consider bolding important information.

I lost a pair of free tickets to a Santana concert because I didn't follow my own advice. When I emailed a friend who had kindly offered me the tickets, I chitchatted for a couple of paragraphs before saying I'd happily take them. After waiting a couple of days and not hearing from her, I emailed her again and found out she'd given them to someone else because she hadn't read the entire email. I learned my lesson. Next time, the subject line will be *Yes! I'll take the tickets.* And then the first line in the email will be *Thanks so much. I'll take the tickets.*

There's nothing wrong with occasional overkill, if that's what it takes.

Email is not designed for immediacy. That's why you have a telephone and a pair of feet. Email is designed for convenience. But for many people, the convenience factor has lost its lustre. A January 2016 article in *The Economist* cited a calculation indicating that Atlantic Media, a mid-sized firm, was spending more than one million U.S. dollars a year on processing emails, with each one costing an average of about 95 cents in labour costs. Tom Cochran, the former chief technology officer of Atlantic Media who made the calculation, commented that "a free and frictionless method of communication has soft costs equivalent to procuring a small company Learjet."

Email savvy: 20 tips

1. **Pause for a moment** before you begin writing to consider what you want the reader to do. Then get organized. Jot down a couple of main points if necessary. **This is Pause No. 1.**

2. **Start with a precise and current subject line.** Look at newspaper and advertising headlines for ideas on how to express ideas quickly and explicitly. Not this: *Meeting tomorrow afternoon.* But this: *Agenda for meeting to discuss party – August 10, 3 p.m., my office.* Help readers respond to emails, find them, and file them. Efficiently.

3. **Keep to one subject per email** if possible. This gives the reader the chance to reply to an email about one thing and not nine.

4. **Wait until the email is ready to send** before filling in the recipient's email address. By doing this, you avoid accidentally sending an unfinished email.

5. **Make your main points quickly**—within the first few sentences. Think like a journalist and get the who, why, what, where, when, and how down first.

6. **Clarify deadlines and other details** so that the reader can get the job done right and on time. Ideally, get any requests in the subject line or first lines of text.

7. **Change paragraphs** when you change topics. One-sentence paragraphs are fine in an email.

8. **Format for easy reading.** Keep paragraphs short with a blank line between them. Big blocks of text are daunting. Daunting = unread. Keep it to one screen, if possible.

9. **Use design elements** when appropriate. For example, if the message is long, use subheadings; if there is an important line the reader must see, bold it or apply colour (but don't underline it—underlining is a holdover from the typewriter age when the only way to emphasize text was to underline it); if there is a list of instructions or steps, use a bulleted or numbered list. But always make sure the email looks professional. (Hint: some people don't like emoticons.) 😜

10. **Craft the email** in such a way that you avoid email ping pong. Consider *if . . . then* statements in any email where you ask a question. Not this: *Would you like to discuss further? Please let me know.* But this: *If you would like to discuss further, then email me a couple of convenient times to phone, and I will confirm one.*

11. **Be true to your word.** Attach documents. Test hyperlinks. Include any necessary details.

12. **Cultivate a warm tone** appropriate to the message and the recipient.

13. **Let people know before sending large attachments.** Sending large attachments can clog up the receiver's inbox, and many servers will not accept more than 10 MB of attachments. One simple solution is to store and share files on a cloud storage service, such as Google Drive or OneDrive.

14. **Check messages before forwarding.** You want nothing that would humiliate you or the reader. And on that note, don't include confidential information.

15. **Keep it tidy.** Don't leave long email threads and excessive carets (>>>>>).

16. **Know the preferences of people you email frequently.** Can you be humorous or chatty with your co-workers? Does your manager dislike sarcasm?

17. **Avoid copying people** on emails they don't need. Know your organization's protocol for using the *cc* and *bcc* designations. Usually people cc'd on an email are included for information only. Narrowcast, don't broadcast.

18. **Use a simple signature** that displays your name, title, and contact info. Again, check your organization's protocol.

19. **Pause again,** and check grammar, punctuation, and spelling— including the spelling of the reader's name. Look for missed words—there's a world of difference between *I did miss the meeting*, and *I did **not** miss the meeting*—and wordiness. **This is Pause No. 2.**

20. **Send! Forgive yourself for any mistakes.** We're not perfect, and we're often writing in a hurry.

Email specifics: openings, closings, and structure

For an email, it's fine to use *Hi Theo,* as your salutation. You may have also seen *Hi, Theo.* as a salutation. Technically speaking, this is correct because *Hi* is an interjection, so it should be followed by a comma. And the entire salutation is a sentence, so the period is also correct. But few people follow this convention anymore. A better strategy is to take your cue from what your colleagues and your manager use.

In your opening, identify the subject, the relevance, and perhaps the main point. This is also the place to set the context: *As we discussed on Tuesday, May 2, . . .* If the reader is unfamiliar with the subject, write an introductory paragraph before you state the main point. When writing your opening, consider the following:

- Give your readers a reason to pay attention. Write an engaging lead. If possible, start with a benefit for the reader to motivate him. Example: *We want the dividend cheque to reach you promptly. Therefore, please complete and return this form by September 15.*

- State your main point so your audience knows what to expect.

- Provide necessary background information, but leave the denser information for later.

- Adjust the length of the beginning to suit the overall message.

- For a lengthy email, begin with a summary.

The closing is the place to emphasize a positive working relationship. It's also the place to let your readers know what you will do or what you expect them to do. Write a strong closing, and be specific. Example: *I will discuss the problem with Emily when we meet this afternoon and let you know by 4 p.m. tomorrow what I intend to do.* When writing your closing, consider the following:

- Repeat your main point(s).

- Summarize your key point(s).

- Refer to a goal stated earlier in your communication.

- Tell your readers how to get more information.

- Tell your readers what to do next.

- Identify any further studies, next steps, and so on.

Here is a suggested organizational structure for emails:

Direct Request	Persuasive Request	Good News	Bad News
Main idea	Attention	Main idea	Buffer
Close	Benefits	Explanation	Explanation
	Action	Close	Decision
	Close		Close

Types of emails

The following samples are some common kinds of emails. Add the openings and closings of emails you generally write to this list, and you'll soon have a handy resource you can draw from when you need it.

The unhappy email This email is written to express your dissatisfaction. If there are personality issues that need addressing, do so in person rather than in an email. In other cases, clearly outline in the email what needs to be done to correct the problem, and be specific and constructive with your criticism.

Begin your email with a positive statement to buffer the bad news, and temper your criticism when necessary. If appropriate, frame the mistake as an example of a department-wide problem, and let the reader know that, criticisms notwithstanding, her contributions are still valued.

Hello Meredith,

You've done an excellent job in handling our landlords and long-term tenants over the past three months. I appreciate the time you've put into this while I get the office ready for the upcoming move.

But you need to be more careful when dealing with new tenants. In the last few weeks, I've received five complaints from new tenants who misunderstood your move-in directions and did not receive a follow-up email when they asked for clarification. I think our communications materials for new tenants do need an overhaul, so I'll set up a team meeting to discuss.

Again, thanks for all your hard work, and please respond to all tenant emails within 48 hours.

Regards,
Luke

If the email is being written to someone outside your organization, state your dissatisfaction clearly for the record. Again, you might have a conversation first, and then follow up with an email summarizing your discussion. But sometimes you have to convey a hard truth quickly in an email. Make it clear what your expectations are and the time frame for a resolution.

Hi Camila,

I was disappointed to read in your email this morning that the repair of the transmitters is going to be delayed until July 15. In our previous communications, you assured me that the repairs would be completed by July 5.

As we discussed last week, a late delivery puts our production schedule at risk and means that we will not meet our obligations to our clients. If you cannot deliver the transmitters by July 5, we expect a 25 percent refund. Let's discuss further when we meet next Wednesday.

Thank you for understanding.
Rachel

The good news email A warm and personal tone generates enthusiasm and motivates people. This is an excellent opportunity to make people feel good about the organization they work for and their role.

Hi team,

Fantastic news for our hard-working team! We finished the project three months ahead of schedule—a company first for any project. I just got word from the CEO that she wants to meet me on September 16 to discuss end-of-year bonuses. Stay tuned for more information.

Regards,
Yuma

The thank-you email People appreciate a thank you for a job well done or for making an effort on their behalf.

Good morning Badru,

Thank you so much for referring me to Peter Bridgestone. We met last week, and he's going to be a great resource; his suggestions on how we could increase our market share were highly creative. I appreciate your taking the time to make the introduction, and I hope to have the opportunity to do business with you sometime soon.

Best regards,
Quinn

Email guidelines for companies

If you have the necessary authority, consider implementing smart and simple organization-wide email guidelines to make everyone's e-life a little easier. Otherwise, it's impossible to solve the problems created by email overload. Establishing guidelines requires frank discussion about concerns and expectations of both employees and management. If your organization has a style guide, you could include these guidelines as an appendix.

Here are some things that could be discussed at an initial meeting. Depending on your organization and your sector, you will probably have other things to discuss. Note that the suggested questions below do not address the organization's or employees' rights or appropriate use of technology at work. This discussion is about how to tame the email beast.

- For internal emails, could we use abbreviations in subject lines as a shorthand to communicate quickly and efficiently? Here are some examples:

  - NNR = no need to respond: *I'm running 15 minutes late. Start without me. NNR*

  - RR = response required: *RR by 2 p.m. December 10*

  - EOM = end of message, which alerts the reader that the entire message is in the subject line, and it's not necessary to open the email: *I picked up the boss's birthday card. EOM*

  - NFA = no further action: *I phoned the bank and cancelled the meeting. NFA*

- What is our policy about the use of the *cc* designation? Does it mean that it's an informational email only? Is it clear that I don't need to respond if I'm cc'd?

- What about group email? Could we agree that people should respond only if they disagree or have new information?

- Do we condone the use of the *bcc* designation? Under what circumstances?

- How do we ensure that employees agree to and follow the following standards?

    - Keep subject lines current.

    - Cut off threads when discussions have become frayed or no longer relate to the original subject.

    - Read a complete thread before contributing.

    - Use *Reply All* with caution.

- What is appropriate email usage outside regular business hours? Should we be emailing each other at 11 p.m. or on Sundays just because we can? Should we email our colleagues when they are on holidays?

- What criteria do we have for deciding which emails are urgent and must be answered when they are received and which ones can wait to be answered during regular business hours?

LETTERS

The letter in all its permutations has proven remarkably sturdy. Once used as a more intimate means of communication—think love letters and letters written to friends—letters are now used mostly for formal business communications. The letter still reigns supreme for official documents, such as employment offers, terminations, contracts, and financial and legal communications.

Although business letters call for a respectful tone, they don't need to be stuffy and overly formal. Aim for a straightforward and natural style. And keep the letter as long as it needs to be, but keep it orderly—with subheadings, if necessary, and tidy sentences.

You can choose to attach the letter in an email as a PDF, and for more impact, you can mail it. A hard copy will definitely stand out from the flurry of email correspondence.

Letter specifics: salutations, openings, and closings

For a letter, address the person more formally than in an email: use his surname, followed by a colon. Not this: *Dear Mr. Raymond Zang,* But this: *Dear Mr. Zang:*

For the opening, set the context and let the reader know why you're writing, just as you would in an email. Example: *Please find enclosed your refund cheque for the defective snow blower. I have also enclosed a 2018 catalogue.*

The closing is similar to that of an email, but, if the situation requires, is more formal than an email closing. Example: *We greatly appreciate your patronage over the years, and we trust we have resolved this matter to your satisfaction.* Don't feel obliged to end with a standard *Should you have any further questions, please do not hesitate to contact me.* You could try this instead: *I hope this letter answers your questions about our shipping policy,* or *We look forward to giving you a tour of our facilities.* Business letters should end with a final closing, such as *Sincerely* or *Yours truly.*

Refer to the advice provided above on email specifics for writing strong openings and closings.

Types of business letters

Depending on your specific profession, you will have to write different types of letters. Here are some common ones:

Types of Letters	Comments
Acceptance letter	■ Thank the reader for the offer. ■ State your acceptance. ■ Confirm any necessary details and terms. ■ Close with a statement of appreciation.
Adjustment letter (Complaint response letter)	■ Begin with a positive statement, expressing understanding. ■ State your intentions. If you accept the claim or complaint, extend an apology and share the corrective actions. If you deny the claim or complaint, explain the reason(s), and if possible, offer some kind of compensation or some friendly advice. ■ Focus on maintaining goodwill and your organization's reputation. Do not respond with a negative or suspicious tone, even if the claim was insulting. ■ Conclude by expressing the hope that you will continue to do business together.
Complaint letter	■ Begin on a positive note, if possible. For example, if you previously had good service, comment on that experience. ■ Be clear and specific about the problem. ■ State the outcome or remedy that will satisfy you, along with the time frame. ■ Attach copies of any supporting documents that prove your case. ■ End on a positive and assertive note. Convey the attitude that you believe the complaint will be resolved.

Types of Letters	Comments
Cover letter	■ See Chapter 6 for more information on the cover letter.
Fundraising letter	■ Personalize the salutation. Do not use *Dear Supporter*. ■ Begin with a strong lead, something that will captivate the reader. Try asking a question or telling a compelling story. ■ Update a current donor on what his last donation helped you achieve. ■ If the reader is not a current donor, then treat him as a friend and encourage him to donate. ■ Highlight a specific program or initiative that you believe will inspire the reader. ■ Close by thanking the reader and telling him how important his contributions will be.
Inquiry letter	■ State clearly what you want, why you want it, and who you are in the first paragraph. ■ Provide details, such as specific questions, in the second paragraph. ■ If there is any benefit to the reader, let her know. ■ Express advance thanks for her help.
Reference letter	■ Make sure you can write a positive letter before you begin; otherwise, turn down the request. ■ Ask for information, such as a current resumé, to help you compose the letter. ■ If the letter is for a specific job, ask to see the job posting. If it is for a specific school, ask for some information about the school and the program the person is applying to.

Types of Letters	Comments
Reference letter (continued)	■ Begin the letter by explaining your connection to the person and why you are qualified to write a reference letter. ■ In the body of the letter, explain why you believe this person is qualified. Be specific and share examples, if possible, that align with the position or school in question. ■ In closing, offer to provide more information or answer any questions.
Refusal letter	■ Begin with a sincere expression of regret, and state exactly what you are refusing. ■ Explain your reasons for the refusal. ■ Offer alternatives to the reader, if possible. ■ Use a diplomatic tone in all instances. ■ End with an expression of goodwill.
Sales pitch letter	■ Complete any necessary research on both the product and the reader to understand how the reader could potentially be interested. ■ Focus the letter entirely on the reader. You might consider writing the first draft using the second-person pronoun *you* in every sentence. You can remove the excessive use of *you* in the revisions. ■ Keep the pitch short and sweet, and make the benefits to the reader crystal clear. ■ Close by specifying when you will follow up.

Sample Letter: full block style

November 18, 2017

Mr. Malcolm Rosenberg
Director of Operations
City of Goldbay
100 39 Street
Goldbay, Prince Edward Island C1A 7J3

> The inside address includes recipient's full name, title, and address.

Dear Mr. Rosenberg:

Final safety report: your file no. 613A

Attached please find our final safety report evaluating the safety measures of the proposed rapid train service between Goldbay and Summerside.

> The opening establishes a professional tone and sets context.

We have revised the safety standards as you requested on October 25. We also met with Ms. Fernandez on November 3 to review her suggested amendments and incorporate them into this report. She has approved the amended report.

> The second paragraph provides any necessary details.

We would like to express our appreciation to you and your team for your assistance in preparing this report. We look forward to meeting you on December 1 at 2 p.m. at your office to review this report. In the meantime, if you have any questions, please contact me at your convenience.

> Appreciation and next steps are expressed in the closing.

Yours truly,

Nicola Achebe

Nicola Achebe
Principal Engineer

c: Ms. Fernandez, City of Goldbay, Finance

> You can use c or cc to indicate that copies of this letter were sent to others.

EXERCISES

A. Reader benefits: Imagine you are going to write three emails based on the scenarios below. First think about the benefit that would motivate the reader. Then write the first two or three sentences for each email keeping the benefit clearly in mind.

1. I want Crystal, my boss, to approve my request for the company to pay for three business communications courses (the core of a professional communications certificate) over the next year. Our company doesn't have a policy on professional development, and I know she will be cautious about the cost and the time off work required. She'll want to see that my request is worth the investment.

2. My supervisor is angry about the dirty staff kitchen. He's asked me to write an email to the team (10 people) emphasizing that the kitchen must be kept clean. He's threatening to shut down the kitchen. But I'm not convinced that the team will take my email seriously. It's not the first time I've had to warn them about this.

3. I work for a property management company, and I have to write an email to a tenant named Jack who works night shifts and sleeps in the daytime. He's upset that we will be sending an electrician to his apartment during the daytime to upgrade the electrical panel. Jack isn't the easiest tenant, so I'm not surprised he's annoyed.

B. Try this.

1. Think about the most common emails and letters that you write. Do you have examples of well-written emails and letters on hand for when you need them?

2. Practise writing informative and tightly written subject lines for the emails you write most often.

3. What organizational techniques do you use to efficiently manage your correspondence?

4. Do you have any useful time-management tips for managing email that you can share with your co-workers?

CHAPTER FIVE

Craft Successful Reports, Proposals, Summaries, and Minutes

Writing is an art. But when it is writing to inform it comes close to being a science.

~ ROBERT GUNNING

Reports, both formal and informal, are written to provide or update information, solve problems, and make recommendations. Reports can be dressed up in various ways: for example, if the audience is internal, an informal report could be written in memo style using *To, From, Date,* and *Subject* lines. In fact, a memo is often called for in place of a series of long emails. A formal report, on the other hand, will be more reserved in tone and include components such as a cover letter and an executive summary.

Proposals are written to persuade someone (e.g., a funding organization, a committee, or an external client) to spend or invest money or resources. A proposal identifies a specific need, explains the need, and recommends how this need can best be met.

Summaries are written to extract the essential points of a piece of writing and rearrange it in a different format to meet a different need. For example, a manager might ask his assistant to take a 20-page report and prepare a 2-page summary and then a 10-minute presentation. Being able to summarize and reframe information is a critically important business skill.

Minutes are the written record of a meeting or hearing. They are an important, but often overlooked, part of business writing. Just like a summary, minutes need to convey information as concisely and as accurately as possible.

REPORTS

Report writing is a business inevitability: many organizations require a steady flow of reports, written for all kinds of reasons. Reports usually follow a standard pattern: first the writer introduces the subject and explains why the report is being written; then she follows up with the body of the report—the who, why, what, where, when, and how; finally, she concludes with a summary of next steps or well-reasoned recommendations or both.

Regardless of whether you are writing an informal or formal report, you need to carry out the steps outlined in Chapter 1:

- Start with a Purpose Audience Context Tone evaluation.

- Generate ideas and gather the information you need.

- Create an outline. Many report writers struggle with structure; it can be challenging to remain focused on the main points if the preparatory work was not done.

- Write the first draft.

- Rewrite and revise as necessary.

- Edit and proofread.

Informal reports or memos

Do you need to bring the supervisor up to date on the team's progress on a project in Q1? Or submit an expense report explaining the $5,000 in over-budget expenses? Reports of this nature are internal communications and usually solicited by someone in authority. The common kinds of informal reports are incident, accident, progress, information, and expense reports. If they are less than three pages, they are often written as memos.

A well-written and tidy memo serves many purposes. A memo often outperforms a series of emails, especially for communicating detailed information. And if formatting is an important consideration (e.g., you want to use headings, tables, and bulleted lists), then a memo saved as a PDF preserves the formatting much better than an email. Finally, if you can envision the message being printed, being sent to several other people (especially executives), or being shared at a meeting, then a memo attached to an email is a better choice than a plain email.

Here is a sample informal progress report written as an internal memo.

Sample Memo

To: Danny Duke
From: Fiona Robbins
Date: April 14, 2017
Subject: Progress Update for Employee Appreciation Day

Summary

The following is a summary of the progress to date on the Employee Appreciation Day (EAD) being held on June 29, 2017.

Background

Building on the success of last year's EAD, an EAD was approved for June 29, 2017. An event committee was struck in January 2017. The 2017 event will be identical to last year's event: four morning sessions, lunch, and four afternoon sessions. Sessions are a mix of personal and professional development activities.

Work to date

- finalized budget ($8,000) and CFO has approved
- completed schedule and description of sessions (see attached)
- booked facilitators for all eight sessions
- secured venue: Rocky Ridge Resort (four breakout rooms and a room for lunch)

Work to be done

- finalize the details of the lunch with the venue
- send a "hold the date" email to all staff on April 15, 2017
- begin planning the logistical details (e.g., promotion, registration, volunteers)

Conclusion

The EAD 2017 is on track, and we anticipate a great turnout this year—about 60 employees. We have an outstanding program of activities lined up. The CEO's recent decision to announce the timeline for the building renovations at the EAD will be welcome news.

If you have any questions, please contact me at extension 333 or by email at frobbins@bubjo.com.

Fiona Robbins

Formal reports

Formal reports are usually written to external clients and provide, for example, a comprehensive overview of a major change or development. Formal reports also provide evidence to support information presented in the report and often include citations for the sources used, visuals, and statistical information. While the structure of informal reports can vary, formal reports usually have a set structure.

Although the content depends on the actual report, most formal reports will incorporate some, if not all, of these components:

Report Component	Description
Title page	List the title of your report and any other necessary information.
Table of contents (TOC)	List the titles of all sections that appear in the report and their corresponding page numbers. The TOC should correspond to the outline.
List of tables	List the captions of all tables and their corresponding page numbers. Prepare this section after the report is complete.
List of figures	List the captions of all figures and their corresponding page numbers. Prepare this section after the report is complete.
List of abbreviations	List all the abbreviations, acronyms, and initialisms used in the report. Prepare this section after the report is complete.

Report Component	Description
Executive summary	Include a summary of your report explaining why the report was written and emphasizing the principal objectives and the major conclusions and recommendations. The executive summary should be no longer than about 10 percent of the entire report and should be written so that it can be read as a stand-alone document. Although this section appears at the start of the report, it's often written last. See page 89 for more information.
Introduction	A key function of the introduction is to establish the significance of the work and outline the report's scope. It may include some or all of the following: ■ A concise purpose statement: List the major objectives of your report and any specific terms of reference. ■ Background: Include any information needed to provide perspective, such as what projects were carried out previously; an in-depth history is seldom required. If the background is extensive, it may require its own section. ■ Scope: Define the topic and any assumptions or constraints that limit the report. ■ Method: If findings were based on a survey, outline the steps. Scientific reports often include an explanation of the methodology used in the investigation. Again, a lengthy section may require its own section.

Report Component	Description
Body	These sections cover the core content of the report and will vary according to the type of report. Present the analysis in a logical and systematic way, and back up claims with evidence. Perform comparisons, if appropriate, and discuss your observations. Include visuals, as needed, to clearly illustrate the results.
Conclusions	The conclusions should identify the major issues and relate specifically to the objectives of the report set out in the introduction. Conclusions should be free from speculation and present no new thoughts. List the conclusions in order of importance, and number them to make them easier to refer to.
Recommendations	The recommendations or next steps point to the future and are action oriented and feasible. They should logically relate to the body and conclusions. List the recommendations in order of importance, and again number them. Be as specific as possible about how each recommendation should be carried out. Caution the reader about any assumptions and limitations.
References	Provide a list of references consulted in writing the report.
Appendices	Provide detailed information that would interest only certain readers, and be selective about what you include.

Differences between informal and formal reports

The following table illustrates some of the key differences between informal and formal reports.

Item	Informal	Formal
Length	Short, with sections	Long (four pages plus), with sections and subsections
Transmittal letter	No	Yes
Title page	Probably in a memo subject line	Yes
Table of contents	No	Yes
List of visuals	Optional	Perhaps
Executive summary	No	Yes
Introduction	Yes	Yes
Body (analysis)	Yes – one or more sections	Yes – several sections
Conclusions	Yes	Yes
Recommendations	Optional	Optional

Item	Informal	Formal
Glossary or list of abbreviations	Probably not	Perhaps
Headings	Seldom more than two levels	Often three or four levels
	Main headings placed where they come on the page	Each main heading placed on a new page
Headers and footers	Seldom	Optional but preferred

Executive summaries

A succinct and clear executive summary provides readers with the highlights of a report. An executive summary should begin with a clear statement describing the purpose of the report, followed by any necessary background information, and should conclude with any results, conclusions, or recommendations.

Here are a few things to remember when writing an executive summary:

- Write a summary that stands on its own.

- Present the main points in the same order they appear in the report.

- Introduce nothing in the summary that wasn't discussed in the main part of the report.

- Aim for about 10 percent of the original text.

Sample Executive Summary

The City of Wolfhaven commissioned this report to examine why public use of Wolfhaven's outdoor swimming pools has declined so dramatically over the last 10 years and to determine the economic feasibility of continuing to maintain and operate these pools.

The City of Wolfhaven has four outdoor swimming pools, open annually from June 15 to September 15: Wolf East, Wolf West, Wolf North, and Wolf South. These pools are maintained and managed by the Wolfhaven Outdoor Swimming Pools Association (WOSPA). WOSPA engages with several non-profit and for-profit organizations to operate the pools. Between 2007 and 2017, the use of these pools, based on the number of people per season, has declined as follows: Wolf East: 12,000 to 9,000; Wolf West: 14,000 to 7,000; Wolf North: 13,000 to 10,000; and Wolf South: 18,000 to 15,000. Overall, this represents a drop in pool usage of approximately 30 percent.

This report examines the reasons for this decline in usage. Without further research and a public survey, it is impossible to definitively understand the reasons for this decline, but the research to date indicates that some factors include increased fear of pathogens, increased use of residential pools, and decreased interest in the sport of swimming in general.

This report also evaluates the benefits that outdoor pools provide to Wolfhaven against the cost to the taxpayer to maintain and operate these pools. The importance of outdoor pools is evidenced by, first, their purpose as a valuable recreational asset that improves the life of city residents, including youth at risk; second, their role in encouraging an active lifestyle and helping to offset health care costs associated with sedentary lifestyles; third, their function as an enjoyable and affordable place for all citizens to enjoy; and fourth, their place in building community and social inclusion.

This report concludes that the value of the outdoor pools to Wolfhaven's civic life is worth the continued investment. It is imperative, however, to find ways to offset the escalating costs and the decline in usage.

Based on these conclusions, recommendations to council are as follows:

1. Provide additional funding of $75,000 in the 2018 Recreation Operating Budget to continue the operation of the pools in the summer of 2018. This funding is additional to the $325,000 currently required to maintain and operate the pools.

2. Work with the communities mostly affected by the potential closure of the pools to determine any solutions to reduce the City's operating and capital expenditures for outdoor pools.

3. Develop an Outdoor Pool Strategy to be approved by city council in January 2019. This strategy will assess future outdoor aquatic needs, examine marketing opportunities to encourage use of the pools by Wolfhaven residents, suggest partnerships with other communities, and explore ways to offset costs.

Team report writing

Writing a report as a team can be a difficult process, but it doesn't need to be. Team writing often means that individuals write their own sections without seeing what the others are writing, and that shortly before the due date, everything is packaged together—with inconsistencies in style, usage, and amount of detail—and given a quick dust and polish. This can be a frustrating experience for everyone involved. Instead, consider a more systematic approach to help the team deliver a cohesive and reader-centred report. Modify this process to suit your team's specific projects.

Get the plan in place

First, assign a project leader who will manage the project from beginning to end; ideally, this person has experience in coordinating team writing projects, either as a writer or an editor. For our purposes here, we'll call this person Harriet.

Harriet will lead a team discussion about the purpose, audience, context, and tone (PACT) that clearly articulates the purpose of the project and identifies the audience (readers, browsers, or users), the context, and the tone of the report. For more information on PACT, see Chapter 1.

Based on the PACT evaluation, Harriet works with the team to create an outline of the project and a workback schedule that includes every phase of the project and indicates the responsibilities and due dates for each team member. Harriet assigns someone to be responsible for front matter (e.g., executive summary) and back matter (e.g., appendices).

When working on a major writing project with other people, always write a workback schedule—a schedule that starts with a final date and works back from that date. A workback schedule will allow you to easily see the tasks, people responsible, and the completion dates. See the conclusion of this section for a sample workback schedule for an annual report that outlines the tasks, person(s) responsible, and due dates.

During this planning phase, the team should also discuss how and when the team will communicate and what style (e.g., in-house style guide, *The Canadian Press Stylebook*) will be used for the report.

Draft, refine, and synthesize

Each writer drafts a comprehensive outline of her contribution and submits it to Harriet. After evaluating the outlines, Harriet brings the teams together again to refine the outlines and make sure they form a cohesive whole. It's important at this stage to identify any gaps in content and redundant material.

Team writers need to agree on the contents of the outline and their contributions before the actual narrative is written.

Complete the first draft

Each team writer now drafts her section of the project, including visuals, and submits it to Harriet by the date set in the workback schedule. Each writer should also include a summary of her section that can be used to write the executive summary.

Harriet reviews the draft contributions and incorporates them into a single draft. She also makes suggestions for revisions to the individual writers. The focus of this first draft should be on the report structure and purpose, although there might also be some copyediting (editing for consistency, correctness, accuracy, and completion).

Prepare the final draft

After the revisions have been incorporated by Harriet, she sends the final draft to the team and any other reviewers for a final review.

After she has received all the revisions back and incorporated them, Harriet assigns an editor for copyediting and style editing. (Although some style and copyediting may have been done before the document was distributed for a final review, another final round of edits has to be done.)

Design and deliver

The document is now ready for Harriet to send for formatting and possibly layout and design, depending on the project. She takes responsibility for the final proofreading once the document has been laid out. Finally, she delivers the document in the correct medium to the interested parties.

Here is a sample informal workback schedule for an annual report; the schedule outlines the tasks, person(s) responsible, and due dates.

Sample Annual Report Workback Schedule

Task	Person Responsible	Completion Date
Distribution of hard copies by mail	Kalila	June 21
Printing and online distribution	Kalila	June 19
Proofread and delivery to Kalila	Mark	June 12
Design and layout of final content and delivery; submit to Mark	Dylan	June 9
Incorporation of final changes; submit to Dylan	Mark	June 3
Approval of content and sign-off; submit to Mark	executive director board chair ARC	May 28
Incorporation of suggested changes from ARC	Kate and Mark	May 19
Draft ready for review and feedback from ARC	Mark	May 10

Task	Person Responsible	Completion Date
Final design approved	ARC	May 8
First draft written; submit to Mark for review	Kate	May 5
Draft layout of design; submit to ARC	Dylan	May 1
Photographs and other images secured	Dylan	April 20
Content gathered from board, department heads, committee chairs; financials received	Mark and Kate	April 20
Key messages and theme finalized	ARC	March 31
First meeting of annual report committee (ARC) to discuss project and draft a schedule	**ARC members** Mark: editor and production manager Kate: writer from marketing Dylan: designer from marketing Kalila: assistant to the executive director and ARC committee chair	March 21

Complex information simplified

Reports often include complex information—details that perhaps not all readers will easily grasp. Exemplary communicators illuminate and provide insight. They don't talk down to their audience and dilute their information. They translate their concepts in a way that deepens the reader's knowledge.

Here are some things to keep in mind when communicating complex information:

- **Plain language** The Australian scholar of plain language Robert Eagleson defines plain language as "clear, straightforward expression, using only as many words as are necessary. It is language that avoids obscurity, inflated vocabulary and convoluted sentence construction." When writing in plain language, consider the following:

    - Keep your language simple, and don't use jargon.

    - Let the sentence be driven by the verbs and not the nouns. Concrete nouns usually work better than abstract ones; active verbs usually work better than passive ones.

    - Keep your sentence structure simple. Aim for shorter sentences (under 30 words) without dependent clauses.

    - Limit the number of messages. Tell readers only what they need to know, and develop one idea at a time.

    - For more information on plain language, see Chapter 11.

- **Terminology** Readers expect technical content in terms they can understand. When technical terms are necessary, they should be clearly defined. Here are some principles:

    - Introduce a concept first and then the term.

- Don't define each technical term within the sentence when writing to a lay audience. Write a new sentence in which you define the term.

- Avoid circular definitions (using a part of the term to define the term itself).

- If possible, make sure the reader doesn't have to look up another term to understand the first term.

- Keep the definition to a couple of sentences.

- Watch out for inconsistent terminology, that is, using different words to explain the same thing. For example, don't use the term *receptacle* in one part of a report and *socket* in another part when referring to the same thing.

- If you have a complex initialism or acronym in a report, redefine it whenever you think the reader might have forgotten it.

- Keep a list of preferred terms and conventions for abbreviations or unique language.

- Consider a glossary or a list of abbreviations. You could also put a list of technical terms in a sidebar so that the sentences aren't bogged down with technical information.

- **Storytelling** Use analogy. Explain the complex information in terms of something that relates to the reader's experience of everyday life. For example, Steve Jobs once described a computer as "the equivalent of a bicycle for our minds."

- **Visuals** Paint a compelling picture if it helps to explain or tell a story. See Chapter 3 for more detail on using visuals to represent data.

- **Tone** When explaining something complicated, visualize talking directly to someone reading the information, and talk to that person using *you* in every sentence.

Not this: *A separate policy will be issued to the resident to cover the replacement costs of the original paintings. There will be a one-time charge of $1,000 for this policy.*

But this: *You will have to pay a one-time charge of $1,000 for a policy to cover the replacement costs of the original paintings.*

In the final draft, you can replace *you* with a more neutral character. Example: *The resident will have to pay a one-time charge of $1,000 for a policy to cover the replacement costs of the original paintings.*

- **Usability testing** Finally, ask a non-technical person to read your draft. Ask him or her to note whenever something is unclear.

PROPOSALS

Just like reports, proposals may be informal or formal. A proposal could be a two-page internal memo proposing the investment of $20,000 in software upgrades or a 10-page grant proposal written by a non-profit organization to a potential funder or a 50-page formal proposal in response to a formal Request for Proposal (RFP).

A proposal has only one purpose: to put a proposition forward and make a sale. Persuasive writing is everything. Enthusiasm is contagious, so share your eagerness and readiness for the opportunity with the reader.

Think about key messages and any stories you want to share. Readers engage in and retain more from a story woven around facts and figures than they do from dense narrative, statistics, and tables. Write strategically by introducing key messages and underlying themes early in the proposal and then elaborating on them throughout the proposal.

If your proposal is a request for financial assistance to launch a project, outline your proposal, and painstakingly follow the RFP or proposal format requirements. Be sure to include these components:

- **Summary** Prepare an umbrella statement of your case and a concise summary of the entire proposal. Explain what you propose to do, and provide the background information the funder will need and want. Provide an overview of the problem, need, or goal, and explain why the funder should care. What will be done by whom and how and over what time frame? Who will the outcomes benefit?

- **Statement of need** Write a statement of need that defines the issue and why it is important. Describe in detail who benefits and why your project fulfills this need.

- **Organizational information** Provide an overview of your primary activities, services, and strengths.

- **Project description** Explain the project details. What are the specific activities? Who will do them? Provide a timeline of activities. What specific outcomes will be achieved? Why are you or your organization the best choice to carry out this work? Give examples of your ability to carry out this project.

- **Budget** Include a budget along with a budget narrative to explain each item. Indicate if there are other funding partners. Identify all sources of revenue.

- **Evaluation** Provide an evaluation that is both quantitative (e.g., how many, how much) and qualitative (e.g., highlights of the project, suggestions for improvement). Outline how you intend to evaluate the project's success.

- **Conclusion** Write a forceful summary of the proposal's main features, and tell the funder how they will be acknowledged. Conclude on a positive note that builds confidence in your ability to complete this project.

- **Appendices** Include any information that will further strengthen your case, such as letters of support. This is also a good place to include any technical details or audited financial statements.

Strong proposals are innovative, offer new insights or benefits, and are inclusive and collaborative. They have the potential to carry on after the grant monies have run out.

Proposal writing is like baking a beautiful cake and entering it in a baking contest. First ask yourself if you have the skills and talent to enter. Then, if you decide you do, find out as much as you can about the judges and their criteria. After you have gathered all the available information, dedicate yourself to the details—from selecting the ingredients to icing the cake with a judicious final flourish. Finally, ask a couple of professionals to sample a slice and provide feedback before you send your cake out to win the award.

— Anecdotal Evidence —

In my role as executive director of a foundation that provided grants twice a year, I screened requests for funding before forwarding them to the board members, who decided which projects to fund. I noticed that at least 30 percent of the hopefuls didn't follow our clearly written requirements. For example, we stipulated: "Send one copy of each of the last two years of annual reports." Eager to impress, some people sent more copies of more years. Their attempts to impress backfired. They had failed to visualize the board: a group of busy executives volunteering on a Sunday afternoon to review these proposals. These executives wanted to read what they had asked for—nothing more, nothing less. Not following the requirements never worked in the overly zealous submitters' favour.

SUMMARIES

One of your job duties may be to occasionally summarize lengthy reports or news articles for management. Summaries can range in length from three sentences to several pages. Remember your target audience, and tailor the language to the audience. Managers are often juggling many projects and don't have time to read detailed information. It's essential to keep your summary lean and focused.

To write a summary, carry out these steps:

1. Skim the original document while deciding what parts are most relevant. You need the complete picture before you begin.

2. Note the most important points, using key words and phrases as headings. Eliminate the non-essential.

3. Organize these main points into paragraphs with one topic each, using your own words. Quote the author only when he expresses a point better than you could or his language is particularly compelling.

4. Write the summary: Start by clearly identifying what you are summarizing, and provide any necessary background information. Follow with the main points. Conclude with a final statement that reflects the significance of the original piece. Use visuals if they make the summary easier to skim.

5. Edit your version, removing all unnecessary words and digressions.

6. Check your draft against the original to confirm that the essential message is still intact.

7. Do one more revision of your draft, including the addition of any necessary transitions. Then carry out a copyedit (accuracy, correctness, consistency, and completeness).

8. Provide any necessary citations. If summarizing another person's work, cite the source below the summary, and place any directly quoted statements within quotation marks.

The following example illustrates a 434-word article quickly turned into a 143-word summary using these steps.

Original Article: New Life for Old Waste

Question: What does a Siberian tiger have in common with the annual paper consumption of an average Albertan? Answer: They're about the same weight—335 kilograms. If you've ever thought about what happens to your "paper weight" after you've recycled all that paper, you'll be pleased to know your recycled tax bill could end up as part of your neighbour's new roof. Now there's a new kind of tax shelter!

Through a partnership with EMCO Limited Building Products, one of Canada's best-known names in the roofing industry and one of the City of Edmonton's oldest customers, one person's paper discard becomes another person's roofing shingle. Since 1955, EMCO has been taking Edmonton's mixed paper waste and transforming it into roofing felt. "Long before most people thought much about recycling, EMCO was busy buying up waste paper from the City," recalls Morley Currey, EMCO's Paper Mill Fibres and Depot Manager.

EMCO is one of the largest recyclers of waste paper in the province. In Edmonton alone, it accepts 30,000 tonnes per year. Not only does this save on landfill space, it also provides much-needed revenues to municipalities. At the EMCO plant, where 170 employees work around the clock 24 hours a day, seven days a week, the mixed waste paper comes in from the City and is mixed with waste wood chips from local sawmills at a ratio of three-quarters paper to one-quarter wood fibre. Final product: a roofing felt that is the first step in a process that eventually results in a roofing shingle.

These shingles last anywhere from 20 to 30 years, greatly extending the lifespan of that initial piece of paper. Waste paper and waste wood chips are transformed into millions of roofing shingles that are sold throughout Western Canada. "The EMCO plant in Edmonton generates 13 million dollars of export sales annually for

Alberta," says Currey. It just goes to show that recycling is not only good for the environment, it's also good for the local economy.

The mixed paper waste that EMCO buys from the City represents close to one-third of what the City collects (by weight). So, next time you're feeling overwhelmed by your paper weight, remember that a new life form awaits your recycled paper. Considering that approximately four billion trees are harvested each year to satisfy the demand for paper, it's critical that we make every effort to get as much value out of paper as we can. Worldwide, our consumption of paper has grown six-fold since 1950, so it's heartening to know that opportunities exist right here at home to prolong the life cycle of paper.

A 143-word summary

The City of Edmonton has a partnership with EMCO to make good use of mixed paper waste. EMCO—one of the largest waste recyclers in the province—has been buying Edmonton's mixed paper waste since 1955 and mixing it with waste wood chips to create roofing felt, which is transformed into a roofing shingle.

These shingles last from 20 to 30 years, extending the lifespan of paper. This is a good thing: four billion trees are harvested worldwide each year for paper, and the annual paper consumption in Alberta is about 335 kilograms per person.

The mixed paper waste that EMCO buys from the City represents about one-third of what the City collects (by weight). This partnership is also a boon for the local economy because EMCO sells these shingles throughout Western Canada, generating 13 million dollars of export sales annually for Alberta.

Source: Written by Margaret Chandler and reprinted with permission from the City of Edmonton, Waste Services Branch. First published in September 2000. The information contained in this article may be outdated.

MINUTES

Minutes are the written record of the meeting for the participants and a source of information for people unable to attend. The amount of detail recorded will depend on the type of meeting and the organization; minutes can range from informal and minimalist to formal and detailed.

Generally, meeting minutes include these items:

- date, time, and location of the meeting
- names of the meeting participants and those unable to attend
- acceptance or amendments to previous meeting minutes
- decisions made about each agenda item, including the following:
  - actions taken or agreed to be taken
  - next steps
  - voting outcomes (e.g., who made a motion; who seconded the motion; and how the motion was approved)
  - items that were tabled
  - new business
- date and time of next meeting

Before the meeting, do as much as possible to ease the task of taking the minutes. Make sure to do the following:

- Create a template based on the agenda to make it easy to take notes under each item as the meeting progresses. Leave space in your hard copy or electronic copy of the template so that you can fill in the details.
- Include some of the information in the meeting agenda, such as the date and time, the chair's name, and the attendees (which can be modified depending on any absentees).

You will be busy during the meeting. Keep the following suggestions in mind:

- You don't need to capture everything verbatim. Focus on recording the decisions, assignments, and next steps. Record action items and decisions directly in your template as they happen.

- When someone makes a motion, write down the exact wording of the motion, who made it, and the final results of the vote. When someone delivers a report, write down who prepared the report, the name of the report, a short summary, and the action taken.

- Don't use people's names except for motions or seconds.

- Ask for clarification, if necessary. You are the minute taker, and you need to understand any decision or next steps.

- If you take regular minutes at a meeting, develop a shorthand that you can use again. For example, you might use abbreviations of common business words such as *P* for *product* or *M* for *management*. Develop a legend for the shorthand you use so that you don't forget what your shorthand code was when you finalize your minutes.

After the meeting concludes, you should wrestle your minutes into final form as soon as possible. It's easy to forget the context of what was said if you don't complete them promptly. Here are some more suggestions:

- Avoid observations and be objective.

- Focus on action items and not the discussion. Your role as the minute taker is to describe decisions made and record actions to be taken, by whom and when.

- Think of future readers as you write your minutes, not just the people who attended the meeting. Will your minutes make sense to someone three years from now? Would they stand up to scrutiny in court?

A strong and complete agenda will help ensure that the minutes are easy to write. Many meetings fail—along with their minutes—because of poorly thought-out and poorly structured agendas. When writing an agenda, consider your priorities, the logical flow of the meeting, and the overall timing. All good agendas contain the following:

- date, time, and location

- attendees

- any guidelines for pre-meeting preparation (e.g., a reading list, items to prepare beforehand, items to bring)

- person responsible for each agenda item

- approximate time per item. This is an important—and often overlooked—item. It also helps participants gauge expectations.

- wrap-up and action items

EXERCISES

Try this.

1. What templates does your organization have for internal documents, such as minutes, memos, or informal reports? Do these templates cover most of the writing scenarios? If your organization doesn't have templates, could you suggest implementing some guidelines and templates to standardize these documents?

2. Take a critical look at a report or proposal that you have recently written. What were the biggest challenges you had when writing it? Looking at it now, what is most effective about the document? What would you improve?

3. Find a short report or article (about three to five pages). Write a summary, reducing the content by about 75 percent. Once you have done that, write one paragraph that encapsulates the original report or article.

4. Do you work on major writing projects as part of a team? If so, do you debrief the projects? How do you find ways to improve the experience for everyone and to create a better process for the next time?

CHAPTER SIX

Navigate the Online Universe: Websites and Social Media

In an online world, our online words are our emissaries; they tell the world who we are.

~ ANN HANDLEY

Many business writers contribute content to their organizations' websites and write blog posts, Facebook posts, or answers for FAQ pages. Much of this kind of writing is considered copywriting, that is, writing text for marketing purposes, rather than business writing. If you find yourself copywriting without a background in marketing or public relations, then familiarize yourself with the genre.

Many of the considerations that go into creating print content are just as valid here: purpose and audience, organization, strong and stylish writing, and correct grammar and punctuation. The virtual world doesn't demand radically different skills than those needed to produce print documents. But online writing does have specific challenges. In this chapter, we explore how these challenges play out in web writing and social media.

WEBSITES

At one time, only certain businesses had storefronts. Today, most businesses have storefronts: their websites. This visual presence needs to engage the potential visitor with lively words and images so that she will come in to check out the goods. The best website is a nuanced balance of pizzazz (the visuals) and pith (the words) that tell the organization's story. For the visuals, hire a great designer. For the words, read on.

Principles of web writing

First, think not so much about how people read but more about how people search. Think of your audience as scanners or browsers. They are not interested, for the most part, in deep reading; web browsers are generally more inclined to dive, scan, and surface. They could even be reluctant to scroll. And these browsers are not stationary. They are roaming from page to page, gathering nuggets of information here and there. And they might land on your website in the middle of a page and miss the preamble. So, throughout your site, provide connective elements. Consider ending each content page with a suggestion of something else to look at (e.g., another product, sales information, a call-to-action).

Second, as we become accustomed to reading on screen, the difference in reading speed and comprehension between print and online is narrowing. It still appears to hold true, however, that people don't make as much mental effort when reading on the screen as they make when reading on paper. As Ferris Jabr points out in an article "The Reading Brain in the Digital Age" in *Scientific American,* many of us approach digital reading with a mindset less conducive to learning and long-term retention.

Part of the problem is that digital media does not offer us the same navigational aids and tactile cues that physical documents do, thus making comprehension more challenging. Therefore, short and descriptive headings and other navigational aids are vitally important. While a headline as dynamic as *Berlin Wall Tumbles* has already been taken, you can still connect with your readers using powerful words.

Focus on clear headings, bold leads, and colour to draw attention. Help the reader navigate the tumultuous seas of web surfing without getting sea sick and abandoning your site. Standing by with a life jacket, and only a click away, is your competition.

Third, browsers are often not as committed as print readers. Their attention span is shorter—a reader might spend two minutes reading a printed page and a browser might spend only ten seconds on a web page. This means that lean writing is even more crucial.

Fourth, ask the same sorts of audience questions posed in Chapter 1, but also think about what features could draw visitors and how they might use these features. Consider your key messages and how best to express them in the virtual world. You can't simply take a brochure that you wrote for print and drop it into a website. The material needs to be reframed for its new home. Questions of structure should also be top of mind. Create outlines, think about how sections and subsections relate to each other, and draft a table of contents to help frame a coherent website.

Chunking information

Long before the arrival of the web, technical writers were applying the concept of chunking information. Chunking means to provide readers with short *chunks* of information to make reading fast and understanding easier. Chunking made an effortless transformation to the web because discrete chunks of information align nicely with web links. And concise chunks of information are suited to the computer screen, which provides a limited view of long documents.

Chunked content usually contains the following:

- short, clean sentences with one idea—two at the most—per sentence
- short paragraphs, even one-sentence paragraphs
- bulleted lists
- short subheadings to break up the information
- easily scanned text, including bolding of key phrases
- design elements to guide the eye or illustrate key points

One of the principles of chunking information is that a unit of information should contain no more than nine separate items of information because this is the limit of what humans can understand and retain at one time. This means that there should be no more than nine bullet points in a list. If you have more than nine, you need to classify the information into smaller, logically related groups and introduce subheadings.

SOCIAL MEDIA

The *Oxford Dictionaries Online* defines social media as "websites and applications that enable users to create and share content or to participate in social networking." Social media platforms that require written content include Twitter, Facebook, and blogs. The discussion below focuses on Twitter and blogs, but if you're writing for other platforms, apply the principles of clear, concise, and dynamic language (the focus of Part Four), and you won't go far wrong. Craft content relevant to your business and your audience, and keep it updated.

It's also helpful to look at how other users of social media use these platforms successfully. The search functions in Facebook,

Twitter, and many other platforms allow you to search for organizations similar to yours. Obviously, you need to sing your own tune, but it's always good to know what tunes are at the top of the charts in this ever-changing and ever-evolving environment.

Twitter

Tweeting is just like any form of two-way communication. Journalist Germany Kent reminds us to "tweet others the way we want to be tweeted." We write well to be well received. The great lesson that Twitter can teach writers is brevity. With 140 characters to convey your message, rambling is not an option.

The danger is that by shrinking and abbreviating language as dramatically as the Twitter universe demands, we are more prone to errors. Punctuation. Who cares? Correct verb tense. Really? Standard English. Get real!

Each of us has to decide if Twitter is simply the place for a casual, in-a-dash thought or if we should apply the standards of clarity and correctness. Does the agility of Twitter outweigh its disadvantages? Is style lost when substance rules? And doesn't the virtue of the confined space create its own wit and verve? There's even been talk of "Twitterature." Let's face it. Oscar Wilde, master of the epigrams, would have loved Twitter. But would he have surrendered to writing *u* for *you* and abandoned proper punctuation and capitals? Perhaps he would have. As he once wrote, "Only the great masters of style ever succeed in being obscure."

If you tweet for business, it should be part of an overall strategy rather than just random tweets hurled out into the ether. Are you promoting a service? Establishing your brand? Sharing company tidbits? And what will interest your readers and build your community?

Your words should be conversational and snappy. Questions work well: e.g., *Why do so many people resist writing from an outline?* Then you can direct your readers to your blog. Lists are also effective: e.g., *Nine superb ways to write headlines*; *Four super editing tools.* These examples would continue with a linked URL, perhaps condensed through http:tinyurl.com or https:bitly.com.

Blogs

Ann Handley, author of *Everybody Writes*, encourages us to see publishing as a privilege. That's wonderful advice. Just because we can all publish a blog doesn't mean we should flout long-standing conventions that exist for good reasons. So respect other people's copyright (words and images); deliver on time (e.g., if you promise to write a blog post every two weeks, don't write one randomly when the mood strikes); have something meaningful to say; and finally, delight the rest of us by making the language shapely and lucid.

One issue that every blogger has to grapple with is word count. If your blog post is 200 words, you may get lots of comments, but it won't rank well on search engines; if it's 2,000 words, it will rank well, but it might not get read. The standard blogging length recommended by many "expert" bloggers is between 300 and 600 words.

Have fun writing a blog post. Be creative with your title, write a captivating lead, find an appropriate image, and conclude with a call-to-action. You may also want to consider optimizing your post for search engine optimization (SEO).

The following is a sample blog post about some words that are no longer useful.

Sample Blog Post: Words Are Not Forever

Words. Never mind how much you love them. Don't hang onto them too tightly. The friendship might not last.

Although we already have more than one million words to play with, our appetite for new ones is insatiable. The *Oxford Dictionary* editors write that "on average, we add approximately 1,000 new entries to *Oxford Dictionaries Online* every year." Words added recently to *The Merriam-Webster Dictionary* include *conlang*, *prosopagnosia*, and *humblebrag*. And the dictionaries only add those they deem fit. According to The Global Language Monitor, we actually create over 5,000 new words a year.

But we lose words too. They linger in the dictionary like an old friend you haven't seen in a very long time. And as much as I applaud all the new friends at the party, I'm sad to see many old friends lost to us. Here are a few words I once loved that I've stopped using.

Penultimate A smart and useful word—and much cleaner on the page than *second-to-last*. Unfortunately, random testing in the classroom indicates that only about 10 percent of working professionals know the meaning of this word. The word *penultimo* is common in Spanish, but even Spanish speakers are surprised to hear it used in English. Unfortunately, people try to guess the meaning of the word and usually arrive at *better than ultimate*. For years, I would arrive at a next-to-last class and greet everyone with this: "Hello, this is our penultimate class." Then I discovered that people thought I was bragging about how wonderful the class was!

Sustainable What happens to a word when it means everything and *ergo* nothing? The UN definition suggested in 1987 was "to meet the needs of the present without compromising the ability of future generations to meet their own needs." But the word has proven too elastic—and now the band has snapped. To some, *sustainable* refers to specific ecological processes; to others, an organization's values; to a chief financial officer (CFO), it could mean fiscal responsibility. I discovered this at an executive board meeting at a college. I had taken on the role of chair of the college's green team and was excited to hear the CFO use *sustainable* so much. *She's really engaged in the movement,* I thought. Unfortunately, she and I had two very different things in mind. My suggestion is to ditch the word entirely or to define what you mean by the word and then be consistent with that usage.

Biweekly, bimonthly, and biyearly These words also mean different things to different people! The publishing industry generally uses *bimonthly* to mean every two months, but a search in any dictionary will tell you that it also means *twice a month*. And the same double meaning applies to *biweekly* and *biyearly*. The only word that you can confidently use to mean twice a year is *semi-annually*. *Biweekly, bimonthly,* and *biyearly* must be scrapped.

What old faithfuls have you stopped using and why? Let us know in the comments. And if you enjoyed this post, I'd be grateful if you'd share it on Twitter, LinkedIn, or Facebook.

EXERCISES

A. This list is disorganized and has too many bullets. Rewrite it by chunking the information into smaller lists with appropriate headings.

Staff Party To-Do List

- Check with the assistant to the president to confirm availability

- Finalize the date

- Secure a good venue that will seat 250 people for dinner

- Liaise with the venue on the logistical details

- Meet once a week with the event committee to discuss entertainment

- Update the event financials from Q1 to see how much money is available

- Contact the finance manager to discuss potential extra funds

- Send staff a "hold the date" email three months before the party

- Meet with the event committee to determine if this party is a free or ticketed event

- Send a formal invite to staff four weeks before the party

- Ask Helen to manage the RSVPs

- Ask Murray to confirm the president has a speech for the event

B. Try this.

Select three to five of your favourite blog posts. Evaluate the titles. Were they dynamic and engaging? Did they set the right expectations? How about the imagery? Did it create an appropriate emotional tone? Did it support the content? Finally, was the content informative and useful? Was it the right length for the subject matter? Was it free of any distracting errors? Would you make any changes?

What can you learn from this exercise and apply to your own writing? Even if you don't write blog posts, you can learn a lot through evaluating the good, the bad, and the ugly.

CHAPTER SEVEN

Customize a Winning Career Package

*The most important tool you have
on a resumé is language.*

~ Jay Samit

An important piece of any job search strategy is creating a well-written and carefully crafted package of materials that includes your cover letter, resumé, and online profile. These pieces, each with its unique purpose, need to demonstrate what position you are looking for and why you are the best candidate for the position. You need to be consistent across the board: your resumé should match your online profile and your cover letter. Once you have developed this package, you can tailor it to a specific job and organization. This package could also include a portfolio of work samples to strengthen your case further.

COVER LETTERS

A cover letter could well be the most important sales letter you ever write. Although it's such an important piece of writing, it's amazing how many writers still do not dedicate the time—or find the help they need—to write a good one. Perhaps they believe that cover letters are passé and that no one reads them. This mindset can be a fatal mistake.

Your cover letter is the first impression you will make. That first impression determines whether you will have the chance to make several more—during an interview. Like any serious piece of writing, the cover letter demands that you devote the necessary time. Before even beginning to write a cover letter, do two things: first, research both the organization and the position, and second, make a list of your qualities that best align with the position. Here are some suggestions for composing a stellar cover letter:

- Use formal language, but try not to sound too proper. Perch on the top rung of your language ladder, but perch with elegance not pomp.

- Use descriptive words, and engage the reader by using enthusiastic language without getting carried away.

- Keep the letter to one page. Don't summarize what's on your resumé.

- Avoid formulaic openings and closings and long, complex sentences.

- Do a careful copyedit, as well as a meticulous proofread (see Chapter 15 for more information).

- Check for repetition of words and phrases: e.g., don't use the adjective *excellent* three times.

- Have a professional email address. An email address such as partyprincess33@hotmail.com will probably not convey the right impression.

Sample Cover Letter

Salutation: Try to find the person's name. If you can't find the name, use a general salutation, such as *Dear Hiring Manager* or *To Whom It May Concern.*

Introductory paragraph: Write a lead sentence that will capture the reader's attention and announce your qualifications. State your reason for applying for the position and describe your background as it relates to the job. Tailor this part of the letter to explain why you want the job.

Paragraph 2: Ask yourself what you would bring to the job. What makes you the best fit? Don't simply list your accomplishments.

Paragraph 3: Close by thanking the potential employer for his or her time and consideration. Repeat your interest in the position, and state that you look forward to hearing from the organization.

Erik Littleton
123 456 Street
Saskatoon, Saskatchewan S7V 6K3

January 10, 2018

Ms. Anandi Kapoor
Bubjo Inc.
789 123 Street
Saskatoon, Saskatchewan S7H 3W1

Dear Ms. Kapoor:

RE: Posting No. 629

As an architect with more than 15 years' experience in commercial and mixed-use building projects, I am excited about the possibility of working for a reputable industry leader. I am a dynamic and highly competent professional who possesses the design flair and project management capabilities to plan, coordinate, and engage in all phases of an architectural project. In particular, I have a passion for environmental design and construction.

For the past five years, I have been employed by Marzipan Construction and have managed projects from the initial design stages through to completion. My resumé demonstrates my strong technical background and my commitment to green building practices. Green construction is rapidly outpacing conventional construction, and I know that your organization wants to be at the forefront of this transformation. I am confident that I could make a significant contribution to that endeavour.

I appreciate your consideration of my application and look forward to discussing this opportunity with you further. I am available for an interview at your convenience and can be reached by phone at 123-456-7890 or by email at eagerarchitect@hireme.com.

Yours sincerely,

Erik Littleton

> ## — Anecdotal Evidence —
>
> I was talking to an American client, an accomplished professional who runs a charity in Berlin. She wanted to hire a U.S.-based communications professional to handle the public relations work stateside. About one-third of the applicants hit the trash pile immediately. Their letters either focused too much on themselves and not the charity, or their letters were poorly worded and had typos and incorrect grammar.
>
> One applicant with a graduate degree from an Ivy League university was upset he wasn't shortlisted for the position and wanted to know why. She agreed to talk to him, and in the call, she told him, "Your cover letter was your one chance to show me how well you express yourself. I could see you had very good qualifications—on paper, but not in practice. Your writing was awkward, and there were several mistakes. I didn't have the confidence you could do the job. You need to improve your writing skills because they're going to hold you back, which is a shame given your credentials. And have someone proofread your letter and resumé."

RESUMÉS

Along with a cover letter, your resumé is your main tool in a job search. Unless you have a lot of experience, you should limit your resumé to one or two pages. Once again, think of organization, ease of reading, and design.

Because there is more than one way to organize your resumé, you should experiment with finding a structure that best highlights your strengths and fits your goals and the requirements of the position. Three common formats are as follows:

- reverse-chronological: lists your work experience, job by job, starting with the most recent

- functional: emphasizes your skills, accomplishments, and responsibilities rather than positions held

- functional/chronological: begins with a functional format and concludes with a brief outline of your work history

Before you begin to write and design your resumé, review as many sample resumés as possible to help you determine what best suits your career aspirations and employment history.

Keep the following suggestions in mind when writing and proof-reading your resumé:

- Ask yourself what information about you would be most important to this employer. Do you know why the employer has posted this job? If you knew, for example, that the position was a maternity leave and a short-term position interested you, you could mention that in your cover letter. And what specific skills do you have that could help the organization the most?

- Consider writing a job objective to frame the beginning of the resumé and help the reader quickly understand who you are and what your career objective is. If you include this objective, use a heading such as *Career Profile* or *Employment Objective*, and tailor the objective to each specific position you apply for.

- Use action verbs: e.g., *supervised* rather than *as the supervisor*; avoid generic verbs such as *led* and *managed*; better choices are *aligned, mentored*, and *motivated*. Avoid phrases such as *exceeded expectations, demonstrated ability to*, and *people person*.

- Avoid the use of the first-person pronoun *I* by using phrases rather than complete sentences: e.g., *promoted to manager* rather than *I was promoted to manager*.

- Be clear and specific about your achievements. Show through examples how you saved time or resources, made money, or created opportunity.

Not this: *Recruited and managed volunteers for a large festival.*

But this: *Organized a recruitment drive and recruited, trained, and supervised 125 volunteers for a three-day visual arts festival with more than 2,000 attendees and 25 workshops.*

Not this: *Demonstrated a track record in sales.*

But this: *Surpassed sales quota by 15 percent for three years.*

- Use the same keywords that appeared in the job description. Even small companies are using digital databases to search for candidates, so the HR department will run search queries based on keywords. If your resumé doesn't have the keywords, you might be immediately eliminated.

- Check for consistency. Be sure to use, for example, the same date formats, punctuation, spelling, and spacing throughout. All bulleted items in a list need to be grammatically consistent. The astute reader will notice inconsistencies.

- Proofread the resumé twice. And ideally, have someone else read it to check for errors.

Your resumé must look visually and functionally appealing. Here are some suggestions:

- Experiment with the design until you find a simple and attractive one. There are many templates available online, and some of them are free.

- Ensure that each section is balanced proportionally on the page.

- Separate each section with sufficient white space.

- Use no more than two fonts, and select fonts for different levels of information: e.g., a sans-serif font for headings and a serif font for text. See Chapter 3 for more information on design principles.

- Use bullets to emphasize individual items such as job responsibilities.

- Know when to keep it simple and when to use visuals and colours. For most resumés, a minimalist design is best.

Sample Resumé (reverse-chronological)

CLARA BUSCADORA

Home: 111-222-3333
cbuscadora@gmail.com
Mobile: 444-555-6666

CAREER PROFILE

Bilingual and accomplished administrative professional with more than 10 years of experience in the public and non-profit sectors in Uruguay and Canada. Strong written and verbal communication skills in Spanish and English. Supported multiple project managers in the IT industry, the construction industry, and the post-secondary sector. Proficient in Microsoft Project, Microsoft Excel, and Adobe InDesign. Seeking a position where I can combine my strong administrative background with my bilingual skills.

PROFESSIONAL EXPERIENCE

West Mountain College, Vancouver, British Columbia   **2014–present**

Program Coordinator, International Student Services

- Conduct market research and needs assessment

- Liaise with potential international summer students

- Advise current students on sensitive and confidential issues

- Work with third-party housing services to arrange housing

- Coordinate the social host program

- Assist with submission of grant applications

Marzipan Construction Inc., Winnipeg, Manitoba   **2011–2014**

Project Assistant, Public Works Projects

- Assisted the project manager in scheduling
- Prepared presentations for management using video editing tools
- Managed the SharePoint team site for projects
- Assigned tasks to team members using MS Project

Verdenu IT Inc., Montevideo, Uruguay   **2006–2010**

Administrative Assistant, Operations Department

- Prepared agendas and coordinated departmental meetings
- Performed data entry using MS Excel
- Researched vendors for equipment availability and pricing
- Assisted in project planning, budgeting, and vendor selection

EDUCATION

- Certificate in Business Communications
  East Prairie College, Winnipeg   **2013**
- BA Business Administration
  University of the Republic, Montevideo   **2005**

LINKEDIN PROFILES

Your LinkedIn profile is another component of your job search package. A strong LinkedIn profile allows you to paint a more comprehensive picture of yourself than you can in a resumé. And it helps you to build your own professional brand and expand your network, two important strategies in today's career market.

Here are some elements in your LinkedIn profile that will make you shine:

- a professional headshot
- a concise and dynamic headline. This 120-character hook is possibly the most important part of your profile. Make it about what you *do* rather than who you *are*.
- a well-written and comprehensive summary of your experience and education
- a healthy list of endorsements
- recommendations from clients, former supervisors, and peers
- participation in LinkedIn groups specific to your industry
- specific projects that you have worked on
- any blogs, videos, articles, and so on that you have written or created

LinkedIn also has some useful articles that will help you create a strong online profile. If you explore the LinkedIn Help section, you will find articles such as "Tips on perfecting your personal profile." For more information, visit www.linkedin.com/help. You can also search job listings in your industry to see what terms other people are using.

Keep a profile handy so that you can use it for different applications in your career search or for promotional purposes. Review your profile every few months to make sure it's still up to date. And like everything else in your career package, have someone from your industry review the content and proofread it for mistakes.

EXERCISES

Try this.

1. Write an advertisement for the job that you have or one that you would like to get. Write a cover letter that responds to this advertisement using the advice provided in this chapter. Have someone proofread it and provide feedback.

2. Write or revise your resumé using the advice provided in this chapter. Make sure it is no more than two pages long. Have someone, preferably familiar with your field, proofread it and provide feedback.

3. If you already have an online profile, could you improve it to better highlight your qualifications? If you don't have a profile, then write one that could be posted to LinkedIn. Also provide a 120-character headline for your profile.

PART THREE

Grammar, Punctuation, and Mechanics

There is a satisfactory boniness about grammar which the flesh of sheer vocabulary requires before it can become a vertebrate and walk the earth.

~ ANTHONY BURGESS

In conversation, you can use timing, a look, inflection, pauses. But on the page, all you have are commas, dashes, the number of syllables in the word. When I write, I read everything out loud to get the right rhythm.

~ FRAN LEBOWITZ

My spelling is Wobbly. It's good spelling but it Wobbles, and the letters get in the wrong places.

~ A. A. MILNE

Does the very thought of grammar and punctuation make you think of flinty-faced English teachers and tedium times ten? Take heart. There is no need to memorize 7,632 rules. That's what the reference materials are for—to look up the rules and apply them. But to use these materials, we do have to learn or relearn some terms and concepts, and that's the focus of this part of the book.

Making sense of grammar and punctuation is, however, not as straightforward a process as it was even 30 years ago. The English language, never one to stand idle for long, has been busy over the last few decades establishing itself as a global language while adjusting to the Internet and social media. Not surprisingly, this evolutionary surge is transforming how we use language. Some of the conventions of Standard English established in the 19th and 20th centuries no longer have the authority they once enjoyed. We will continue to see the emergence of competing norms and the erosion of certain standards that once dominated the language.

We see these changes everywhere: in the abbreviated forms people use for texting; in the casual banter of many emails, even business ones, including the use of emoticons; in the preference for the sparing use of capitals; and in the repurposing of punctuation marks to convey a range of emotions. Fortunately, these innovations are mostly in usage (that is, the way language is actually used) rather than in rules. For business writing, the existing rules still hold. The mindful writer, however, keeps current with changes in language usage.

— CHAPTER EIGHT —

Appreciate Grammar: The Language of Language

People associate grammar with errors and correctness. But knowing about grammar also helps us understand what makes sentences and paragraphs clear and interesting and precise.

~ ASSEMBLY FOR THE TEACHING OF ENGLISH GRAMMAR

I t's a curiosity of language history that the words *grammar* and *glamour* came from the same source word. Over the centuries, *glamour* has transformed into meaning all things fun and sexy. For many people, *grammar* has transformed into the polar opposite.

What is grammar then, you ask? The Linguistic Society of America defines it as "the collection of principles defining how to put together a sentence." A grammar grump might tell you it's all about "good" grammar (usually the grump's) versus "bad" grammar (usually yours). Sometimes, this grump might be correct; sometimes, not. It all depends on the context and the writer's intention. And then there are the people who use the term loosely to define anything they don't like about writing standards, especially all the rules.

Here's a useful definition: grammar is the language of language. If you don't speak the language—for example, you don't know what a verb or a run-on sentence is—you won't be able to use the reference materials, fix your mistakes (and the mistakes of others), or significantly improve your writing.

Imagine Gwen attempting to read music without any knowledge of chords, sharps, or flats. She wouldn't progress very far because she would lack the right words, the right understanding of these words, and the right application. The same holds true for grammar. It's impossible to have a decent discussion about any aspect of writing without a common vocabulary.

You'll find lots of detail about this vocabulary in this chapter, some of which is quite technical. Whether you read it from beginning to end or use it as reference material, the information will help you understand the underpinnings of the language and put that understanding to good use. Ultimately, grammatical misdemeanours reflect poorly on the writer and distract the reader.

Before turning to a review of common grammatical problems and some potential solutions, let's take a look first at the parts of speech and sentence structure.

PARTS OF SPEECH

Learning the vocabulary of grammar begins with a review of the parts of speech. The table on pages 133 and 134 outlines the traditional eight parts, along with some characteristics. This orthodox classification, which we inherited via Latin from the ancient Greek grammarians, is considered inadequate by many linguists. But, for better or worse, it's the model taught in schools and used in dictionaries and reference books. Therefore, it's the most useful model for most of us.

Before diving into the parts of speech, a couple of things need mentioning. Many words can belong to more than one part of speech: how the word functions in a sentence determines how it is categorized. For example, *after* can be an adjective, an adverb, a conjunction, or a preposition as the following examples illustrate:

- The *after-dinner* remarks were unsettling. (compound adjective)

- I left shortly *after*. (adverb)

- *After* he returned from living in Bruges, William Caxton set up the first printing press in England in 1476. (subordinating conjunction)

- I went to the gym *after* work. (preposition)

Furthermore, we distinguish between open and closed classes, a fancy way of specifying whether we can add new words to a category. The open classes allow new members: these are the nouns, verbs, adjectives, adverbs, and interjections. The closed classes rarely allow new members: these are the conjunctions, prepositions, and pronouns. A visit to the always amusing website http://www.wordspy.com shows us that we can add the adjective *fappy*, meaning "overweight and happy with one's life," to our lexicon. But good luck adding *buzat* as a new preposition to mean a vigorous version of "through," as in *The ball went* buzat *the window*.

Language reflects culture, and these open and closed classes have cultural implications—as classes always do! Because pronouns are a closed class, it's difficult to introduce a new gender-neutral, singular, third-person pronoun to refer to someone whose gender is unknown or who chooses not to identify as male or female. At our disposal, we have *he*, *she*, and *it*. The pronoun *he* once served as a stand-in for everyone, but it's now regarded as sexist to use *he* in this way. The closed-class business isn't the only reason it's challenging to introduce a new pronoun, such as *hesh* (a blend of *he* and *she*) or *ze*, but it's definitely part of the problem.

The Eight Parts of Speech

PART	FUNCTION	CHARACTERISTICS	EXAMPLES
NOUN	A noun defines a person, place, thing, or concept.	COMMON NOUNS	bean, beauty, bugs, garlic, giraffes, girls, lipstick, lobster, luck
		PROPER NOUNS	Advil, Dark Ages, Dr. Lin, Earth Day, Judi, Peace River, Twitter
		COLLECTIVE NOUNS	committee, family, flock, group, staff, team
PRONOUN	A pronoun replaces a noun.	CASE subjective	I, you, he, she, it, they
		objective	me, you, him, her, it, them
		possessive	mine, yours, his, its
		PERSON first, second, third	I, we, you, she, he, it, they
		NUMBER singular or plural	anyone, each, some, all
		GENDER masculine, feminine, neuter	he, she, it, they
VERB	A verb expresses an action, state of being, or condition. Sometimes the main verb is preceded by one or more helping verbs (e.g., *did* eat, *must* go, *can* extract, *will* help).	THREE KINDS transitive	hold, lay, pick, raise
		intransitive	lie, rise, sit
		linking	become, feel, is
		TWO VOICES active	eat, write
		passive	eaten, written
		THREE MOODS indicative	argue, cherish, sleep
		imperative	go, leave, sit, take
		subjunctive	be, were

PART	FUNCTION	CHARACTERISTICS	EXAMPLES
ADJECTIVE	An adjective describes, qualifies, or limits nouns or pronouns. The articles *the, a, an* are adjectives. Numbers are also considered adjectives.	**DEGREES OF COMPARISON** Positive Comparative Superlative Absolute (no comparison)	brilliant, ferocious, few, good, hopeless, needy, many, purple, wrong sweet, young sweeter, younger sweetest, youngest round, perfect, unique
ADVERB	An adverb describes, qualifies, or limits adjectives, adverbs, and verbs.	**DEGREES OF COMPARISON** Positive Comparative Superlative	often, sometimes, slowly, soon, perhaps, especially quickly more quickly most quickly
PREPOSITION	A preposition links a noun or pronoun to other words in a sentence.	Usually precedes a noun or pronoun to form a phrase	at, before, from, in, into, like, of, over, through, under, up
CONJUNCTION	A conjunction joins words, phrases, and clauses and indicates the relationship between the elements joined.	**COORDINATING** **CORRELATIVE** **SUBORDINATING** **CONJUNCTIVE ADVERB**	for, and, nor, but, or, yet, so either . . . or not only . . . but also although, because, if, until, unless, while besides, consequently, however, therefore, thus
INTERJECTION	An interjection is a short exclamation.		Jeepers. Ugh. Wow!

The noun

A noun is the name of a person, place, thing, or concept. Nouns are classified as follows:

- **Common** nouns refer generically to people, places, and things: *opera, president, miracle*. They are not capitalized.

- **Proper** nouns are names of people, specific places, and particular groups and events: *Ethan, Jamaica, Chinese New Year*. They are capitalized.

- **Collective** nouns stand for an entire group: *gang, herd, troupe*.

- **Concrete** nouns refer to nouns you can experience with your five senses; you can feel them, smell them, hear them, taste them, or see them: *cotton, incense, music, potatoes, sunset*.

- **Abstract** nouns refer to qualities and concepts that you cannot experience with your senses: *dignity, materialism, relaxation*.

The pronoun

A pronoun is a word used to replace a noun. Usually the pronoun replaces a specific noun, known as its antecedent. Here are some of the key characteristics of the pronoun:

- **Case** shows the relationship of the pronoun to other words in the sentence. The three cases are subjective (the pronoun is used as a subject), objective (the pronoun is used as an object of a verb or preposition), and possessive (the pronoun expresses ownership). The sentence *Joey loves Zoe* would be replaced with *He loves her* (the subjective pronoun *he* replaces *Joey*; the objective pronoun *her* replaces *Zoe*, the object of the verb *love*). The sentence *Go with Hafiz!* would be replaced with *Go with him!* (the objective pronoun *him* replaces *Hafiz*, the object of the preposition *with*).

The sentence *That is my book* would be replaced with *That is mine* (the possessive pronoun *mine* replaces *my book*).

- **Person** is specific to personal pronouns and indicates whether the pronoun refers to the speaker (first person—*I*, *we*), the person spoken to (second person—*you*), or the person or thing spoken about (third person—*he, she, it, they*).

- **Number** makes the pronoun either singular (*he*) or plural (*they*).

- **Gender** refers to whether the pronoun is masculine (*he*), feminine (*she*), or neuter (*it*).

Pronoun classes

There are eight classes of pronouns:

- **Personal** pronouns refer to specific persons or things. They change form according to person, number, and case.

Singular	Subjective	Objective	Possessive
First person	I	me	my, mine
Second person	you	you	your, yours
Third person	he, she, it	him, her, it	his, her/hers, its

Plural	Subjective	Objective	Possessive
First person	we	us	our, ours
Second person	you	you	your, yours
Third person	they	them	their, theirs

- **Relative** pronouns point back to another noun or pronoun and function as the subject or object of a dependent clause. Common relative pronouns are *who, whom, whose, which,* and *that. The ballerina **who** was in the movie was amazing.* (The relative pronoun *who* refers back to the ballerina.)

- **Reflexive** pronouns, also known as mirror pronouns, name a receiver of an action identical with the doer of the action. Singular reflexive pronouns are *myself, yourself, himself, herself,* and *itself,* and plural ones are *ourselves, yourselves,* and *themselves. Martin cut **himself**.*

- **Intensive** pronouns have the same form as reflexive pronouns and are used to emphasize a noun or another pronoun. *You might have seen aliens, but I **myself** have never seen them.*

- **Interrogative** pronouns are used to introduce questions: *which, who, whom, whose,* and *what. **Who** invented all these rules?*

- **Reciprocal** pronouns are used to express mutual action or relationship. The reciprocal pronouns are *each other* and *one another. Our two dogs love **each other**. The students cooperate with **one another**.*

- **Indefinite** pronouns are vague; they don't stand in for specific nouns. That's why getting the gender and number right can be tricky. The indefinite pronouns include *all, any, anybody, anything, both, each, either, enough, everybody, everything, few, less, many, more, much, neither, none, nothing, one, plenty, several, some,* and *someone. **Neither** of the files is mine. **All** of the files are mine.*

- **Demonstrative** pronouns point to and identify a noun or pronoun. The demonstrative pronouns are *this, that, these,* and *those. **This** is my new office.*

The verb

A verb is a word that expresses an action, a state of being, or a condition. A sentence always has a main verb and may also have one or more helping verbs. A few helping verbs, namely *have*, *do*, and *be*, can also be main verbs, but several can be helping verbs only: *can*, *could*, *may*, *might*, *must*, *ought*, *shall*, *should*, *will*, and *would*.

The verb is such an important part of speech that it's worth exploring some of its qualities. Here are a few of the key ones.

Three kinds: transitive, intransitive, or linking

A **transitive** verb has an object that answers *whom?* or *what? He is reading his email. American visionary Noah Webster championed the natural rules of English. The Vikings first invaded Britain in the late eighth century.* (The objects in these three sentences are *his email, the natural rules of English*, and *Britain*.)

An **intransitive** verb has no object. *The sun rises at 6:30 a.m. Sit here. Achak talked all the time.* The words *at 6:30 a.m., here*, and *all the time* are not objects because they do not answer *whom?* or *what?*

A **linking** verb requires a complement that reflects back on the subject. The complement is usually an adjective that describes the subject or a noun that could substitute for the subject. *The coffee smells divine. Rumi is a poet. The shortest "ology" is oology, the scientific study of eggs.* (The subject complements in these three sentences are the adjective *divine* and the nouns *poet* and *oology*.)

Sometimes, a verb can be transitive, intransitive, or linking, depending on the context. Transitive: *He felt the dog's dry skin. (Skin is* the object of the verb *felt*.) Intransitive: *I felt in my purse for my house keys*. (There is no object.) Linking: *I feel bad about missing your party.* (The adjective *bad* is more information about the subject *I*.)

Two voices: active or passive

The voice of the verb determines whether the subject (who or what the sentence is about) has performed the action (active voice) or is acted upon (passive voice). *In 1828, American lexicographer Noah Webster **published** the groundbreaking American Dictionary of the English Language.* (active) *In 1828, the groundbreaking American Dictionary of the English Language **was published** by American lexicographer Noah Webster.* (passive)

Only transitive verbs can be transformed into passive voice constructions. The passive voice formula is this: a noun or pronoun + a conjugation of *to be* + past participle + phrase that begins with *by*. (The past participle is a form of the verb that usually ends in *–ed*, e.g., *investigated*.) Example: *He was loved by many*. The *by* phrase can be omitted, in which case the performer of the action is not explicitly stated. Examples: *My car has been stolen. The plums were eaten.*

Do not mistake the passive voice for a passive, or inactive, style. In the sentence *The ball was kicked forcefully down the field by the soccer player*, there is an action—the ball was kicked. But the ball was acted upon; it was kicked by the soccer player who is at the end of the sentence. The sentence contains a conjugation of *to be* (*was*) and a past participle (*kicked*) and a phrase that begins with *by* (*by the soccer player*). Therefore, this sentence is in the passive voice, but the fact it's in the passive voice is not a comment on its style.

For more information on using the passive voice, see Chapter 12.

Three moods: indicative, imperative, or subjunctive

The verb mood is the form of the verb that indicates the manner in which a thought is expressed.

The **indicative mood** expresses facts, opinions, assertions, and questions. Most verbs are in the indicative mood. *What is your kitten's name? Shakespeare introduced about 1,600 new words into the English language. Did you know that the word* leg *is a Viking word?*

The **imperative mood** expresses a command. *Please make me a cup of tea. Please pick the cherries.*

The **subjunctive mood** expresses advice, suggestions, a wish in a clause beginning with *if* or *that*, or a request in a clause beginning with *that. If Webster were alive today, he'd be delighted with the vibrancy of modern English. I suggest that you be on time tomorrow. We asked that she speak more slowly.*

In the subjunctive mood, present-tense verbs do not change form to indicate the number and person of the subject: I *eat*; we *eat*; you *eat*; he, she, it *eat*; and they *eat*. In the subjunctive mood, *be* has only one past tense form, *were. I recommend that he read more carefully. If he were more honest, I would like him more.*

Three tenses: present, past, or future

The verb has three primary tenses: present, past, and future. Each verb has a progressive form, indicating ongoing action; a perfect form, indicating completed action; and a perfect progressive form, indicating ongoing action that will be completed at some definite time.

	Simple	Progressive (ongoing action)	Perfect (completed action)	Perfect Progressive (ongoing action to be completed at some definite time)
Present	write/s	am/is/are writing	have/has written	have/has been writing
Past	wrote	was/were writing	had written	had been writing
Future	will write	will be writing	will have written	will have been writing

Regular verbs (e.g., *talk*) form the past tense (*talked*) and past participle (*have talked*) by adding –*d*, or –*ed* to the present form, but the root (*talk*) doesn't change. Irregular verbs don't form the past tense and past participle by adding –*ed* or –*d*. Either the spelling changes (e.g., *begin, began, begun*), or nothing changes (e.g., *set, set, set*).

Verb tense consistency Unnecessary or inconsistent shifts in verb tense can create confusion: e.g., moving from present tense (*he examines*) to past tense (*he examined*). The general rule is to maintain one primary tense—typically the simple past or the simple present—and express changes in time by changing tenses relative to that primary tense. Here are some guidelines:

- Do not change the tense if the time frame for each action or condition remains the same. But shift tense if there is a change in the time frame: *I am* (simple present) *pleased with this book, which I wrote* (simple past) *last month*. And sometimes a series of events requires a mix of verb tenses: *He **mentioned*** (simple past) *that the move **had been going*** (past perfect progressive) *smoothly before the transit strike, but **is** now **proving*** (present progressive) *challenging.*

- Use the past tense to narrate past events, previous conditions, or completed processes: *In 1399, Henry IV **became** the first English-speaking monarch since the Norman invasion of 1066. Did you know that there **was** a word in Old English,* uhtceare, *that **meant** "to lie awake at dawn, worrying"?*

- Use the present tense to express anything happening at the present moment, facts, ongoing or habitual actions, or your ideas or the ideas of others: *It **is** important to master grammar if you **wish** to become a skilled writer.*

- Use the present tense to describe action in a book, movie, and so on: *In the book* The Glamour of Grammar, *Roy Peter Clark **encourages** us to "embrace grammar as powerful and purposeful."*

- Use the past perfect tense (*had delivered, had seen*) for an action already completed by the time of another past action. *By the time the parcel arrived, the CEO **had** already **left** town.* Do not use the past perfect for two past actions that happened at the same time. *The parcel **arrived** when she **was** in the boardroom.*

- Use the future tense to express actions that will occur in the future. There are several ways to express the tense, including the use of *will, shall, is going to,* and *are about to. I am going to respond to the offer next week.*

Verbals

The verbals may look like verbs, but they are not. Verbals are verb forms without the power of a verb, so they cannot serve as the verb of the sentence. Instead, they function as nouns, adjectives, or adverbs. They come in three flavours: gerunds (used as nouns), participles (used as adjectives), and infinitives (used as nouns, adjectives, or adverbs).

Gerunds usually end in *–ing* and always function as nouns, typically as a subject or object. *Singing helps me relax.* (*Singing* functions as a noun and is the subject.) *I enjoy* **singing***.* (Here, *singing* is an object.)

Participles usually end in *–ing* or *–ed* and always function as adjectives. They are either present participles (*talking*) or past participles (*talked*). *The* **giggling** *children ran out of the room. She received an award* **designed** *in the style of an Olympic medal. I was* **bored** *with the* **boring** *movie.*

Infinitives are usually introduced by *to* plus the base form of the verb. **To drive** *rapidly is a great thrill for her.* (*To drive* functions as a noun and is the subject.) *The best time* **to swim** *is early in the morning.* (*To swim* functions as an adjective modifying *time*.) *Agnes phoned the supervisor* **to discuss** *her complaint.* (*To discuss* functions as an adverb because it answers the question of *why* Agnes phoned the supervisor.)

The adjective

An adjective is a descriptive word, such as *financial*, *global*, and *romantic*. It describes or modifies nouns or pronouns.

Many adjectives can express degrees of modification. For example, you can be poor, or you can be poorer than your great-aunt (unfortunately). The adjective has three forms that indicate degrees.

The positive form is the base form of the adjective. The comparative form is used to compare one thing to another. *My computer is quieter than your computer.* The superlative form is used to compare one member of a category to all the others. *My computer is the quietest computer in the office.*

Positive	Comparative	Superlative
light	lighter	lightest
smart	smarter	smartest

Some adjectives (often those of three syllables or more) become too cumbersome if we add *–er* or *–est*, so we use *more* as the comparative and *most* as the superlative. Let your ear be the guide. *He is more handsome than his son. This is the most incredible story I've ever heard.*

Some adjectives are absolute: they don't have a comparative or superlative form. Someone or something is either *dead, essential, harmless, perfect, round, unique* or not. Advertisers abuse these adjectives all the time, but that's no excuse for us to indulge.

Adjectives that describe *how much* or *how many* are often used incorrectly. For things that can be counted, use *fewer* or *many*; for things that cannot be counted, use *less, a lot of,* and *much.* Example: *fewer dollars, less money; many friends, much joy.* Another easy way to remember this is to use *less* with singular nouns (e.g., *less candy*) and *fewer* with plural nouns (e.g., *fewer candies*).

Do not use adjectives to modify a verb or to modify another adjective. Not this: *He is a real keen bridge player.* But this: *He is a really keen bridge player.*

The adverb

An adverb is a descriptive word that can modify a verb (*drive carelessly*), an adjective (**often** *miserable*), another adverb (**too** *carelessly*), or an entire sentence (**sometimes** *he writes all night long*). An adverb often, but not always, ends in –*ly*. Think about function when deciding if a word is an adverb because adverbs often tell where, when, or how: *there, early, incessantly*. Remember that an adverb can never modify or describe a noun or pronoun. *She was a **little** rude.* (The adverb *little* modifies the adjective *rude*.) *I have a **little** dog.* (The adjective *little* modifies the noun *dog*.) *The apple smells **sweet**.* (adjective) *The girl sings **sweetly**.* (adverb)

Adverbs have the same forms as adjectives when used to make comparisons.

Positive	Comparative	Superlative
late	later	latest
abruptly	more abruptly	most abruptly

When using adverbs, place the adverb as closely as possible to the word being modified. One particularly pesky word is *only*, which can be an adverb, an adjective, or a conjunction. According to *The Chicago Manual of Style*, *only* is probably the most poorly placed word in a sentence. Make sure to place it right before the word or phrase you want to emphasize. Consider the difference between the following: *I drink coffee only in the morning* (meaning I don't drink it in the afternoon) versus *I only drink coffee in the morning* (meaning I don't drink anything else in the morning).

The preposition

A preposition is a word placed before a noun or pronoun to form a phrase modifying another word in the sentence. The word *preposition* means literally "a setting before." English has several dozen prepositions; the most common ones are *at, by, for, from, in, of, on, to,* and *with*. Some prepositions are more than one word long: *apart from, as well as, in addition to, next to,* and *with regard to*. And sometimes they combine with verbs and adverbs in interesting ways to create multi-word verbs. See Chapter 11 for more information on multi-word verbs.

Prepositions can be especially challenging for non-native speakers of English because the differences can be subtle and idiomatic.

The conjunction

A conjunction is a word that connects words, phrases, or clauses; it indicates the relationship between the elements joined.

Coordinating conjunctions link grammatically equal elements. The coordinating conjunctions are easy to remember as the FAN BOYS: *for, and, nor, but, or, yet, so. All the files **and** the memory sticks are missing. We have enough money **but** not enough time. Wu doesn't like to waste paper, **so** he always prints on both sides of the page.*

Correlative conjunctions are coordinating conjunctions that come in pairs: *both . . . and, either . . . or, neither . . . nor, not only . . . but also, whether . . . or*. The elements they connect must be grammatically equal. *Stella **not only** speaks Arabic **but also** speaks Russian. Stella speaks **not only** Arabic **but also** Russian.*

Subordinating conjunctions link unequal or unbalanced sentence parts and introduce dependent clauses. Common subordinating conjunctions include *after, although, because, before, if, in order that, since, than, though, until, when, where,* and *while. Don't discuss it with Sophia **until** you've discussed it with your boss. **After** he's given his permission, you can talk to her.*

Conjunctive adverbs are a subset of conjunctions. They connect independent clauses and indicate the relationship between the clauses. They can be used with a semicolon to join two independent clauses, or they can be used alone with an independent clause. Common conjunctive adverbs include *finally, however, nevertheless, then, therefore,* and *thus. I must finish this presentation by 3 p.m.; **therefore,** I'm not going to join you for lunch today. She went back to university to study dentistry. **However,** she found that she missed teaching.*

The interjection

An interjection expresses surprise or emotion and is often used on its own or at the start of a sentence. It has no grammatical function in a sentence, but it does communicate emotion and tone. Common interjections include *Hey! Oh. Ow!*

SENTENCE PARTS AND TYPES

With this understanding of how words are categorized into parts of speech, let's explore how words relate to each other to form sentences. Consider the parts of speech as a community, with each member working (hopefully harmoniously!), according to its capacity, with other members to create sentences.

Every complete sentence contains two elements: a **subject** and a **predicate.** Let's begin by looking at the subject.

The subject

The subject names who or what the sentence is about. The core of the subject is always a noun or a pronoun; the entire subject can consist of only the core word (*peonies bloom in May*) or a group of words built around this core (*the 35-page report* landed on my desk this morning). Two more examples: *In January, the abandoned house* burned to the ground. *Felipe* gave Jude an ultimatum. To find the subject, first ask *who?* or *what?* Then insert the verb and finish the question. What burned to the ground? *The abandoned house.* Who gave Jude an ultimatum? *Felipe.*

A **compound subject** is two or more subjects that are joined by a conjunction, such as *and* or *or*, and that have the same predicate (e.g., *the goat and the donkey*; *Uma nor Lola*).

A **simple subject** is the *who* or *what* without any additional description. The complete subject is the *who* or *what* including all the modifiers. In the sentence *The old computers in the warehouse were of little value*, the simple subject is *computers*, and the complete subject is *the old computers in the warehouse.*

The predicate

The predicate consists of the verb and any objects, complements, and adverbial modifiers. The predicate might be a simple verb indicating some action (e.g., *I laughed*), but it could have other functions, such as modifying the subject (e.g., *he is my friend*).

There are two kinds of **objects**. The most common is the **direct object**—a word or word group that follows a transitive verb and names the receiver of the action. *Colin sold his 1962 Cadillac. Natalie loves her three children.* In other words, a direct object answers *whom?* or *what?* What did Colin sell? *His 1962 Cadillac.* Whom does Natalie love? *Her three children.*

The **indirect object** comes before a direct object and indicates *to whom* or *for whom* the action is done. *When Sebastian sobs, his mother gives **him** chocolate. I made **Annette** a wonderful dessert.*

Like the subject of the sentence, an object is always built around a core word—a noun or a pronoun. The object may consist of only the core (*him* and *Annette*), or it may be a word group built around the core (*his 1962 **Cadillac*** and *her three **children***).

There are two kinds of **complements**. The most common is the **subject complement**—a word or word group that follows a linking verb and completes the meaning of the subject by describing it or renaming it. *His email was **clear and direct**. It's **a beautiful day**. I am **an accountant**. One of the most unique features of spoken Canadian English is **the expression "eh."*** The less common **object complement** is a word or word group that describes or defines the object. *Sasha considers this restaurant **the best in the city**.*

Adverbial modifiers may also be added to the predicate. *Arjun worked **hard**. She ran **in circles**.*

Sentence patterns

Subjects and predicates combine in familiar patterns to create sentences. English sentences usually begin with the subject, followed by the verb, followed by any objects or complements. Most sentences follow one of the five patterns illustrated in the following table:

Sentence Patterns			
Subject	**Verb**		
It	rained.		
Subject	**Verb**	**Direct Object**	
Teddy	loves	the rain.	
Subject	**Verb**	**Indirect Object**	**Direct Object**
Teddy	gave	his wife	an umbrella.
Subject	**Verb**	**Direct Object**	**Object Complement**
The rain	drove	his wife	mad.
Subject	**Verb**	**Subject Complement**	
The rain	was	intense.	

Variations of these patterns—for example, in questions or commands or in passive voice constructions—are common.

Being able to recognize subjects and predicates helps writers fix sentence fragments and run-on sentences and avoid grammatical blunders such as subject–verb agreement problems and incorrect pronoun cases (discussed later in this chapter).

Phrases and clauses

Words combine to create word groups—phrases and clauses.

A **phrase** is a group of related words without a subject and a predicate. The two main kinds of phrases are prepositional and verbal.

■ **Prepositional phrases** begin with a preposition (e.g., *in, with, to*) and end with a noun or pronoun, which is the object of the preposition: *to Botswana, through the door, behind him, at the factory, on the Internet, by us, with mercy.* Prepositional phrases almost always function as adjectives or adverbs. *The boxes **in the storage room*** (functioning as an adjective) *are mine.* ***During the meeting*** (functioning as an adverb), *he paid attention.*

- **Verbal phrases** begin with a verbal—a verb form that functions as a noun, adjective, or adverb—and end with an object, complement, or modifier. ***Living without fear*** *is a good thing.* ***Listening carefully**, I could follow his instructions. We study grammar **to improve our writing**.*

A **clause** is a group of related words containing a subject and a predicate. There are two types of clauses: independent and dependent.

- An **independent clause** can stand alone as a complete sentence and expresses a complete thought. *I am studying editing. Owen was promoted. The proposal is due tomorrow. The three most significant differences between American English and British English are vocabulary, pronunciation, and spelling.*

- A **dependent clause** depends on an independent clause for its meaning and cannot stand alone as a sentence. There are three kinds of dependent clauses: adjective clause, adverb clause, and noun clause.

  - **Adjective clauses** modify nouns and pronouns and begin with the relative pronoun *who, whom, whose, which,* or *that. Tomatoes, **which are actually a fruit**, can be grown in Siberia.* The dependent clause *which are actually a fruit* is an adjective clause modifying the subject *tomatoes.* This clause is a non-essential clause—sometimes referred to as a non-restrictive clause—because it could be omitted from the sentence without changing the meaning. It's merely extra information about all tomatoes. That's why it's set off in commas.

  But consider this sentence: *Tomatoes that are grown in Siberia are some of the best early producing tomatoes in the world.* Like the clause *which are actually a fruit* above, the dependent clause *that are grown in Siberia* is also an adjective clause modifying the subject *tomatoes.* But now it's an essential clause—sometimes referred to as a restrictive clause. It cannot be omitted from the sentence without changing the meaning. And it's not set off in commas. The writer is not referring to all tomatoes, just the ones grown in Siberia.

When deciding between *that* or *which*, ask yourself if you can drop the clause without losing the meaning of the sentence. If you can, then use *which*, and put the *which* clause inside commas. If you cannot, then use *that* and no commas. *Declan's car, which is a 2010 Ford, needs an oil change.* The clause *which is a 2010 Ford* is extra information and not essential to the meaning of the sentence. *Cars that are fuel-efficient appeal to many people.* The clause *that are fuel-efficient* is essential to the meaning of the sentence.

- **Adverb clauses** give information about the sentence's main verb: When? Where? Why? Under what conditions? *Wilma moved to Drumheller **because she is intrigued by dinosaurs**.* Why did Wilma move to Drumheller? *The full moon rose **as the sun set**.* When did the full moon rise?

- **Noun clauses** are dependent clauses that serve as nouns and often as sentence subjects. Noun clauses usually begin with the subordinating conjunction *that.* Other words that begin a noun clause include *how, what, when, where, whether, who,* and *why.* ***That he did such a thorough job** didn't surprise me at all.* The noun clause *that he did such a thorough job* is the subject of the sentence.

Grammatical sentence types

There are four types of grammatical sentences: simple, complex, compound, and compound-complex.

Simple	Complex	Compound	Compound-Complex
One independent (main) clause	At least one independent clause and at least one dependent clause	Two or more independent clauses joined with a coordinating conjunction	Two or more independent clauses and at least one dependent clause
Example	**Example**	**Example**	**Example**
Australians like to shorten words.	When words get shortened in Australian English, they almost always end with a vowel.	These shortened words are used to express informality, and they often express a verbal playfulness.	I really like *arvo* for *afternoon*, but Ian likes *Tassie* for *Tasmania* because he used to live there.
Look for a clause that expresses a complete thought. This clause can vary in complexity and length.	Look for subordinating conjunctions, such as *after, because, unless,* or *when,* or relative pronouns, such as *which.*	Look for one of the coordinating conjunctions: *for, and, nor, but, or, yet,* and *so.*	Look for both subordinating and coordinating conjunctions.

Sentence fragments and run-on sentences

A **sentence fragment** is an incomplete sentence: *Left work at 3:30 p.m today. When she never phoned me.* The first example is a predicate with no subject. The second example begins with a subordinating conjunction, so it's a dependent clause without an independent clause to complete it. To fix a sentence fragment, rewrite the phrase or clause to include a subject and a verb or add the fragment to an independent clause. *I left work at 3:30 p.m. today. I was hurt when she never phoned me.*

Run-on sentences are independent clauses that have not been joined correctly, like bones without ligaments. There are two types of run-on sentences: fused sentences and comma splices.

- A **fused sentence** has no punctuation between the independent clauses. *I moved to Halifax in 2006 I lived in Cambodia for two years before then.*

- A **comma splice**, which is more common, is two independent clauses joined with a comma. *There are about 6,000 languages in the world, half the world's population speaks only 10 of them.* The most common type of comma splice is joining two independent clauses with a conjunctive adverb like *however* and using a comma instead of a semicolon. *I wanted to study Italian, however I never had the opportunity.*

There are several ways to correct a run-on sentence, such as this one: *Heather worked all weekend, she completed the audit.*

- Separate the two independent clauses with a period. *Heather worked all weekend. She completed the audit.*

- Use a comma followed by a coordinating conjunction. *Heather worked all weekend, and she completed the audit.*

- Separate the two independent clauses with a semicolon (only if the ideas are closely related). *Heather worked all weekend; she completed the audit.* You could also add a conjunctive adverb. *Heather worked all weekend; therefore, she completed the audit.*

- Make one clause dependent by adding a subordinating conjunction. *Heather worked all weekend because she wanted to complete the audit.*

- Transform one clause into a verbal phrase, and attach it to the independent clause. *Working all weekend, Heather completed the audit.*

GRAMMATICAL PROBLEMS AND SOLUTIONS

The good news is that the structure of the English language is simpler than many other Indo-European languages. Verbs, nouns, and adjectives in English, for example, do not change form depending on their sentence function. And unlike German speakers, we don't have to determine whether a chair is masculine, feminine, or neuter—for which we are thankful.

There are many reasons for English being less complex than some of its relatives. English has long been an accommodating language. For example, when the Vikings invaded and settled in England, the Old English speakers needed to communicate with the Old Norse speakers. As a result, many prefixes and suffixes that complicated English were simply dropped.

The bad news is that English can be maddeningly inconsistent, and although the grammar may appear simple at first glance, many entrenched problems still plague writers everywhere. Here are some of the key challenges that writers often struggle with.

Grammar Blunders

Sign at a dry cleaner

Anyone leaving garments here for more than 40 days will be disposed of. (Wow, that's a no-nonsense dry cleaner!)

Try this: *Garments left here for more than 40 days will be disposed of.*

Or you could change the passive voice to active:

We dispose of any garments left here for more than 40 days.

Instructions for wildlife viewers

Tigers please stay in your jeep. (What are the tigers doing in the jeep?)

Try this: *Caution! Tigers! Please stay in your jeep.*

First words in an email

Can you believe how fast time fly's? (The only time you would ever use *fly's* is if you were writing about something like the fly's lunch or the fly's wings. The apostrophe is running amok all over our words leading to disasters like this.)

Try this: *Can you believe how fast time flies?*

Final words in an email

I look forward to see you next week. (This mistake signals that English is probably not your first language.)

Try this: *I look forward to seeing you next week.*

Subject–verb agreement

The rule: In the present tense, verbs agree with their subjects in number (singular or plural) and in person (first, second, third). *The dog howls*, and *the dogs howl*. *The lake is beautiful*, and *the lakes are beautiful*. *The company has no emergency planning in place. Many companies have emergency planning in place.*

Subject–verb agreement can be problematic in the following situations:

Compound subjects

Use a plural verb when the subject is composed of two or more nouns or pronouns connected by *and*. *Oliver and I are friends* (compare with *Oliver is a friend of mine*). *Pippa and I love* dancing (compare with *Pippa loves dancing*).

Exception: When the parts of the subject create a single unit or when they refer to the same person or thing, the subject is singular not compound. *Three and three is six. Xavier's friend and mentor is amusing.*

Expressions such as *with, together with, including*, and *as well as* do not change the number of the subject. *The astronaut, as well as her husband, is coming to our party.* If you want to emphasize that both of them are equally important, then use *and* instead: *The astronaut and her husband are coming to our party.*

Subject–verb separation

Watch out for sentences where the subject is separated from the main verb by one or more long modifying phrases or clauses. Don't lose track of the core noun in the subject. *The **potential** for collective gains for the many affected minority interests **appears** to have been lost in the ongoing debate. The executive officers' **determination** to proceed with the layoffs in spite of the suggestions of their HR advisers **is** incomprehensible.*

Prepositional phrases following the subject usually do not affect agreement. Watch especially for prepositional phrases that begin with *of*: *The **weight** of the five filing cabinets **was** shocking. The **man** with the three umbrellas **is** the new manager.*

Reversed sentence order

Make the verb agree with the subject even if the subject follows the verb, such as in sentences beginning with *here* or *there*. *Here **are two proposals** for Tara. There **was a variety** of reasons why our company did not win the bid. When **are James and his friends** coming?*

Subject complements

Make the verb agree with its subject, not the subject complement. *A **significant problem** in modern politics **is** the many people who don't bother to vote.* Because it's generally better if the subject and its complement agree in number, you could rewrite this as ***Voter apathy** **is** a significant problem in modern politics.*

Co-related subjects

For a compound subject containing *or* or *nor* (or *either . . . or*, or *neither . . . nor*), make the verb agree with the part of the subject closest to the verb. *A passport or **a birth certificate is** required. Either the program coordinators or **the manager was** at the conference. Neither the manager nor **the program coordinators were** at the conference.*

Collective nouns

Treat collective nouns as singular subjects unless the meaning is clearly plural. ***The class is** happy that no homework was assigned. **The class are** discussing the importance of good grammar.*

Plural nouns

Words such as *athletics, statistics, dollars, news,* and *measles* are usually singular unless they clearly have a plural meaning. ***Statistics is** a tedious subject. **The statistics** on cyberbullying **are** sobering.*

Twenty dollars is not a lot of money. The silver dollars designed by the Royal Canadian Mint are an excellent investment.

Some words that were once plural have become singular over time (e.g., *agenda* and *stamina*). The words *data* and *media* are technically plural, but are often treated as singular. *The data is stored on my computer. The media plays an important role in society.*

Indefinite pronouns

Indefinite pronouns refer to nonspecific persons or things. Treat indefinite pronouns that mean *one* as singular: *anybody, anyone, each, either, everybody, everyone, everything, neither, none, no one, someone, something. Each of the writers has to consult the company style guide. Everybody at the college needs to take a writing course. Each dog and cat was immunized.* An exception to this rule is when *each* follows a compound subject. *André and Darren each have their own laptops.*

Treat indefinite pronouns such as *few, many,* and *several* generally as plural. *Many of the employees are going to the party.*

But for some indefinite pronouns, such as *all, any,* and *some,* the choice depends on whether the indefinite pronoun refers to a singular noun or plural noun. *All of the report is finished. All of the reports are finished. Some of the chocolate was mine. Some of the chocolates were stolen.* This rule is contrary to the general rule that the verb agrees with the grammatical subject and not the object of the preposition.

None can be either singular or plural. Most authorities maintain that it is plural when it is closer in meaning to *not any* and singular only when it means *none of it. None of the scientists were at the conference. None of the water was drinkable.*

Relative pronouns

The relative pronouns (e.g., *who*, *which*, and *that*) take verbs that agree with their antecedents (the noun or pronoun that the pronoun refers to). *Read a **book that makes** you happy. Read **books that make** you happy.* *I was one of the **employees who were** transferred to Denver.* (The antecedent is *employees*.) *I was the only **one** of the employees **who was** transferred to Denver.* (The antecedent is *one*.)

Fractions or units of measurement

When fractions or units of measurement are used with a singular noun, make the verb singular; when they are used with a plural noun, make the verb plural. ***Two-thirds of the cake has been devoured** by the children. **One-half of the students have been practising** for the exam.*

Gerund phrases, words mentioned as words, *the* number versus *a* number

Treat gerund phrases as singular (a gerund phrase is an *–ing* verbal that functions as a noun). ***Keeping many things in mind is** taxing for the brain.*

Words mentioned as words take a singular verb. ***"Alternative facts" is** a contemporary expression for lies.*

The phrase *the number* takes a singular verb; *a number* takes a plural verb. ***The number** of songbirds **is** declining. **A number of people are** coming to the workshop.*

Pronoun challenges

Many writers struggle to use pronouns correctly—for them, pronouns are the champion grammar grief givers. If it's any consolation, mastering the pronoun and all its complexities is relatively easy in English compared with some other languages. We have only three cases, whereas Czech, a Slavic language, has seven. Watch out, in particular, for the following indiscretions. In some of these examples, you will see that it's not always possible to use a pronoun.

Ambiguous reference

Make sure that the pronoun's antecedent (the noun or pronoun that the pronoun refers to) is clear.

Not this: *The adviser told the president, but **she** made no announcement.* (Who made no announcement? The adviser or the president?)

But this: *The adviser told the president, but **the president** made no announcement.*

Not this: *Najim gave me a watch for my graduation, but **it** wasn't that great.* (What wasn't great? The watch or the graduation?)

But this: *Najim gave me a watch for my graduation, but I didn't like **the watch** that much.*

Implied reference

Make sure the pronoun refers to a specific antecedent, not to a word that is implied but not explicitly stated.

Not this: *We phoned the police station and reported the road rage incident to **them**.*

But this: *We phoned the police station and reported the road rage incident to **the officers**.*

Possessive modifiers cannot serve as antecedents.

Not this: *In **Annie Dillard's book** The Writing Life, she explores the joys and travails of the writer's craft.*

But this: *In her book The Writing Life, **Annie Dillard** explores the joys and travails of the writer's craft.*

Indefinite reference

Do not use the pronoun *they* to refer to persons who have not been specifically mentioned.

Not this: *Some suggested ways to help new students are included with the orientation kit. For example,* **they** *suggest giving them a tour of the campus.*

But this: *Some suggested ways to help new students are included with the orientation kit. For example,* **the orientation team** *suggests giving them a tour of the campus.*

In the same vein, the pronoun *it* should not be used indefinitely in constructions such as *In the report,* **it** *says that . . .*

Not this: *In the journal article,* **it** *stated that Abraham Lincoln understood the power of brevity.*

But this: *The journal article stated that* **Abraham Lincoln** *understood the power of brevity.*

Broad reference

Ensure that the pronouns *this, that, it,* and *which* refer clearly to earlier word groups or ideas.

Not this: *Annie Taylor, a 63-year-old widow and non-swimmer, was the first person to go over the Niagara Falls in a barrel,* **which** *was amazing.* (What was amazing? Her age, her marital status, her inability to swim? All of these?)

But this: *Annie Taylor, a 63-year-old widow and non-swimmer, was the first person to go over the Niagara Falls in a barrel, an amazing feat for a non-swimmer.*

Pronoun and antecedent agreement

Make sure the pronoun agrees with its antecedent. This is straight-forward when the pronoun is replacing a gender-neutral antecedent.

Not this: *The **company** released **their** market research in February.* (The noun *company* is singular; the pronoun *their* is plural.)

But this: *The **company** released **its** market research in February.*

But when the antecedent is a human, it gets more complicated. In the sentence ***Everybody** has paid **their** fees*, the question inevitably arises: Is *their* correct?

A prescriptive grammarian, someone who believes there are long-standing rules that define how language should be used, might respond this way: *Everybody* is a singular pronoun, and *their* is a plural pronoun; therefore, this sentence is incorrect and should read *Everybody has paid **his or her** fees.*

Someone of a more descriptivist bent—that is, someone who believes language is defined by how people use it—might respond that *they* and *their* have been used as gender-neutral singular pronouns since the 14th century, even by Shakespeare and Austen. Therefore, *everybody has paid **their** fees* is just fine.

Many of us prefer using *their* to refer to *everybody* because we want to avoid using either *his* (to refer to males and females collectively) or *his* or *her.*

In formal writing situations, however, it's best to side with the prescriptivists and avoid treating *everybody* as plural. But here's the problem. We don't want to use *he* as a generic pronoun referring to a person of either sex, and it has become common in speech and informal writing to use *they, them, their,* and *themselves* in these situations. *Has **each manager** submitted **their** test results?*

Here are some suggested ways to resolve this problem and keep both the prescriptivists and the descriptivists happy:

- Pluralize the antecedent. Not this: *Every student has paid his or her fees.* But this: *All the students have paid their fees.*

- Use an article. Not this: *Each employee can ask to have his union representative at the meeting.* But this: *Each employee can ask to have a union representative at the meeting.*

- Use an imperative. Not this: *Everybody must file their complaints by 5 p.m.* But this: *File your complaints by 5 p.m.*

- Use *he or she* or *his or her* occasionally. Not this: *A passenger can request a refund if their flight is delayed.* But this: *A passenger can request a refund if his or her flight is delayed.*

Pronoun case

Use personal pronouns in the correct case.

- Use the subjective case (*I, you, he, she, it, we, they*) for subjects.

  Not this: *Reg and me went shopping.* But this: *Reg and I went shopping.*

- Use the objective case (*me, you, him, her, it, us, them*) for objects.

  Not this: *Let Beryl and I help you.* But this: *Let Beryl and me help you.*

  Not this: *Between you and I ...* But this: *Between you and me ...*

- Use the possessive case (*my, mine, our, ours, your, yours, his, her, hers, its, their, theirs*) to indicate possession.

  Not this: *The chances of you winning are slim.* But this: *The chances of your winning are slim.*

- For *we* or *us* before a noun, choose the pronoun case you would use if the noun were removed.

  Not this: *Us business owners are unhappy with the increase in taxes.* But this: *We business owners are unhappy with the increase in taxes.*

- For pronouns used as appositives (noun phrases that rename nouns or pronouns) use the same case as the original noun or pronoun.

  Not this: *The winners of the dance marathon, Lazaro and me, will now get free lessons.*

  But this: *The winners of the dance marathon, Lazaro and I, will now get free lessons.*

Who versus *whom*

The use of *whom* is fading. But many careful writers tend to agree with writer and editor Mary Norris's comment: "*Whom* may indeed be on the way out, but so is Venice, and we still like to go there." *Who* is a subject pronoun, and *whom* is an object pronoun. An easy way to remember this—if you would use *he*, use *who*; if you would use *him*, use *whom*. **Who** *is responsible for this?* (He is responsible for this.) **Whom** *did they choose?* (They chose him.)

Not this: *You gave the ticket to **who**?* But this: *You gave the ticket to **whom**?*

Shift in person

Don't shift unnecessarily between first person (*I* or *us*), second person (*you*), and third person (*he, she, it,* or *they*), or the indefinite pronoun *one*. Keep the point of view consistent.

Not this: *One can succeed as an editor if you are willing to work hard.*

But this: *You can succeed as an editor if you are willing to work hard.*

Muddled modifiers

Modifiers—which can be words, phrases, or clauses—describe, clarify, or provide more detail about a concept. Modifiers need to be used with care to avoid confusing the reader.

Dangling modifiers

A dangling modifier is a word or phrase that modifies a word not explicitly stated in the sentence.

Not this: *While washing the dishes, a tarantula trundled across the floor.*

But this: *While washing the dishes, Steven watched a tarantula trundle across the floor.*

Not this: *The morning passed quickly, editing a manual and sending it to the client.*

But this: *The morning passed quickly; I edited a manual and sent it to the client.*

Misplaced modifiers

A misplaced modifier is too far from the item it modifies. Watch out especially for the modifiers *only* and *just*.

Not this: *The inventory can only be finished today if you help me.*

But this: *The inventory can be finished today only if you help me.*

Not this: *Isabella served lunch to her guests on plastic plates.*

But this: *Isabella served her guests lunch on plastic plates.*

Squinting modifiers

A squinting modifier squints because it can modify either the words that precede it or the words that follow it.

In the sentence *Employees who miss work frequently lose their jobs*, it's unclear whether employees miss work frequently *or* they frequently lose their jobs. In the sentence *People who fret rarely are happy*, it's unclear whether people fret rarely *or* they are rarely happy. If the writer wrote *Employees who frequently miss work lose their jobs* or *People who rarely fret are happy*, then the meaning is clear.

Absolute modifiers

An absolute modifier cannot be comparative or superlative. Examples: *absolute, adequate, final, perfect, unique, universal.* Marketers might trumpet *whiter than white,* or tell us a certain product is *very unique,* but the careful writer does not fall into this trap.

Not this: *Jasmine is my **most favourite** scent.*

But this: *Jasmine is my **favourite** scent.*

Verb problems

Use the subjunctive mood when it is called for, and watch out for unnecessary mood, tense, and voice shifts.

Mood error

The subjunctive mood is used for impossibilities, suggestions, recommendations, or advice.

Not this: *The board recommended that the motion **is** passed.*

But this: *The board recommended that the motion **be** passed.*

Not this: *We asked that she **drives** more carefully.*

But this: *We asked that she **drive** more carefully.*

Mood shift

Don't shift the mood unnecessarily.

Not this: ***Remove** the back of the remote, and then you **should insert** the battery.*

But this: ***Remove** the back of the remote and **insert** a battery.*

Tense shift

Don't shift the tense unnecessarily.

Not this: *Esra **delivered** the presentation, and then he **takes** questions.*

But this: *Esra **delivered** the presentation, and then he **took** questions.*

Tense shift is more common in a paragraph or section than in a sentence.

Not this: *Hi Yolanda, I would like to discuss an issue that came up after our meeting last Tuesday. At the meeting, we **have agreed** to complete the amendments to the policies before December 15. I now realize that by the time December 15 **will arrive**, it **will have become** too late to do this.*

But this: *Hi Yolanda, I would like to discuss an issue that came up after our meeting last Tuesday. At the meeting, we **agreed** to complete the amendments to the policies before December 15. I now realize that by the time December 15 **arrives**, it **will be** too late to do this.*

Voice shift

Don't shift the voice (passive or active) unnecessarily.

Not this: *He **inspected** the building, and the parking lot **was** **inspected** by him too.*

But this: *He **inspected** the building and the parking lot.*

Adjective and adverb conundrums

The role of adjectives is to modify, describe, and limit nouns and pronouns; the role of adverbs is to modify, describe, and limit everything else. Because their job description is identical, but they modify, describe, and limit different parts of speech, it can be tricky to tell them apart and to know which one is best for the situation at hand.

Bad and *badly*

After a linking verb, use the adjective *bad*. *I feel **bad** about missing your party. I feel **bad** for always using* badly *when I should be using* bad. And if someone tells you it's correct to say *I feel **badly** about handing the report in late*, tell that person that now you feel *worsely*. That's all you should need to say to shut down this conversation.

Safe and *Safely*

Why is it okay to say *drive fast* but not *drive careful*? It's because of flat adverbs, which are adverbs that have the same form as a related adjective. Some of these adverbs never have an *–ly* suffix— e.g., *seldom, fast, straight, thus*—or they have an *–ly* suffix, but the adjectival form may be just as good, especially in an informal context: *drive safe, hold me tight*. In a more formal context, *drive safely* would be preferred. The flat adverb can also have an entirely different meaning from the *–ly* adverb. Consider the difference between *Jackson is **trying hard*** and *Jackson is **hardly trying**.*

Well and *good*

Use the adverb *well* when referring to performance, manner, and action. *Leave **well** alone! I wish you **well** in your future endeavours! We worked **well** together.* The adjective *good* must refer to a noun or pronoun, not a verb: *I'm a **good** swimmer*, and *I swim **well**.*

Although this is a book about writing, not speaking, many people ask if it's acceptable to say "I'm good" in response to "How are you doing?" The answer is that informally it's common, and Grammar Girl, among others, encourages us to say "I'm good" with "absolute confidence." If you want the most formal reply, then say "Fine, thanks" or "I'm doing well, thanks." Of course, if you're neither fine nor well, then tailor your answer accordingly, but use an adverb: "Not that splendidly."

More potential quicksand

Here are some final issues to watch out for when checking for grammatical errors.

Faulty comparison

A comparison between two or more things must be complete, consistent, and clear.

To be complete, there must be at least two things to compare.

Not this: *The moon is smaller.* (What is the moon smaller than?)

But this: *The moon is smaller **than Earth**.*

To be consistent, the basis of comparison must be logical.

Not this: *The **delays** in April were more problematic **than March**.* (This sentence compares *delays* to *March*.)

But this: *The **delays** in April were more problematic **than the delays** in March.*

Not this: *Connie writes better **than anyone I know**.* (The *anyone I know* includes Connie; therefore, it's illogical.)

But this: *Connie writes better **than anyone else** I know.*

To be clear, there can be no ambiguity in the comparison.

Not this: *Louisa helped me **more than Kim**.* (Does this mean that Louisa helped me more than she helped Kim? Or does it mean that Louisa helped me more than Kim helped me?)

But this: *Louisa helped me **more than she helped Kim**.*

Or this: *Louisa helped me **more than Kim did**.*

Faulty parallelism

If two or more ideas are parallel, they must be expressed in parallel grammatical form to avoid faulty parallelism. In other words, balance single words with single words, phrases with phrases, clauses with clauses. *A kiss can be a comma, a question mark, or an exclamation.* ~ Mistinguett

Not this: *We want to hear your ideas on **motivating** employees and how **to introduce** change.*

But this: *We want to hear your ideas on **motivating** employees and **introducing** change.*

This can be especially tricky with correlative conjunctions, such as *not only . . . but also.*

Not this: *We disagreed **not only** with the results **but also** we disagreed with the research.*

But this: *We disagreed **not only** with the results **but also** with the research.*

Faulty predication

The subject and the predicate (the verb and its attendants) must make sense together. When they don't, the mistake is known as faulty predication.

Not this: *The cost of health insurance protects people from onerous medical bills.*

But this: *Health insurance protects people from onerous medical bills.*

For the same reason, avoid constructions such as *is when, is where,* and *the reason . . . is because.*

Not this: *A simile is when you make a comparison using as or* like.

But this: *A simile is a comparison introduced by the words as or* like.

Garden path sentences

A sentence that leads the reader down a path, but not the path he thought he was on, is known as a garden path sentence. It tricks him into reading one element in a sentence as another.

Not this: *The boy pushed through the door tripped.*

But this: *The boy who was pushed through the door tripped.* (In the first version, the reader must read the entire sentence to realize that the boy wasn't pushing but that he was tripped because he was pushed.)

Not this: *Have the new hires who missed the orientation take it tomorrow.*

But this: *Please have the new hires who missed the orientation take it tomorrow.* (The problem with *Have the new hires . . .* is that the reader initially might think that a question is being posed; the *please* takes care of this problem.)

To *that* or not to *that*

If you eliminate *that* when it's necessary, the reader can be led astray, either temporarily or permanently.

Not this: *Sean told me on Sunday he would pay the invoice.*

But this: *Sean told me on Sunday that he would pay the invoice.* (The problem with *Sean told me on Sunday he would . . .* is that we're not sure if he told you on Sunday or if he told you he planned to pay on Sunday.)

Writers and editors don't agree on whether *that* should always be added to a sentence. Always use it when it's essential for clarity. And many verbs, such as *feel, find, think, hope, say,* and *wish,* sound better when they're followed with *that.*

It's versus *its*

Don't mix up *it's* and *its.* Remember, *it's* always means either *it is* or *it has,* whereas *its* is a possessive pronoun. *It's snowing. It's been a wonderful holiday so far. The lizard relishes its time in the sun. Ah, the challenges of the English language—especially its infinite spelling variations.*

i.e. and *e.g.*

The abbreviation *e.g.* (from the Latin, *exempli gratia*) means "for example." It's always followed by a comma. *There are many fascinating town names in Canada: e.g., Witless Bay, Vulcan, and Skookumchuck.* You can also put this information in parentheses. *There are many fascinating town names in Canada (e.g., Witless Bay, Vulcan, and Skookumchuck).*

The abbreviation *i.e.* (from the Latin, *id est*) means "namely," "that is," or "in other words." Like its cousin, *e.g.,* it's also always followed by a comma. *I love the capital of Quebec—i.e., Quebec City—even though I am not a Québécois. An independent clause— i.e., a sentence—always has a subject and a verb.* You can also put the abbreviation in parentheses. *An independent clause (i.e., a sentence) always has a subject and a verb.* This mnemonic may help you remember the difference:

e.g. = example given   i.e. = in essence

But here's my advice. After asking thousands of writers if they understand the difference between *i.e.* and *e.g.*, I am sorry to report that about 75 percent tell me they don't. Therefore, in the interest of reader-centred writing, I suggest not using the abbreviation *i.e.* Instead, write it out: *Our backup drives—namely, drives E and D—do not have sufficient storage.*

I, me, and *myself*

Mixing up *I, me,* and *myself* has become so rampant that it deserves special mention. The pronouns *I, me,* and *myself* are not interchangeable. They're not even in the same categories. *I* and *me* are both personal pronouns, in the subjective case (**I** *admire Emile*) and the objective case (*Emile admires* **me**), respectively. The pronoun *myself* is a reflexive pronoun (*I look at* **myself** *in the mirror—nice haircut!*) that reflects back on the subject pronoun *I.* It is also used as an intensive pronoun to intensify the *I: You might use this pronoun incorrectly, but I* **myself** *would never do that!*

No matter who it is, never believe anyone who tells you that *myself* is a formal version of *I* or *me.* It is not. Instead of arguing with this person, make him an outrageous bet that he will never find this rule in any reputable grammar reference. And then enjoy your winnings!

Not this: *Obi, Selma, and **myself** attended the conference.*

But this: *Obi, Selma, and **I** attended the conference.*

Not this: *Please contact **myself** by 4 p.m. today.*

But this: *Please contact **me** by 4 p.m. today.*

Not this: *Please file this for Michelle and **myself**.*

But this: *Please file this for Michelle and **me**.*

Courtesy of texting

If we allow our busy little texting thumbs to write with abandon, soon enough here's the sad result that shows up everywhere:

Not this: *Dear nut supplier: I don't know **whose** the person I should direct this complaint to, so I'm hoping you can help me. **Your** the best supplier of cashews in Canada, but the last shipment had many rancid ones. **Their** usually so fresh, so I was surprised that **they're** were so many bad ones. Please let me know if **your** able to issue me a refund. Thanks.*

But this: *Dear nut supplier: I don't know **who's** the person I should direct this complaint to, so I'm hoping you can help me. **You're** the best supplier of cashews in Canada, but the last shipment had many rancid ones. **They're** usually so fresh, so I was surprised that **there** were so many bad ones. Please let me know if **you're** able to issue me a refund. Thanks.*

Five common grammar myths

Time to bust some myths again! Don't think of English as a weedy pond with stagnant water and too many bugs. It's more like a mighty river, aggressively carving out new routes and never standing still. Rules that you learned in school might no longer hold true. Here are some myths well past their expiry dates.

Caveat: The more formal your tone (the top rungs on your language ladder), the more likely it is that your audience will be relatively prescriptivist about grammar. When writing in a very formal tone, it is still best not to split infinitives and not to end sentences with prepositions.

Myth No. 1: Don't end a sentence or a question with a preposition.

If we took this myth seriously, we wouldn't be able to write questions or sentences such as *Which building does he work in?* or *He certainly has a lot to worry about.* Luckily, ending a sentence with a preposition is just fine.

A popular story tells us that Churchill once retorted, "This is the sort of bloody nonsense up with which I shall not put" in response to a clumsy edit. Although the anecdote is probably not true, the point is well made.

It's okay to end your questions and sentences with prepositions. What are you waiting *for?*

Myth No. 2: Don't split infinitives.

This is another rule drilled into us by fuddy-duddy grammarians. An infinitive is a verb in its base form preceded by the word *to: to devise, to eat, to work.* To split an infinitive means to put a word or several words in between *to* and the verb itself: *to automatically update* an account.

This rule comes to us courtesy of 19th-century linguists who based their English grammar rules on Latin. But the smart money knows that English is not a Latin language; it's a German one.

I want to tell you *to boldly go* ahead and split infinitives when it sounds better to do so.

Myth No. 3: You can't start a sentence with a conjunction.

Here's the good news: yes, you can. A persistent belief that you can't start a sentence with a conjunction still lingers in the air, but it's a stylistic choice. And, as author Bryan Garner points out, *and* and *but* are superb transition words. Therefore, if the sentence reads better starting with a conjunction, use it. But if it would function just as well without it, then reconsider.

And that's all there is to say.

Myth No. 4: Don't start a sentence with *however* or *because*.

Wrong! Go ahead and start a sentence with *however*, but remember to use a comma after it when it means "nevertheless." *However hard you're finding this grammar, it's worth learning. However, I would encourage you to read this chapter a few times, maybe as bedtime reading.* And if you start a sentence with *because*, make sure you complete the sentence. So, for example, *Because I am tired* is not a sentence, but *Because I am tired, I went to bed early* is.

We tolerate prescriptivists. *However,* the only thing we're tired of is people who think you can't start a sentence with the word *however.*

Myth No. 5: Passive voice is always wrong.

Another myth bites the dust. There's nothing wrong with the occasional passive voice, and in some cases—for example, when you want to avoid blaming a specific person—it's perfect. Instead of telling your new boss "You've broken the espresso maker," why not be more subtle and use the passive voice: "Oh, the espresso maker has been broken."

Mistakes *were made.* But not by your boss (or you).

— Ask Maggie —

My boss is a dinosaur! She learned English 40 years ago and won't accept that the rules have changed. I tell her it's okay to occasionally start a sentence with *and* or to end a sentence with a preposition. But it's her fossilized way or the highway. Any advice?

Signed,

Frustrated Frances

Dear Frances,

I can relate to this. I ran a workshop a few years ago, and in the workshop description I said, "This workshop will help you to effectively prepare for a major writing project." Here was the client's response:

"Hi, Margaret—I was reviewing your description and the split infinitive *to effectively prepare* bothered me. Why didn't you write *to prepare effectively*? In my days as a teacher, I could fail a paper for including such a breach of grammar. Someone must catch you for having one in the workshop description. What do you think? Regards, Charlotte"

Well, I didn't share with her what I thought, but I was glad I never had her for a teacher. And split infinitives are not considered a breach of grammar. But I was grateful that she reminded me that I should not have forgotten my audience (I already knew she was a grammar grump) and committed what to her was a serious writing crime.

So, Frances, I suggest that when writing to your boss, you keep her old-school philosophy in mind. And maybe find a way to share one or two books on contemporary language usage with her, if possible. A gift, perhaps?

EXERCISES

A. What are five things (nouns) that you feel strongly about? Be as specific as you can, e.g., not *food*, but *Mexican food*.

B. Now provide five descriptive and unusual adjectives for one of these things. Try to get beyond common words like *exciting*, *good*, and *interesting*.

C. Label the part of speech for every word in the following sentences. Use these labels: N for noun, PRO for pronoun, V for verb, ADJ for adjective, ADV for adverb, CON for conjunction, PRP for preposition, and I for interjection.

1. I drove slowly to the workshop although I was late.

2. The closest languages to English are Frisian and Dutch.

3. She gave us a remarkably difficult exercise.

4. Some critics scorned Webster because he allowed slang and jargon in his dictionary.

5. The shortest and most commonly used word in English is the word *I*. Amazing!

D. Answer the following questions about this sentence: *In 911, the French ruler Charles the Simple had reluctantly given the pugnacious Vikings land in northern France.*

1. Is there a pronoun? If so, which word is it?

2. What is/are the adverb/s?

3. What is/are the adjective/s?

4. Is the verb active or passive?

5. What is the subject of the sentence?

6. What is the direct object of the verb?

7. What is/are the preposition/s?

E. **Identify the simple subject, the verb, and any direct object in each clause below by drawing one line under the subject, two lines under the verb, and circling the direct object. Put any prepositional phrases in parentheses. Then identify whether the sentence is simple, compound, complex, or compound-complex.**

1. They met. They fell in love. She abandoned him.

2. William the Conqueror, who was the first Norman king of England, never learned English.

3. Meiling went to the bank, and she met the manager.

4. *The pen is the tongue of the mind.* ~ Cervantes

5. When the people arrived at the ski hut, some of them built a fire, and others cooked dinner on the gas stove.

6. Since he was always late for meetings, they demanded his resignation.

7. In South Africa, there are 11 official languages.

F. **Put parentheses around the dependent clause, and label it as a noun clause, an adjective clause, or an adverb clause.**

1. When everyone was in the living room, Claire and Mateo brought in the birthday cake.

2. The party, which was supposed to be on the previous Saturday, had been rescheduled.

3. What had caused the party to be rescheduled was not completely clear.

4. Because the party was now on Tuesday evening, many of the guests were reluctant to stay long.

5. All the guests went home after the presents were opened.

G. The Dreaded Grammar Quiz

Fix the grammatical errors in each of these sentences. Give your-self a bonus point if you can name the error.

1. There's many opportunities in Western Canada for someone eager to live here.

2. A characteristic I dislike is a person who is dishonest.

3. After reading several books, cybersecurity is still as puzzling as ever.

4. Let Dmitri and I help you with that heavy box.

5. Magda respects me more than Fay.

6. Neither of your suggested solutions are going to get your boss's approval.

7. The winners of the tournament, Jamila and me, will now receive our awards.

8. Esmahan is smart, creative, and works hard.

9. The reason I love grammar is because it is so fascinating.

10. If Cornelia was sensible, she would never take that job.

11. Although nearly completed, the analysts stopped working on the report to talk to Jill and myself.

12. Here comes the winners. Please tell them I feel badly about being such a poor loser.

13. Running down the path, my wig flew off.

14. She did real well on her exam.

15. To find our office, you can either go right on Broadway Avenue or left on Rosewood Street.

16. Gareth removed the brush from the pot and washed it carefully.

17. Please contact either Peng or myself if you have any questions.

18. Freight costs for the second quarter were 15 percent higher.

19. No one was allowed to store anything in the attic except the landlord.

20. Of the group, only her and I attended the seminar.

21. The reviewer's online comments were aggravating to me and caused much embarrassment for all of us.

22. Molly told Helen that she hated her new haircut.

23. The executive assistant scheduled a meeting with a software company using a newly released web platform.

24. If Jabari would have attended the meeting, he would have met the new manager.

25. Chess is the hardest of any other game.

26. Craig likes playing banjo, collecting antiques, and to ski; it's due to the fact that he likes to keep busy.

27. A dictionary is where you look up the definition of words.

28. If you checked the questionnaire again, you will find less mistakes.

29. I insist that he attends the workshop tomorrow.

30. The manager and the engineering team examined the test results carefully because of their focus on cost savings and efficiency.

CHAPTER NINE

Make Peace with Punctuation: Marks and Remarks

If it were all a party, the periods would be by the bar,
drinking whiskeys and politely discussing the price of
daycare, the commas chiming in at just the right moment,
while the exclamation points pretend to dance, nodding
furiously at anything anyone says, smiling so hard their
eyes look crazy, taking way too many photos,
teetering on their impractical shoes.

~ STEVE MACONE

Grammar and punctuation have much in common, which is why they often appear closely aligned in books on writing. Both are fundamental to establishing sentence clarity and meaning, and both are challenging in their scope and complexity. And the debates about "correct" usage rage as fervently for punctuation as they do for grammar. In fact, punctuation standards can be even more confusing than grammar rules because, contrary to what you might think, there is no single correct answer for every punctuation question. Is it *Carlos' book* or *Carlos's book*? Is it *pups, cubs, and kits* or *pups, cubs and kits*? Answer: both versions are correct.

As June Casagrande explains in her book on punctuation, sometimes you can make a choice, sometimes the style manual you use (e.g., *The Associated Press Stylebook*) will determine the choice, and sometimes there is only one correct choice, and if you don't choose it, you end up with sentences like the infamous "Let's eat Grandma."

Professional writers and editors keep a well-thumbed reference book or two close by and know how to handle common punctuation conundrums. Although it's impossible to provide all the punctuation rules for all occasions, the standard rules and principles outlined below will work for most situations. When you have more detailed questions, consult your reference materials, and use your best judgment.

APOSTROPHE

The main function of the apostrophe is to indicate possession. For most singular nouns, add an apostrophe and an *–s* (e.g., *the boy's toy*). For most plural nouns (except for irregular plurals that do not end in *–s*), add an apostrophe only (e.g., *the two clients' files*, but *the men's files*). To form the possessive of singular nouns that end in a sounded *–s* or *–z*, add an extra *–s* if you can pronounce it (e.g., *Chris's crisis, Sophocles' plays*). (Although this convention is the norm in Canadian English, it is not incorrect to write *Sophocles's plays*.)

To show joint possession, use *–'s* with the last noun only; to show individual possession, make all the nouns possessive: *Chen and Vida's new house* (they jointly own one house); *Max's and Parvin's expectations of work* (they individually have different expectations).

None of the possessive pronouns (e.g., *my, ours, yours, his, hers, its, theirs*) take an apostrophe.

The apostrophe is also used to mark omissions in contractions and numbers (e.g., *can't, the '70s*). Generally, do not use an apostrophe to form the plural of numbers, abbreviations, and words mentioned as words (e.g., *figure 8s* not *figure 8's*, *1990s* not *1990's*,

GHGs not *GHG's*, *PhDs* not *PhD's*). However, you can use an apostrophe to form the plural of letters as in these examples: *There are two* r's *and two* s's *in the word* embarrass. *Johnathon's name has two* o's *in it.*

Do not use an apostrophe to make people's names plural. If the name ends in –*y*, add an –*s*. If the name ends in –*s*, –*x*, –*z*, –*ch*, and –*sh*, add an –*es*. Example: *the three Larrys, the Foxes,* and *the Churches.*

Certain people hold passionate views about the apostrophe. In Britain, there is an Apostrophe Protection Society, whose specific aim is to preserve "the correct use of this currently much abused punctuation mark in all forms of text written in the English language."

COLON

The colon focuses the reader's attention on what is to follow and therefore should be used to introduce a list, a summation, or an idea that fulfills an expectation raised by the clause preceding the colon. The colon must be preceded by an independent clause—that is, a group of words that can stand alone as a sentence. Examples: *Samara visited three cities in Nepal: Pokhara, Kathmandu, and Birganj. Kaleb had but one thing on his mind: finding a new job.*

Never use a colon to separate the verb from the rest of the sentence.

Not this: *Harry bought: a compact fluorescent, a low-flow shower-head, and a rechargeable battery.*

But this: *Harry bought a compact fluorescent, a low-flow shower-head, and a rechargeable battery.*

A common error is to place a colon, incorrectly, after the word *include* or *including*. You'll see it in print everywhere, but it's just plain wrong.

Not this: *The amenities in the building include: an exercise room, two meeting rooms, and a rooftop patio.*

But this: *The amenities in the building include an exercise room, two meeting rooms, and a rooftop patio.*

When a colon is used within a sentence, the first word following the colon is lowercased unless it is a proper noun. However, use uppercase when the colon introduces two or more sentences, a quotation, or a question.

COMMA

By giving readers a reason to pause, this versatile, and sometimes vexing, punctuation mark helps readers grasp the rhythm of the sentence and understand its meaning. Without the comma, sentence parts would bang into each other like bumper cars run amok. We can all appreciate the difference in meaning between *Sabine maintained Akio had lost the lab results* and *Sabine, maintained Akio, had lost the lab results.* Here are some of the key ways that the unassuming, but powerful, comma helps create sentence meaning.

Commas between independent clauses

Use a comma to separate two independent clauses connected by one of the seven coordinating conjunctions: *for, and, nor, but, or, yet,* or *so. Water conservation is especially important in the summer months, but year-round water conservation also counts.*

If the clauses are short, you can omit the comma. *I walked to the bank and I cashed a cheque.* You can also omit the comma for imperative sentences, in which the subject (*you*) is omitted but understood, if the clauses are short. *Take this book and give it to Helga.*

In general, do not use a comma if these conjunctions connect groups of words that are not independent clauses. *Many people conserve water in the summer by collecting rainwater and reusing the water.*

Don't confuse the coordinating conjunction *so* with the subordinating conjunction *so that* which introduces a dependent clause. Example: *I want to finish the business plan by Friday so that I can take a three-day break.* *So that* can be confusing because the *that* is optional. Even when the *that* is missing, don't mistake it for *so* and add a comma.

Commas with introductory phrases and clauses

Commas signal that introductory word groups have come to an end as the following examples illustrate:

- to separate introductory participial phrases from the independent clause: *Hoping to talk to my boss, I walked over to his office.*

- to separate introductory prepositional phrases: *Without Sadie's help, I won't finish this expense report in time.*

- to separate introductory dependent clauses: *When Harlan was ready to eat, his dog was too.*

When prepositional phrases or dependent clauses are short, the comma may be omitted if there is no danger of miscommunication. *In 2016 Rebecca moved to Florida.* And when they follow the independent clause rather than precede it, do not use a comma if the concluding phrase or clause is essential to the meaning of the sentence. *Don't talk to Dan this morning until he's had a coffee.*

Commas in non-essential elements and appositives

A non-essential element (also known as a non-restrictive element) is a word, phrase, or clause that is not essential to the meaning of the sentence. It is parenthetical information and is set off with commas. Here are some examples:

- to set off a non-essential clause: *My rain barrel, which I purchased three years ago, does a great job of collecting rainwater.* Do not use commas to set off an essential clause: *Rain barrels that are made locally are hard to find.*

- to set off a non-essential phrase: *His new office, with its beautiful carpet, will be ready next week.* Do not use commas to set off an essential phrase: *The office with the beautiful carpet is on the seventh floor.*

- to set off a non-essential appositive (a noun phrase that renames a noun or pronoun): *David Crystal, a British linguist, maintains that texting improves children's writing and spelling.* Do not use commas to set off an essential appositive: *The movie* Arrival *features a linguist as the hero.*

Commas in a series

When three or more items are presented in a series, separate these items from one another with commas: *Baruti's favourite flowers are daisies, irises, and orchids.*

The comma after the second-last item (in the sentence above, the comma after *irises*) is referred to as either the serial comma or the Oxford comma. Using it or not is a matter of style; neither choice is incorrect. *Winona purchased a laser printer, a carton of paper and 20 three-ring binders.*

However, the omission of the serial comma can create confusion. *I went to the opera with my parents, Marisol and Umberto.* Do you mean two people—your parents Marisol and Umberto—or four people—your mom, your dad, Marisol, and Umberto?

The Chicago Manual of Style recommends using the serial comma. It is also the style choice for this book. If you work for an organization, the choice to use the serial comma or not should be consistent and noted in the in-house style guide or style sheet.

In a series of adjectives, use a comma if the adjectives could also be separated by *and*. *The beautiful, elegant jacket was a pleasure to wear.* But in this example, *white* and *cotton* cannot be separated by *and*: *The man's white cotton shirt was filthy.*

Commas with transitional and parenthetical expressions

Transitional expressions include conjunctive adverbs, such as *however*, and transitional phrases, such as *for example*. When a transitional expression is placed between two independent clauses, it is preceded by a semicolon and followed by a comma. *I didn't understand the instructions; therefore, I asked Ojal to help me.* Generally, if a transitional expression is placed at the beginning of a sentence or in the middle of an independent clause, it is set off with commas. *Furthermore, I had to take an online tutorial. I still found, however, the program difficult to run.*

Parenthetical expressions are distinct asides and should be set off by commas. *Many studies indicate, by the way, that about 90 percent of the punctuation marks we use are commas or periods.*

Commas with quotations

Use a comma to introduce a quotation of a complete sentence and to substitute for a period at the end of a quotation if the sentence continues after the quotation. *Jinjing said, "That's ridiculous!" "I've never heard such trash," said Jinjing.*

Commas with assorted short elements

Use a comma to set off contrasting elements, direct addresses, tag questions, and interjections. *We told Latif, not his sister, to help us on Friday. Wendy, are you going to the conference next week? Monique was washing her hair when I phoned, wasn't she? Gosh, I thought you were going.*

Commas with dates, addresses, and titles

Use a comma to set off dates. *We flew to Mozambique on Saturday, March 18, 2017, to attend a conference.* But never separate a date consisting of only the month and year. Not this: *We went there in March, 2017.* But this: *We went there in March 2017.*

Use commas to separate the elements of a place name or an address. *He was born in Madison, Wisconsin, in 1984. Please return this book to R. Popov at 123 Red Street, Winnipeg, MB R2C 0A1.* Do not put a comma before a postal code.

Use a pair of commas to separate a title from the rest of the sentence if it follows a name. *Chen Hong, PhD, recently joined our organization.*

Disobedient commas

We'll conclude with some examples of commas that frequently make an appearance where they don't belong:

■ Do not use a comma to separate a subject from its predicate.

Not this: *Registering for the business writing webinar before May 15, will ensure that you have time to prepare.*

But this: *Registering for the business writing webinar before May 15 will ensure that you have time to prepare.*

- Do not use a comma after a coordinating conjunction.

  Not this: *Patsy really likes her job, and, she wants to stay with the organization.*

  But this: *Patsy really likes her job, and she wants to stay with the organization.*

- Do not use a comma after *although*.

  Not this: *Although, he went to bed early, he was still tired the next day.*

  But this: *Although he went to bed early, he was still tired the next day.*

- Do not use a comma with a question mark or an exclamation point.

  Not this: *"I finally know how to use commas!," she exclaimed.*

  But this: *"I finally know how to use commas!" she exclaimed.*

DASH

The em dash (long dash) is an emphatic mark of punctuation best used to indicate a sudden interruption in thought, a sharp break, or a shift in thought. It's a vigorous piece of punctuation that should be used sparingly. Usually the em dash is a substitute for the colon, semicolon, or comma; it indicates a more abrupt break in the sentence or a less formal style. *We decided to update our materials— even though we had little time—because we wanted them to be as useful as possible.*

Some writers also use the en dash (wider than the hyphen but shorter than the em dash) to replace *to*, *through*, or *until* when they feel that the flow of words is not important: *the 2014–2015 season, pages 33–37, the Los Angeles–Lisbon flight.* If *from* or *between* is used before the first of a pair of numbers, do not use the en dash; instead *from* is followed by *to* or *through*, and *between* is followed by *and*. Examples: *from 33 to 99; from June 1, 2017 through May 31, 2019; between 12 and 49.*

ELLIPSIS MARK

An ellipsis mark is three spaced periods with a single space on either side. Use this punctuation mark to indicate omitted words from a quoted passage. Place a space between the ellipsis and surrounding letters or other marks. The ellipsis can also be used to express hesitation or breaks in a writer's train of thought. But when using it this way, use it sparingly. *There was not much to say . . . so I kept quiet.*

EXCLAMATION POINT

Use an exclamation point to express strong feeling or to provide emphasis. *That's fantastic!* A quotation that ends with an exclamation point is not followed by a comma. *"I'm so happy I'm going on holidays!"* Deidra said.

In formal writing, the exclamation point is generally considered inappropriate. Some writers maintain, however, that it lends a friendly and enthusiastic tone, especially useful for informal emails. Because we interact with people electronically more than we do in any other medium, these writers argue that exclamation points serve to replace other cues, such as tone of voice, facial expressions, and physical gestures. They contend that these spirited punctuation marks can convey a range of meanings, including apologizing, thanking, agreeing, and showing solidarity. Obviously, this is a personal choice, but if you use them, do so infrequently and only when the sentence needs a boost. The sentence *I look forward to meeting you next week* doesn't need an exclamation point, but a single word such as *Great* would convey more excitement as *Great!* But keep it to one exclamation point, not five.

HYPHEN

The rules for using the hyphen correctly are complex and dictated by the dictionary and style manual you use. Here are some basic principles:

- Compound words may be written as one word (*fireplace*), left open as two words (*fact sheet*), or hyphenated (*fuel-efficient*).

- A compound modifier is two or more words that function as a unit to modify a noun. If it is placed before a noun, hyphenate the words: *a frost-resistant strawberry*. If it is placed after the noun, hyphenation is usually not necessary: *a strawberry that is frost resistant*.

- Hyphenate any compound modifier if there could be confusion without the hyphen: *small-business seminar*.

- Do not hyphenate a compound modifier if the meaning is instantly clear because of the term's common usage: *acid rain threat, sales tax increase*.

- A two-word compound modifier that begins with an adverb ending in –*ly* is not hyphenated: *a bitterly contested debate*.

- Hyphenate most well-known compounds of three or more words: *mother-in-law*.

For more complex decisions, use your reference materials. *The Chicago Manual of Style* has a 10-page hyphenation table. Yes, 10 pages. But this table will allow you, as a witty student once said, to become The Hyphenator.

— Anecdotal Evidence —

You might be reading some of this grammar stuff and thinking *Did I sleep that heavily through this in school?* or *Was I ever taught this?* That's how I felt when I learned German and had my first inescapable head-on encounter with grammar. I was staggered to find that I didn't know the foundations of my own language, let alone German. So if you haven't learned another language, then grammar might feel quite foreign. And it's an acquired taste for most of us. But it does grow on you—just like salty licorice or kimchi does. One day grammar will be palatable, even pleasing.

Think of practising grammar like practising scales on a piano. You may have to practise when no one is around at first, but soon enough you'll be playing a harmonious tune. Mastering grammar and punctuation in your own language or another language is all in the practice.

PARENTHESES

Use parentheses (like these) for words that are less vital to the sentence than material that would be set off with dashes or commas. If a punctuation mark applies only to the words inside the parentheses, put the mark inside the closing parenthesis. *Most employees appreciated the workshop. (But I didn't.)* Use brackets [like these] to enclose material that does not belong to the surrounding text (e.g., in quoted matter, reprints, editorial interpolations, explanations, translations, or corrections). *The official insisted, "We foresee no change in [Canadian] policy in the next 15 years."* Brackets are also used to insert parenthetical information within parentheses. *See Crown's latest article ("Canadian foreign policy [2017]").*

PERIOD

The period signals the end of a sentence. Use a period to end a declarative sentence (statement) and even an imperative sentence (command) if the exclamation point would be too strong. *Darwin liked his new boss. Please file this.* Although a sentence fragment is frowned upon in most formal writing because it does not qualify as a complete sentence, it still needs a period if used. *Another brutal deadline. Makes you wonder.* If a polite request is written in the form of a question, you can use a period. *Would you please remember to email me tomorrow.* Use a period instead of a question mark after an indirect question. *I was wondering how much the new software would cost us.*

A period comes before a closing parenthesis or bracket when the parenthetical item is a complete sentence. *The workshop is tomorrow. (We need to bring flipcharts.)* When the parenthetical item is inserted into another sentence, do not place a period before the closing parenthesis or bracket. *The workshop is tomorrow (we need to bring flipcharts).*

When an abbreviation ends with a period and comes at the end of the sentence, do not add another period. *I'll see you tomorrow at 6 a.m.* When a quotation that would otherwise end with a period is used as a quotation within a larger sentence that ends with a question mark or exclamation point, omit the period. *Do you agree that, as Cedric maintains, "Vancouver would be the best place to hold our conference"?*

If an ellipsis comes after a complete sentence, place a period before the ellipsis. *I come from an Italian family. . . . The slamming door was our punctuation mark.* ~ Mario Batali

Do not put two spaces after a period. This rule also holds true for the colon, the exclamation point, and the question mark.

QUESTION MARK

A direct question should be followed by a question mark. *Do you enjoy hiking as much as I do? Why not?* Question marks are quite straightforward unless you have to combine them with quotation marks. A quotation that ends with a question mark is not followed by a comma: *"Do you live in Colorado?" he asked.* At the end of a sentence, a question mark always replaces a period, regardless of whether the question mark is within quotation marks, not in quotation marks, or part of a proper name. *Who said, "Commas, like nuns, often travel in pairs"?* (Answer: writer and editor Mary Norris) *Leo asked me, "Why didn't you sign up for that grammar class?" I just finished the book* Do Androids Dream of Electric Sheep?

QUOTATION MARKS

Quotation marks are primarily used to identify exact language (spoken or written) taken from another source. Use double quotation marks, and reserve single quotation marks only for quotations within quotations. *Ian replied, "I was told, 'The meeting is in Ottawa.'"*

Place commas and periods inside closing quotation marks. Place semicolons and colons outside closing quotation marks. Context determines whether question marks and exclamation points are placed inside or outside closing quotation marks. *Who said, "The structure of every sentence is a lesson in logic"? She warned, "Be careful!"*

Quotation marks can be used sparingly to enclose words used ironically or to draw attention to certain words, such as slang or technical terms in non-technical writing. Do not use them just for emphasis. If a restaurant has a sign that reads *"Brunch" Served Here*, the reader might wonder what exactly is being served.

SEMICOLON

Many people are uncertain how and when to use the semicolon, but it's actually one of the easiest marks to learn to use. Avoid problems by using it only in these two instances.

The first use: Use a semicolon as a transitional device to link two independent clauses closely related in meaning. *Abdominal exercises help prevent back pain; proper posture is also important.* Also use it to link independent clauses joined by a conjunctive adverb such as *therefore* or *however. More than 60 percent of all English words have Greek or Latin roots; however, 96 of the 100 most frequently used words in English have Germanic roots.*

The second use: Use it to separate elements in a sentence if the elements have commas or other punctuation marks within them. In this application, the semicolon serves as a super comma. *The exhibition presented diverse styles and artists: sculptures from Moore, Quinn, and Rodin; paintings by Dali, Klee, and Monet; and antiques from the Ming Dynasty.*

SLASH

The slash can be used occasionally to separate paired terms, such as *student/teacher* and *producer/director.* Do not use a space before or after the slash. The slash is considered informal; therefore, use it sparingly and avoid the use of *and/or* or *he/she.*

EXERCISES

A. Insert apostrophes where necessary, and delete any that are incorrectly placed. You also might have to remove a letter or change a word.

1. There are several boys skates in the locker room, but the mens are by the rink.

2. Alexs' car, a 92 Mustang, is actually his fathers.

3. Who's laptop is this?

4. Johns and Jareds car needs a new transmission.

5. Kiera lived in Iqaluit in the 90's and managed her brothers-in-laws' company.

B. Make any necessary changes to show possession.

elephants foot   six years experience   10 weeks' notice

job requirements   its properties   bachelors degree

policy cash value   the Joneses condo   a week vacation

C. Identify which of the following sentences are run-on sentences.

1. Cassandra loves her husband, that's why she puts up with his annoying nieces.

2. I wanted to phone my girlfriend, and I also wanted to phone my sister.

3. That ad always makes me laugh, it's so funny.

4. I wish I could help you with this exercise; however, I cannot.

5. His memo is quite brief, he didn't have much time to work on it.

6. My dog was unhappy all day he didn't get a walk.

7. When you're through writing the speech, please check with Zelda.

8. I will continue to monitor the situation, let me know if you would like an update.

D. Correct the punctuation mistakes in these sentences, and change words if necessary.

1. Each weeks menu featured a different African countries cuisine.

2. We visited Europe last year and went to: Madrid, Spain, Venice, Italy, and York, England.

3. The company held a one day retreat on Nov 24 2017.

4. The wholly-owned subsidiary is in Chicago which is one of Americas largest cities.

5. The reduction in expenditures was due to several factors; a reduced number of project teams, fewer employees in Q1 and the delayed recruitment of a new Executive Director.

6. Can you believe, Neville asked me, that it has been almost a year since we've seen each other.

7. But, we still need to revise the budget, and preliminary estimates of additional work required.

8. After eating the baby always slept soundly.

9. Sally the new editor is really helpful, therefore you should ask her what she would do.

10. The suspect in the lineup, who has red hair, committed the crime.

11. The two Harries had breakfast with the Joneses' and the Alvarezes'.

12. Who's writing down the pro's and con's of hiring a full time assistant?

— CHAPTER TEN —

Explore Mechanics: Conventions of Print

Rules of proper usage are tacit conventions. Conventions are unstated agreements within a community to abide by a single way of doing things—not because there is any inherent advantage to the choice, but because there is an advantage to everyone making the same choice.

~ STEVEN PINKER

Writers usually have many questions about mechanical issues—the somewhat technical parts of writing, such as capitalization, abbreviations, numbers, symbols, and spelling. Is it *June 1st* or *June 1*? Should I spell out a number? Are we having *French fries* or *french fries* for lunch? Yes, these are details, but the sophisticated writer attends to the details too.

Mechanics are conventions of print: we don't think of them when we're speaking. But in our written language, they are important signals to the reader because, like grammar and punctuation, they help determine meaning and clarify intent. These conventions are agreements more than rules—agreements about how written language will be interpreted when it is read.

CAPITALIZATION

Capital letters are primarily used to emphasize key words and to differentiate proper nouns and adjectives from common nouns and adjectives. Actual practice will vary considerably depending on the degree of formality and intended readership.

Many editors advocate a shift toward less capitalization and less punctuation. The Canadian Press refers to this as the "modified down style" and defines it as follows:

> Capitalize all proper names, the names of departments and agencies of national and provincial governments, trade names, names of associations, companies, clubs, religions, languages, nations, races, places, addresses. Otherwise, lowercase is favoured where a reasonable option exists.

The following rules are based on *The Canadian Press Caps and Spelling* and *Editing Canadian English*. You and your organization may decide to modify some of them, but it's good to be aware of common conventions. For more detailed information on capitalization, consult your reference materials.

Proper nouns Capitalize specific persons, places, or things: *Pavarotti, Lorraine Many Feathers, House of Commons, the Fraser River, Geology 201, Adobe InDesign.*

Specific groups Capitalize the names of religions, ethnic groups, and nationalities: *Buddhism, Romani, Slovenians.*

Formal titles Capitalize formal titles if they precede a name, but lowercase them when they are standing alone or are plural: *Prime Minister Justin Trudeau; the prime minister of Canada; the premiers Rachel Notley and Kathleen Wynne.*

Job descriptions Do not capitalize job descriptions: *managing director Imogen Birtwistle, chair Hsin Ting, administrative assistant Raj Khanna.* If you're not comfortable with this, ask yourself if you would write *Wheat Farmer Pip Sanderson* or *wheat farmer Pip Sanderson.* You'd prefer the latter one, correct? So why use one convention for business job descriptions and another one for other occupations?

Even so, some companies will want to make exceptions, and certainly in an email signature line or a business card, *Team Lead Arthur Pettie* would be preferable. And *Irene Hodgers, Regional Manager* is acceptable too. But use lowercase here: *The regional manager is visiting our office in Montreal on June 10.*

Always consider context, and whatever you decide, remember to be consistent.

Historic events, specific eras, holidays, months, and days of the week Capitalize all these, but do not capitalize seasons: *the Mexican Revolution, the Middle Ages, Remembrance Day, April, Tuesdays, summer.*

Government departments and agencies Capitalize federal and provincial departments and agencies: *Health Canada, Ministry of Transportation.* Municipal government departments and boards are lowercased: *public utilities department.*

Geographical regions and features Capitalize geographic regions (e.g., *Eastern Canada* and *the Far North*), but not their derivatives: *a northern Canadian, the western provinces.* Do not capitalize *north, south, east,* and *west* and derivatives (*southeast*) when they refer to directions: *I will travel west this summer to visit the West Coast.*

Common words derived from proper nouns and adjectives If these words have become household names, they are lowercased: *french fries, brussels sprouts, xerox.*

First words should be capitalized in the following situations:

- The first letter of the first word in a sentence is always capitalized. *Pigs are highly intelligent animals.*

- The first word of a complete sentence in quotation marks is capitalized. *Bob Wootton said, "Clarity, brevity, narrative and pace are axiomatic to creative writing, yet are seldom applied to business writing—to its great cost."*

- The first word of a complete sentence enclosed in dashes or parentheses is not capitalized when it appears as part of another sentence. *I think this is a strange rule (many other writers do too).*

- In correspondence, the first word in the salutation and complimentary close are capitalized: *Dear Ms. Pickles, Yours truly, Sincerely yours.*

ABBREVIATIONS

There are three types of abbreviations: true abbreviations, acronyms, and initialisms. Although they have different meanings, people often use the terms interchangeably. A **true abbreviation** is a shortened form in which either the end of the word is dropped (e.g., *eng.* for *engineer*), or the middle of the word is omitted: *Dr.* for *doctor*. An **acronym** is a word formed as an abbreviation from the initial letters in a phrase or word: *PIN (personal identification number), laser (light amplification by stimulated emission of radiation).* Be careful not to be redundant: *a PIN* not *a PIN number*. An **initialism** is an abbreviation consisting of initial letters pronounced separately: *CPU (central processing unit), ATM (automated teller machine).*

Unless they are well known to the audience, spell out all abbreviations on first use, with the abbreviation following in parentheses. Examples: *the Canadian Securities Commission (CSC),* but *the RCMP*. But remember that *RCMP* would only be clear to a Canadian audience; if you have any doubt, spell it out.

The trend is to drop the periods in abbreviations: *IBM,* not *I.B.M.* Academic degrees may appear with or without periods, but again the tendency is to remove periods: *PhD,* not *Ph.D. The Chicago Manual of Style* recommends periods with lowercase abbreviations (e.g., *a.m.*) but not with uppercase abbreviations (e.g., *FBI*).

Business terms usually follow this convention: *mgmt.* for *management* and *POS* for *point of sale.* Sometimes a term is lowercased when spelled out, but capitalized in the initialism: *standard operating procedures (SOPs).* Don't use an apostrophe before an abbreviation in parentheses. Not this: *The Canadian Securities Commission's (CSC) 2018 report was lengthy.* But this: *The 2018 report issued by the Canadian Securities Commission (CSC) was lengthy.*

Latin abbreviations are usually lowercased. Here are some common ones:

a.m./p.m.	ante meridiem, post meridiem (before/after noon)
c. or ca.	circa
cf.	confer (compare)
e.g.	exempli gratia (for example)
etc.	et cetera (and so forth). Note: Don't use *etc.* at the end of a list that begins with *e.g., such as,* or *including.* In general, limit the use of *etc.*
i.e.	id est (that is). As mentioned in Chapter 8, be careful with *i.e.* Many people do not understand what this abbreviation means.

Dates and times There is no international agreement on using numeric abbreviations for dates. Generally, Canadians follow the day/month/year format: *24/06/2006 = 24 June 2006*. Americans follow the month/day/year format: *06/24/2006*. Many other countries follow the International Organization for Standardization (ISO) standard: *2006 06 24* or *2006-06-24*. To prevent confusion, you must define the chosen sequence in the first occurrence or spell the month out and use all four digits for the year.

For times, use *d* for *day*, *h* for *hour*, *min* for *minute*, and *s* for *second*: *3 h 16 min flying time*.

Eras To designate eras, it is best to de-emphasize the Christian origin and use the following abbreviations, which are also often set in small caps:

BP   before the present
BCE   before the Common Era
CE   of the Common Era

Plurals of abbreviations Do not use an apostrophe before the *–s* unless it is needed for clarity.

Six MPs
14 RSVPs
two SIN's

ITALICS

Italics is a style of type used to denote emphasis and to distinguish published documents, foreign expressions, and other elements. Do not overuse italics for emphasis.

Foreign words and phrases If they have not been assimilated into common speech, italicize them: *sine qua non, carpe noctem, ex nihilo nihil fit.*

Titles Italicize the titles of published documents, such as books, periodicals, newspapers, brochures, legal cases, and movies. Also italicize the titles of compact discs, plays, long poems, paintings, sculptures, and musical works.

Words, letters, and **numerals** discussed as such are italicized. Example: A spell-checker won't point out that you wrote *skeptic* when you meant *septic.*

NUMBERS

Here are some guidelines to follow when expressing numbers in business writing:

Words or numerals Spell out whole numbers from zero to nine (unless followed by an abbreviated unit: *2 cm*), and use numerals for 10 and above. When several numbers modifying the same or similar item(s) appear in the same sentence or even the same paragraph, disregard this rule and write them all as either words or numerals: *The company leases 14 breweries and owns 5 wineries.* Do not spell out a number and then follow it with the digit in parentheses, unless you are writing legal documents. Not this: *seven (7)* But this: *seven*

Never begin a sentence with a numeral. Either spell out the numeral or recast the sentence.

Not this: *2015 was a fantastic year for our company.*

But this: *Our company had a fantastic year in 2015.*

Ordinals (ranked numbers) should be treated the same way as other numbers (e.g., *seventh*, *101st*). In formal writing, avoid ordinals in dates. Not this: *March 31st* But this: *31 March* or *March 31*

Money Use numerals to express exact amounts of money: *His book costs $29.95.* Use words to express indefinite amounts: *The new software system will cost thousands of dollars to implement.*

In numbers more than four digits long, use commas to separate the number into groups of three, starting from the right. In numbers four digits long, a comma is optional. *7,600 or 7600; 240,000; 17,000,000; The population of Canada, based on the latest estimates by the United Nations, is 36,557,808 as of April 2017.*

Times Use numerals with the time of day when exact times are being emphasized or when using a.m. or p.m.: *3:30 a.m.* However, use *noon* and *midnight* rather than *12:00 p.m.* and *12:00 a.m.* With *o'clock*, the number is always spelled out: *eleven o'clock.* Some companies write time using the 24-hour clock: *12:00, 23:33.*

Large numbers Numbers in the millions or higher are written as a numeral plus a word: *More than 435 million people worldwide speak Spanish as their first language.*

Documents Page numbers are expressed as numerals; chapter and volume numbers may appear as either numerals or words: *page 3, Chapter 6,* or *Chapter Six.* Figure and table numbers are expressed as numerals: *Figure 6, Table 10.*

Measurements and percentages Exact measurements should be followed by symbols or abbreviations: *30 km, 15 cu. yd.* Percentages should be expressed as *5 percent* (in a visual, a table, or technical writing, use *5%*).

SYMBOLS

Ampersand   Use the ampersand (&) only when it forms part of a corporate name: *the lawyers Lewey & Howe.*

Currency   Can$, CDN$, or CAD (the ISO system); US$20; $0.25 (not 25¢)

Degrees   30° to 40°, 22 °C, 33°N lat.

Numbers   When abbreviating the words *number* or *numbers* within the body of a text, use *no.* or *nos.*, not the symbol #, which is generally reserved for tables and statistics. Not this: *#s 33–42 are still incomplete.* But this: *Nos. 33–42 are still incomplete.*

Section and   The symbols § and ¶ are generally used only in legal
paragraph   and technical writing.

Metric units   These are based on the International System of Units (SI, from the French *Système international d'unités*). They never take an *–s* in the plural and are separated from a number by a space (e.g., *3 kg, 15 m line).*

SPELLING

Many English words are notoriously difficult to spell. For starters, English spelling is not phonetic: English doesn't have an alphabet that represents speech sounds in a way that is close to how the words sound. And the spelling rules almost always have exceptions—not surprising, given the hundreds of ways to spell the language's 40-plus separate sounds. Here's one quick example that would confound someone learning the language: *you* and *ewe* have the same pronunciation but share no letters in common.

The confusion began with the missionaries who first wrote English—in those days, an Anglo-Saxon language—using the Roman alphabet. Then, in 1066 CE, the French arrived with their own spelling dictates. By the Middle Ages, the situation was desperate: at one stage, there were more than 60 ways to spell the word *night*. Even today, linguist David Crystal reckons that if we added up all the spelling variations in a dictionary, 15 percent of the words would have alternative spellings.

Over the centuries, there's been much talk of spelling reform. In fact, George Bernard Shaw willed part of his estate to fund the creation of a new alphabet, including a competition for the best submission. But the winning system soon fell into obscurity. Public resistance to spelling reform has remained consistently strong, and given that English is spoken in so many different countries already wrestling with their own spelling standards, it would now be almost impossible to implement any global reform.

We have to accept that there's no easy fix to the quagmire that is English spelling. But misspellings will definitely distract your reader. Of course, use your computer's spell-checker, but never depend solely on it. You still need to read through the document because the spell-checker will not capture incorrect pronouns, homophones (words that that sound the same but have different meanings and often different spellings), and misspelled proper nouns.

Use a dictionary as your first point of reference—and everyone in an organization should use the same dictionary. Even with the help of a dictionary, every writer has some words that will always confound her. Keep track of these words, perhaps in a style sheet—see Chapter 16 for more info on style sheets. Appendix B provides a list of words that are commonly confused: *affect* and *effect*; *principal* and *principle*.

Here's a list of commonly misspelled words that plague writers from Alaska to Adelaide.

Commonly Misspelled Words

acceptable	definite(ly)	lightning	receive
accidentally	embarrass	maintenance	relevant
accommodate	foreign	millennium	schedule
acquire	fourth	noticeable	separate
argument	immediate	occasion	success
calendar	independent	parallel	twelfth
category	indispensable	pastime	until
changeable	irresistible	privilege	vacuum
commitment	knowledge	publicly	vicious
conscience	liaise/liaison	questionnaire	weird

As if things weren't thorny enough already, Canadians must also contend with Canadian English. Canada is linked historically to Britain and is a member of the Commonwealth of Nations, but it shares its borders with the United States. In like fashion, Canadian spelling tends to vacillate between British and American, and fixing a Canadian standard is as easy as forecasting the weather six months from now.

But the hybrid quality of Canadian spelling does allow for a fair degree of flexibility, as *Editing Canadian English* points out. The same book also recommends maintaining consistency within these categories of spelling variants: *–or/–our*, *–er/–re*, *–ize/–ise*, *–yze/–yse*, and *–l/–ll* before endings. In other words, if *colour*, then *labour*; if *theatre*, then *centre*; if *analyze*, then *catalyze*; and if *installed*, then *travelled*.

If you want your English to be impeccably Canadian, you need to use these three resources:

Canadian Oxford Dictionary, 2nd edition, 2004
Editing Canadian English, 3rd edition, 2015 or online
The Canadian Press Caps and Spelling, 21st edition, 2015 or online

EXERCISES

A. Correct the mistakes in the following sentences.

1. 2013 was a good year for me. I won first place in 3 spelling bees.

2. I want to travel East this summer.

3. Kelley holds a Ph.D. in biology.

4. Did you finish the layout & design of the document yet?

5. From 2012–2016, the crime rate decreased by ten percent.

6. I travelled to St. Johns, Newfoundland in the Fall of 2017 to give step by step instructions to 3 Board Chairs.

B. Correct the punctuation and mechanical mistakes in these two emails. You may decide to tidy them up a bit more too.

1. Hi Dean

   Thank-you for your e-mail of January 19th. I discussed your long term plans to cut costs with Dr. Beckett and he wants to meet with you to discuss further. I need at least 2 weeks notice to set-up a meeting with him, therefore I wanted to know if you're available on February 2 at 3 pm.

   Regards,
   Jane

2. Hi Nguyen;

   I have not been able to process your claim for $27532.50, there are still several line items missing. Do you remember that I asked you to fill in three line items before submitting it. Once I have received the completed claim I can process it right away. If you need additional information, please contact me at (416) 123-4567.

   Best Regards,
   Ruth

PART FOUR

Style in Action

Take advantage of every opportunity to practice your communication skills so that when important occasions arise, you will have the gift, the style, the sharpness, the clarity, and the emotions to affect other people.

~ Jim Rohn

You do not create a style. You work and develop yourself; your style is an emanation from your own being.

~ Katherine Anne Porter

An attractive style requires, of course, all kinds of further gifts (beyond clarity and brevity)—such as variety, good humour, good sense, vitality, imagination. Variety means avoiding monotony of rhythm, of language, of mood. One needs to vary one's sentence length; to amplify one's vocabulary; to diversify one's tone.

~ F. L. Lucas

Crafting beautifully plain and lucid prose is our primary task as business writers and our greatest challenge. Perhaps you can write a meticulous outline, fix a run-on sentence, or design a handsome table. Unfortunately, this is not worth five minutes of your time if your words are not read. If you can't charm the reader to keep reading, all your efforts have been in vain.

Many readers are under no obligation to read your hard-won writing. Visualize Zara, a hotel manager and potential reader of your report on cybersecurity in the hospitality industry. Zara has a mighty heap of things demanding her attention; she's trying to juggle them all, with limited success. She's interested in your report, and she's made the time to read it. But if it is clumsily written, she'll soon turn her attention elsewhere. How do you deliver clear and expressive prose that keeps her engaged? How can your report stand out as a fine example of stylish writing? Answering these questions is the focus of this part of the book.

Rules won't help us much. Instead of rules, we need to hone what author John Trimble calls a "writer's sense." This concept is explored through a discussion of four fundamental qualities of style: clarity, energy, concision, and flow. These qualities enjoy a natural synergy. For example, if you attend to concision by trimming sentence fat, the sentence springs to life, becoming more energetic.

We'll start with clarity. For many of the most accomplished stylists, it is the supreme virtue.

CHAPTER ELEVEN

Express Yourself with Clarity and Sparkle

*Have something to say, and say it as clearly as you can.
That is the only secret of style.*

~ MATTHEW ARNOLD

I f the reader cannot understand your message, you have wasted your time and his. You have failed to communicate. Even if he manages, after some exertion, to grasp your meaning, your writing says much about you: it can signal muddled thinking, uncertainty about your message, or an inability to express your ideas. According to critic and writer F. L. Lucas, when Napoleon was assessing someone for appointment to a particular post, he asked, "Has he written anything? Let me see his *style.*"

We don't write to pass on our confusion but to convey a message that we consider valuable. Confusing prose insults your reader because the not-so-subtle message is *I'm too busy,* or *I don't respect you very much.* Whatever your reason, you're leaving it to the reader to do your job.

Unfortunately, a lack of clarity diminishes a writer's credentials in the eyes of the reader. You might be a brilliant scientist, but if you cannot articulate your insights, the brilliance is lost. It's floating out there in the universe, disconnected and distraught.

Clarity establishes credibility. Make your mantra this: everything clear on first reading. How do you accomplish this? The first step is to look closely at the verb because its force—or lack thereof—shapes every sentence.

VERB POWER

Every proficient writer appreciates the power of the verb. Author Constance Hale writes, "A sentence can offer a moment of quiet, crackle with energy or it can just lie there, listless and uninteresting. What makes the difference? The verb." Choose your verbs with care! Use verbs that express definite actions rather than vague ones. Shun weak verbs and the host of other words, such as adverbs, prepositions, and nouns, that accompany them, flittering like moths around a dim lightbulb. Here are some tips for choosing the best, most precise verb.

Favour more vigorous verbs than the linking verb *to be*. (Note that the following discussion is not about the verb *to be* as a helping verb: *I am helping Neil with the report.* Nor is it about the verb *to be* when it means "to exist": *Let it be.*) The linking verb *to be* (conjugated as *am, is, are, was, were, been,* and *being*) is, by its very nature, a weak verb. It functions as an equal sign (e.g., *I am an astronaut; I = astronaut*), and there's not much vigour in an equal sign. Of course, *to be* performs a useful and essential service when you need to identify or describe the subject or express a relationship: *This report is excellent. We have been friends for 17 years.* And it's used to convey colloquialisms: *We be stylin.*

Although the linking verb *to be* is sometimes necessary, it should never be the only verb in your repertoire. Some writers, however, use it almost exclusively: *The blah-blah were important. The purpose of blah-blah was blah-blah.*

Instead of *Timoteo is always on time*, try *Timoteo always ar-rives on time*. Instead of *The presentation was awful*, try *We didn't like the presentation*. Instead of *Our products are superior to your products*, try *Our products devour your products for breakfast*.

Caution: Although linking verbs lack action, they are not passive voice verbs. In the sentence *Before Edith moved to Canada, she had never been in a blizzard*, the verb *had been* is in the past perfect tense but not the passive voice. Do not confuse tense (the time something happens) with voice (active or passive).

Exercise caution with generic verbs. Imprecise verbs, such as *address, concern, become, come, give, make, provide,* and *take,* can describe many potential actions. For example, the second edition of the *Canadian Oxford Dictionary* has 29 definitions of the verb *go.* Ask yourself if you've named a specific action when you use one of these verbs.

Take this sentence: *I will address your complaint immediately.* What does that mean? Not much, unfortunately. If you didn't intend to be evasive, then you would communicate more by writing *I will discuss your complaint with the team manager this afternoon.* If you plan to fire the complainer on Friday, then evasion might be a good choice. Sometimes, of course, these all-purpose verbs are necessary. *Dr. Wootsi has office hours tomorrow from 8:00 a.m. to 1:30 p.m. Ingrid gives me a lot of grief.*

Watch out for multi-word verbs. These are verbs that need another word to complete them. The most common kind consists of a verb and one or more prepositions or adverbs. (Technical note: Prepositions or adverbs that combine with verbs in this way are not being used as ordinary prepositions or adverbs. When used this way, they are called particles.) There are also some idiomatic expressions that are multi-word verbs: e.g., *make do with* and *get moving.*

Multi-word verbs are often unnecessarily wordy, they can have multiple meanings (e.g., *make up* can mean *to lie, to restore,* or *to compensate*), and they are especially challenging for non-native speakers of English. Multi-word verbs are an important element in conversation, but in formal writing, they are used less frequently than single words unless they are matched to certain verbs: e.g., *refer to, apply for*. There are three types of multi-word verbs; sometimes the term *phrasal verb* is used to refer to all three types:

1. **Phrasal verbs** consist of a verb and an adverb particle: *break down, take off, give away*. The most common adverb particles used to create phrasal verbs are *around, at, away, down, in, off, on, out, over, round*, and *up*. The following examples illustrate how you can replace a phrasal verb with a single word, thus saving a word, expressing more formality, and being clearer.

   Not this: *Sales have **picked up** over the last few weeks.*

   But this: *Sales have **improved** over the last few weeks.*

   Not this: *My book **came out** in 2017.*

   But this: *My book **was published** in 2017.*

2. **Prepositional verbs** consist of a verb and a preposition particle: *deal with, look for, lead to*. Many prepositional verbs are not idiomatic and make good sense to use: *My cat **jumped on** the computer. I will **wait for** you at the bus stop.* However, you can occasionally replace a prepositional verb with a single word, such as in these examples:

   Not this: *Antonio **looked after** her accounts while she was gone.*

   But this: *Antonio **managed** her accounts while she was gone.*

   Not this: *Let's **talk about** this on Friday.*

   But this: *Let's **discuss** this on Friday.*

3. **Phrasal-prepositional verbs** combine the characteristics of phrasal verbs and prepositional verbs. They consist of a verb, an adverb particle, and a preposition particle: *look down on, look forward to, get away with*. They are often informal, and their meaning can be difficult to guess from their individual parts. Sometimes they can be replaced by single words, such as in these examples:

    Not this: *I cannot **put up with** his bad moods any longer.*

    But this: *I cannot **tolerate** his bad moods any longer.*

    Not this: *We all **looked up to** her.* But this: *We all **respected** her.*

    But sometimes no satisfactory replacement with a single word exists, such as in these examples: *I **look forward to** meeting you tomorrow. You think you can **get away with** anything!*

Don't disguise the verb. Make sure the action—which should be expressed by the verb—isn't hiding somewhere else in the sentence, perhaps lurking as a noun. Converting another part of speech—usually a verb—into a noun is known as **nominalization**. The writer too fond of nominalization will bore the reader with insipid and long-winded sentences. The sentences bumble along because the action of the sentence has been transformed, or even disguised, as a thing. Here are some examples:

Verb	Nominalization
assess	assessment
construct	construction
develop	development
establish	establishment
evaluate	evaluation
recommend	recommendation
submit	submission
transmit	transmission

Notice how removing the nominalization in these examples allows the writer to trim words and end the sentence more emphatically.

Not this: *Staff parties that require minimal input from management are the only ones that our boss will give his **endorsement** of.*

But this: *Our boss **will endorse** staff parties that require only minimal input from management.*

Not this: *My **advice** is that upon your **return**, you carry out a **review** of the data.*

But this: *I **suggest** that when you **return**, you **review** the data.*

Nominalization does have its uses and should not always be avoided. Not this: *She is not sure what he **intends** to do.* But this: *She is not sure of his **intentions**.* And nominalization can sometimes help smooth the transition between two sentences: *We have discussed this situation endlessly. **These discussions** are not helping us find a solution.*

VERB VOICE

The writer's choice of active or passive voice is another style decision that affects overall clarity and readability. An astute writer knows how and when to strike the energetic and personal note using the active voice and the authoritative and impersonal note using the passive voice. Chapter 8 details the difference between these two voices, but here's a quick reminder.

In the active voice, the subject is the agent of action, and in the passive voice, the subject is acted upon. Active voice: *After the audit is complete, Jason **will hire** a project manager. Maria **submitted** the report three weeks ago.* Passive voice: *After the audit is complete, a project manager **will be hired** by Jason. The report **was submitted** by Maria three weeks ago.* Jason and Maria (the agents of the action) can be removed from these examples while keeping the verb's passive voice: *After the audit is complete, a project manager **will be hired**. The report **was submitted** three weeks ago.*

As also discussed in Chapter 8, don't confuse the passive voice with a passive style. They are two different things. A writer might have a weak style; that is, he might rely heavily on linking verbs instead of action verbs, writing *My decision **was** to wait until Friday to file the incident report* rather than *I **decided** to wait until Friday to file the incident report.* But neither of these sentences is in the passive voice. Nor is the sentence *Hatsu **remained** passive during her arrest,* although the sentence might be better expressed as *Hatsu **did not resist** arrest.*

In most situations, the active voice is a much better, more concise, and more direct choice. Here are some tips for avoiding—and using—the passive voice:

■ Try to avoid using the pronoun *it* along with the passive voice; the result is an awkward sentence. Instead, make the sentence active by making the subject the agent of action.

  Not this: *It **was concluded** that the therapy had not been helpful.*

  But this: *We **concluded** that the therapy had not been helpful.*

■ Never use the passive voice habitually, sentence after sentence. People relate to people. The reader will lose interest if you use the passive voice excessively. *This report **was written** during the last three months of 2016. The report **will be distributed** widely throughout the community.* Who wrote and distributed the report?

■ Specify the agent of action when necessary. Passive voice verbs are handy for omitting the agent of the action, but sometimes the agent needs to be specified.

  Not this: *An apology **was made** to the vice-president.* (Who apologized?)

  But this: *The board chair **apologized** to the vice-president.*

- Many researchers prefer to use the passive voice to imply objectivity: *The subjects **were questioned** . . . The results **were measured** . . . The samples **were taken** . . .* Just remember that using the passive voice doesn't make the researcher's work more objective. A person is still doing the questioning, the measuring, and the taking; this person will not be absolved from blame if something goes wrong.

  Researchers also often prefer the passive voice when describing work that anyone could perform: *The test **was performed** at 8:00 a.m.* But if the action is unique to the writer, then active voice is a much better choice. *As part of my post-doctoral work, I **analyzed** soil samples from the Yucatán peninsula to determine the role of climate change in the collapse of the Mayan civilization in the ninth century.*

- Don't use the passive voice to avoid responsibility: own up to your transgressions. *The 2017 financials **have been misplaced.*** (But I don't want to tell you that I am the culprit.)

- Avoid using the passive voice as a hedging device. Hedging means to couch claims in cautious or tentative language and is a common feature of scientific and academic writing. Passive voice is only one type of hedging. Other hedging devices include unnecessary qualifiers and imprecise quantifiers: *to some extent, a fraction, arguably, supposedly.*

  Although a scientist might want to qualify her certainty about an experiment or an observation, excessive hedging strips a sentence of its vitality and clarity and the writer of her authority. In the following example, the writer has combined an unnecessary qualifier with the passive voice.

Not this: *The **presumed** hypothesis for apparent depression **was validated** in the study and indicated that patients with dementia were more likely to suffer depression.*

But this: *The study **validated** the hypothesis that patients with dementia were more likely to suffer depression.*

■ When using the passive voice, be careful not to combine it with a dangling modifier: *After analyzing the soil, the growth of the plants **was measured**.* Obviously, the plants did not analyze the soil; some unknown agent of action did.

As other writers have noted, the impersonal scientific style that favours the passive voice is a recent invention. Williams and Bizup, the authors of *Style: Lessons in Clarity and Grace*, cite a lively first-person account written by Isaac Newton in a 1672 paper titled "New Theory of Light and Colours." Every clause except one is in the active voice:

I procured a triangular glass prism, to try therewith the celebrated phenomena of colours. And for that purpose, having darkened my laboratory, and made a small hole in my window shade, to let in a convenient quantity of the sun's light, I placed my prism at the entrance, that the light might be thereby refracted to the opposite wall. It was at first a very pleasing diversion to view the vivid and intense colours produced thereby.

Although many style books and language pundits encourage us to *never* use the passive voice, the passive voice does have value. Here are some situations where the passive voice works well:

■ You know that the agent of action is irrelevant, unknown, obvious, or implied. *About 30 percent of the water consumed in homes **is used** to flush toilets.* (We understand the agent of action to be the person flushing the toilet.)

- You wish to avoid blaming someone. For example, your boss emails you asking where the sales report for Q1 is. You know that your co-writer, Frankie, is having a rough day. A diplomatic response to the boss might be this: *My apologies. I know you're waiting for the report. It **will be submitted** to you tomorrow morning.* And not this: *My apologies. I **will submit** the report tomorrow; I have been waiting for Frankie to complete her section.*

- You want to position important information at the beginning of a sentence rather than after the verb. *We must decide if we are going to open a branch office in Fredericton. This decision **will be made** once we have reviewed the cost-benefit analysis.* The passive voice works well for the second sentence because the subject, *this decision,* is more important than the implied agent of *will be made.*

- You want to focus the reader's attention on a specific character. In this example, the writer wants to explain the history from the point of view of the conquered.

*In 55 BCE, Celtic Britain **was invaded** by the Romans under Julius Caesar, but the Britons **were** not **conquered** by Caesar and his legions. In 43 CE, however, the Britons **were** finally **subjected** to Roman domination by the Roman emperor Claudius. In 61 CE, the Celtic tribal queen Boudicca led a revolt against Roman rule, but after some early victories, she **was defeated,** and Roman rule **was restored.***

NOUN FLAIR

If the verb is king, then the noun is queen. The verb drives while the noun calls out the names. As much as possible, choose concrete and specific nouns that engage the senses and help the reader "sense" the meaning. We can't sense a situation, but we can sense a forest fire.

All-purpose nouns are akin to all-purpose verbs. They are not always weak, but they can be imprecise at times. Some abstract nouns that lurk in business and scientific writing include the following:

ability	character	environment	nature
activity	degree	factor	process
approach	design	issue	role
area	development	kind	situation
case	effect	matter	thing

Consider these sentences: *These **aspects** are invaluable **considerations** for this **area**. The existing **nature** of the temperature variations was handled through computer modelling **capabilities**.* Yikes!

Also watch for noun stacks, which are lengthy noun phrases consisting primarily of nouns modifying other nouns, becoming adjectives in the process: *energy efficiency strategy planning, student loan repayment reliability study.* Fix these perilously balanced stacks either by moving the main noun in front of the stack and introducing prepositions as necessary or by breaking the stack up over two sentences.

Not this: *Install a **hazardous materials dispersion monitoring system**.*

But this: *Install a **system** for monitoring the **dispersion** of hazardous materials.*

INCLUSIVE LANGUAGE

Inclusive language respects all people's cultural, racial, ethnic, and national backgrounds; gender identity; religion; sexual orientation; age; or physical condition. The inclusive language guidelines of Queen's University define inclusive language as "vocabulary that avoids exclusion and stereotyping and is free from descriptors that portray individuals or groups of people as dependent, powerless, or less valued than others."

Biased language, on the other hand, includes expressions that demean people because of ethnicity, gender, political interests, race, sexual orientation, social class, or specific mental or physical traits.

One of the most common forms of biased language is based on gender: referring to doctors and lawyers generically as *he* or *him*, while nurses, admin assistants, and homemakers are *she* or *her*; making special mention of *female surgeons* or *female hockey players*; and drawing attention to those who have taken on traditionally female roles, like *male secretaries* or *male nurses*.

Keep references to individuals and groups as neutral as possible. When referring to members of a specific culture, be as precise as possible—instead of *Latin American* or *Asian*, use *Cuban* or *Japanese*. Avoid judgmental expressions: instead of *Third World country* or *underdeveloped nations* or the *Far East*, use *newly industrialized* nations or *East Asia*. Use *Ms.* instead of *Mrs.* or *Miss*, unless you know the reader prefers *Miss* or *Mrs.*

When referring to someone with a disability, avoid pitying or overly euphemistic terms, such as *victims*, *unfortunates*, *challenged*, or *differently abled*. Focus on the individual instead of the disability: instead of *blind person*, use *person who is blind*. In general, avoid expressions that demean people with medical conditions: *insane idea*, *lame excuse*, *the blind leading the blind*, etc.

In Canada, the term *Indigenous Peoples* refers to the Indigenous population in Canada collectively, including First Nations, Métis, and Inuit. Indigenous Peoples come from different nations with separate languages, cultures, and customs; therefore, use the specific nation, community, or band when possible. The term *First Nation(s)* is also widely used; it refers to both status and non-status people, but excludes Métis and Inuit people. The term *Eskimo* has been replaced by *Inuit*. *Inuk* is the singular form of *Inuit*.

Respectful Language

Avoid	Use
business man	business person
chairman	chair or chairperson
stewardess	flight attendant
housewife, house husband	homemaker
manpower	human resources
the disabled	person with a disability
police man	police officer
waiter or waitress	server
foreman	supervisor

SIMPLICITY

As business writers, we shouldn't be experimenting with complex sentence structure and revelling in verbal gymnastics. Our job is to inform, not to impress. It's about making sure that our readers can easily comprehend our intended message. As author Somerset Maugham points out, the only thing to be said against simplicity is "the possibility of dryness." But for Maugham, this risk is worth taking "when you reflect how much better it is to be bald than to wear a curly wig."

This simple, unadorned style is often referred to as plain language. How can we best achieve this deceptively simple style? Dress the words to suit the occasion. Think of business writing as a plain but pleasing dress, navy blue with a modest aesthetic. Clean and classy. Don't dress the words up in a flashy party outfit, ruby red with a beaded brocade. But don't dress the words down in sweatpants and a grubby t-shirt, either.

Here are some suggestions for dressing your words appropriately. These are general guidelines only and are not applicable to every situation. Sometimes that simple dress needs a little accessorizing!

- Engage directly with your reader when the context allows. Consider using first-person (*I, we*) and second-person (*you*) pronouns. Show that you're interested in two-way communication.

- State your major point(s) first, then provide the details. Think like a journalist, and get the most important information up front. And limit the number of dependent clauses, phrases, and parenthetical information.

- Don't be afraid to issue instructions in the active voice and imperative mood, when appropriate. Not this: *The amendments to the procedures must be filed in the online policy folder.* But this: *File the amendments to the procedures in the online policy folder.*

- Use straightforward and plain words. Multi-syllabic words are more difficult to grasp. What you consider sophisticated might just be pretentious. Instead of *utilize*, write *use*. Instead of *terminate*, write *end*.

- Prefer single words to phrases or pairs. Instead of *negative investment increment,* write *loss. A career in the medical profession* is *a career in medicine.*

- Use headings, lists, and visuals to make your documents more readable and interesting. See Chapter 3 for more information on this subject.

For more information on simplifying complex information, see Chapter 5.

EXERCISES

A. In which of these sentences is the verb in the passive voice?

1. Procrastination is said to decrease efficiency.

2. Table 18 shows the increase in procrastination in the control group.

3. The control group's level of procrastination was measured seven times using a highly innovative measurement tool.

4. The scientists challenged the findings, however, because the data was inconclusive.

5. If Jeannie had been able to participate in the control group, she would have understood more about her own struggles with procrastination.

6. Although her manager had given her permission to participate, she did not submit the necessary forms in time.

7. The experiment was conducted in 2017.

B. Change the passive voice into active voice. Add a subject if necessary.

1. It is our understanding that she was recruited by Kasem.

2. To save time, the agreement was sent by courier.

3. Please note that any changes to these balance sheets must be recorded by fiscal year-end.

4. Extensive training in the new procedures will be required by all staff.

5. Every evening, our offices are vacuumed and dusted.

C. **Improve these sentences by applying the principles reviewed in this chapter.**

1. Maurice seems to be ready for a holiday.

2. Please make a decision by November.

3. These are the recommendations of the chairman of the committee, who is an outstanding member of the community.

4. The role of an editor is to correct grammar and improve style.

5. I just wish my boss would provide an explanation of the new benefits package.

6. The request for an amendment to the project scope has arisen due to both a change in cost and also in the timing.

7. This manual gives instructions to end users.

8. Our field operations are in conformity with the association's standards.

9. Did Patrick finish editing the employee orientation manual updates?

10. How do I quote an editing job? This is a question that I am often asked by junior editors.

CHAPTER TWELVE

Energize Your Writing with Dynamic Words and Sentences

I recited my articles of faith:
humanity, clarity, simplicity, vitality.

~ WILLIAM ZINSSER

Good writers engage readers through dynamic, crisp prose. A natural connection springs up between the writer and reader because the writer has found the best words for the occasion and placed them carefully into a well-defined and shapely sentence. Knowing this is one thing; learning how to do it another. Fortunately, there are techniques for mastering the art of the finely crafted sentence that writers can use to strengthen their everyday writing.

When we invigorate our writing, we serve our readers well. We spare them the tedious chore of reading yet another feebly written email or memo. Your efforts to liven up the language and deliver meaningful sentences provide a welcome relief. Your deftly written letter might be the first piece of strong writing that Eleanora has seen all week. She might leap for joy!

Unfortunately, we're swimming in a murky sea of sluggish and indifferent writing; in fact, some of us are barely managing to stay afloat. Every well-written and lively passage is a life jacket; it provides hope to writers and readers everywhere.

In this chapter, we'll take a closer look at two things: words and sentences. Why do we have so many words to choose from in the English language? And given this abundance, why do many stylists still recommend the short word, above all? Then we'll turn our attention to sentences, because as scholar and author Stanley Fish reminds us, the formula goes like this: "Sentence craft equals sentence comprehension equals sentence appreciation." Let's rouse our stodgy sentences from their undeserved slumber with a strong cup of coffee: power words and power sentences.

A WEALTH OF WORDS

Short. Sharp. Smart. These words are the Anglo-Saxon heart of the English language. As children, we use these words instinctively. We call out *Need! Drink! Hungry! Help!* not *Require! Imbibe! Famished! Assistance!* Why does the fabric of the English language contain so many instances of two—or even more—words for the same thing? Why is the English language never at a loss for words?

To answer this question, let's take a quick jaunt down history's lane, specifically the history of the English language. The earliest inhabitants of the British Isles whom we know much about are the Celts, who moved in around 600 BCE. The Celts named the land *Albion.* They were followed by the Romans who by 43 CE had made Albion part of their empire and introduced some Latin words, including the name *Britain.* By the middle of the fifth century CE, the Roman Empire was disintegrating. The Romans withdrew from Britain, leaving the small island weakened and vulnerable to attacks.

On the heels of the Roman retreat, tribes of Germanic-speaking people—the Angles, the Jutes, and the Saxons—began arriving as invaders and settlers. These Anglo-Saxons, as these Germanic tribes were collectively known, gradually established permanent settlements and displaced the Celts. The southern part of the island was reborn as *Engla-land*, the land of the Angles. The fusion of the closely related Germanic dialects gave birth to the language known as Old English.

Many beautiful poems and stories—about 400 texts—survive from this Anglo-Saxon period. But more importantly for us, many of the most common words used today have their roots in Old English: *be, bread, drink, fish, food, he, house, milk, mother, night, she, sleep, strong, water*, and *you*. Many of our common swear words are also an Anglo-Saxon legacy.

By the late eighth century CE, the ferocious Vikings (or Norsemen) began their raiding expeditions. Although the Viking expansion was finally halted, about 1,000 Norse words were permanently added to the English lexicon, including words such as *again, anger, berserk, egg, law, race, skill, sky*, and *want*. The Viking invasions also led to a simplification of Old English, which was a heavily inflected language (inflection refers to the modification of a word to express a different meaning or relationship).

Old English is, however, radically different from Modern English, thanks to one more invasion. In 1066, with the Duke of Normandy at the helm, the French-speaking Normans successfully conquered England at the Battle of Hastings. The Norman duke, later renamed William the Conqueror, influenced the evolution of the English language more than anyone before or after him—quite an accomplishment for an illiterate noble who never learned English!

For more than 300 years after what became known as the Norman Conquest, French was the language of power in England, spoken by royalty and officials. It was not until 1399, at the coronation of Henry IV, that a king claimed his throne using English—albeit with about 30 percent of the lexicon being French in origin. Amazingly, Old English had not died out; instead, over the centuries, Norman French merged with Old English to create Middle English, the bedrock for the Modern English we speak and write today.

Some 10,000 French words were absorbed into the English language, and about 75 percent of them are still in use. But the heart of the English language remains Anglo-Saxon. When Churchill wrote "Short words are best, and old words, when short, the best of all," the old words he was referring to are the Anglo-Saxon ones. He used these words to great effect in his rally to the English people in 1940: "We shall fight on the beaches, we shall fight on the landing grounds, we shall fight in the fields and the streets, we shall fight in the hills; we shall never surrender..." All the words in this passage are Old English, as it was spoken before the Norman Conquest, except the last one, *surrender*, which is a French word that arrived with the Normans in 1066.

Never be afraid to use the short word, and never think it undignified. Respect the Germanic heart of the English language!

This list outlines some Old English (Anglo-Saxon) words and their French counterparts to illustrate some of the choices available to us.

Old English	French	Old English	French
answer	reply	green	verdant
belief	faith	help	assist
buy	purchase	homesick	nostalgic
forgive	pardon	smell, stench	odour
freedom	liberty	unwilling	reluctant
ghost	phantom	weird	strange
And some words specific to business writing:			
ask	enquire	fix	repair
because of	due to	give	provide
book (verb)	reserve	job	occupation
check	verify	needs (noun)	requirement

As English has evolved over the centuries, it has become more rigid in word order: the roles of the nouns in the sentence, marked with suffixes before Old English made contact with Old Norse, are now identified by their place in the sentence. We have to write *The dog loves the woman* in that order and that order only if we wish to convey that the dog is doing the loving.

But what we lose in flexibility of word order, we win back a thousand times over in the beauty of the language's extraordinary vocabulary. This extravagance, due in no small part to the Norman Conquest, is a wellspring from which our novelists, poets, playwrights—and, yes, even adept business writers—drink gratefully from. The best style balances Anglo-Saxon with French. If you rely too heavily on Anglo-Saxon, your voice will be too monosyllabic. If you rely too heavily on French and Latin, your voice will be too ornate.

Not this: *Prior to the termination of the project, we facilitated a workshop to encourage people to utilize the new software.*

But this: *Before the project ended, we delivered a workshop to encourage people to use the new software.*

SENTENCE SENSIBILITY

A jumble of expressive words does not a powerful sentence make. To craft meaningful and eloquent sentences, we have to analyze our writing at the sentence level. Here's how we do this:

Reinforce meaning with the sentence core. Place the main idea of your sentence in the core—namely, the subject and verb of the independent clause. Don't waste that prime real estate!

Not this: *The expected result of the use of organic fertilizers is an increase in the profitability of the greenhouse operations.*

But this: *Using organic fertilizers should increase the profitability of the greenhouse operations.*

Let's take a closer look at this example:

Original Sentence	Improved Sentence
The expected result is the simple subject. The verb is the linking verb *is*.	*Using organic fertilizers* is the subject. The helping verb and main verb are *should increase*.
The subject complement is *an increase in the profitability of the greenhouse operations*. This complement includes a nominalization: *increase*.	The object of the verb is *the profitability of the greenhouse operations*. There is no nominalization.
The subject and verb do not convey the main idea.	The subject and verb convey the main idea.

In *Style: Lessons in Clarity and Grace*, authors Williams and Bizup make this helpful suggestion: "The two most general principles for clear sentences are these: make main characters the subjects of your verbs; make those characters' important actions your verbs." Readers appreciate subjects and verbs that match character and action.

Not this: *The magician's card trick enchanted the audience.*

But this: *The magician enchanted the audience with her card trick.*

Not this: *The committee's plan is to amend the outdated bylaws.*

But this: *The committee plans to amend the outdated bylaws.*

Watch out for dummy subjects. Notice how dummy subjects (formally referred to as expletives) also weaken the sentence core. Dummy subjects are the pronouns *it* or *there* used at the beginning of the sentence simply to fill the subject position: they do not have an antecedent (a noun the pronoun refers to) and are therefore empty of meaning. These constructions delay meaning and waste the core of the sentence on a simple declaration.

Not this: *It is often the case that a solar panel installation will last for years.*

But this*: A solar panel installation will often last for 25 years.*

Notice that cutting the unnecessary lead *it is often the case that* allowed the writer to add the detail of 25 years, which is a useful detail because *years* is vague—it could be 3 years or 393. The writer has anticipated potential questions.

In the following sentence, *there* is the dummy subject, and the true subject is *a discussion*. In the improved sentence, *we* becomes the subject.

Not this: *At the next meeting, there must be a discussion about the cost overrun.*

But this: *At the next meeting, we must discuss the cost overrun.*

Avoid too many interruptions between the subject and the verb. Get to the main subject as quickly as possible, and connect the main subject to its verb. If you need to extend the subject, do so after the verb.

Not this: **The employees**, *despite their interest in listening to the presentation on Friday afternoon,* **were** *eager to start their weekend.*

But this: **The employees were** *eager to start their weekend despite their interest in listening to the presentation on Friday afternoon.*

Not this: **An amendment** *to the standard operating procedure, which means that moving forward vacation requests must be approved at least three months beforehand,* **has been approved** *by the team lead.*

But this: **The team lead has approved** *an amendment to the standard operating procedure, and vacation requests must now be approved at least three months beforehand.*

— STYLE IN ACTION —

Position the main verb close to the beginning of the sentence. This is especially problematic with technical information written in the passive voice. In the sentence below, the passive voice and the parenthetical information have forced the verb to the end of the sentence. In the suggested fix, the verb is closer to the beginning of the sentence.

Not this: *The team's evaluation of the permeability of the Bluesky Formation sandstones—namely, the sandstones' ability to transmit fluids—**was discussed** at the meeting.*

But this: *At the meeting, the team **discussed** its evaluation of the permeability of the Bluesky Formation sandstones—namely, the sandstones' ability to transmit fluids.*

Scientists are not the only guilty parties. Lawyers often compose unnecessarily difficult sentences.

Not this: *If any member of the board retires, the company, at the discretion of the board of directors and after notice from the board chair to all the members of the board at least 40 days before exercising this option, **may buy** the member's interest in the company.* (47 words)

But this: *The company **may buy** any retiring board member's company shares. This option will be exercised at the board's discretion after the chair has given all board members at least 40 days' notice.* (32 words)

Sequence your information appropriately. Readers best understand carefully sequenced information. In the first part of your sentence, place the old information that links backward and sets context; then follow with the new information that you want to emphasize. Provide context for your readers before asking them to consider anything new.

Not this: *Athletes can improve their performance by paying attention to what they eat. Plant-based foods contain many valuable vitamins and minerals that provide optimal nutrition.*

— 237 —

But this: *Athletes can improve their performance by paying attention to what they eat. One way they can optimize their diets is by eating plant-based foods, which contain many valuable vitamins and minerals.*

Prefer positive constructions. Negative constructions slow the reader down and delay comprehension.

Not this: *It is not possible to reduce demands for energy when the government does not introduce conservation measures.*

But this: *Demands for energy will decrease when the government introduces conservation measures.*

Watch out for strings of prepositional phrases. Too many prepositional phrases can confuse the reader.

Not this: *We determined that there was a very real threat from the lack of disposal sites for the waste from the nuclear plants at locations outside the province.* (Six prepositional phrases: *from the lack, of disposal sites, for the waste, from the nuclear plants, at locations, outside the province*)

But this: *We determined that the lack of nuclear waste disposal sites at locations outside the province posed a significant threat.* (Three prepositional phrases: *of nuclear waste disposal sites, at locations, outside the province*)

In his book *Editing Prose*, Richard Lanham observes that "two prepositional phrases in a row turn on a warning light, three make a problem, and four invite disaster. . . . The *of* strings are the worst of all. They seem to re-enact a series of hiccups."

Start well and end well. The lead and close of a sentence carry the most weight and will have the most impact on the reader. The beginning of a sentence defines the topic the sentence will cover; this part of the sentence is referred to as the topic position. The end of a sentence emphasizes the main point; this part of the sentence is referred to as the stress position. In the sentence *Engineers do their calculations using complex software*, the sentence emphasizes *complex software*. In the sentence *Using complex software, engineers do their calculations*, the sentence emphasizes *calculations*. Once you know what you want to emphasize, position it at the end where readers expect it.

Author and teacher Roy Poynter illustrates these concepts of sentence leads and ends using this line from Shakespeare's *Macbeth*: "The Queen, my lord, is dead." Thanks to the commas, the sentence has a carefully defined beginning, middle, and end. But what Poynter really appreciates about the sentence is that the subject, *the Queen*, appears at the start, and the most significant phrase, *is dead*, is placed at the end, where the natural power of the sentence resides.

Not this: *Without your assistance, we would not be able to carry out the important work that we do.*

But this: *Without your assistance, we would not be able to carry out our important work.*

Not this: *The need to find renewable sources of energy in the next decade is becoming clear to everyone.*

But this: *In the next decade, we must find renewable sources of energy.*

Keep sentences short and simple. Write relatively short sentences. Try not to exceed 30 words per sentence, and aim for an average of 20 words. You can check your average sentence length by using the reading tools available in Microsoft Word and Outlook. For more information on this test, see Chapter 18.

Your sentence structure, too, should be reasonably simple. Too many ideas crammed into one sentence will not please your reader. Place the main information in the main clause, and keep less important information for phrases and dependent clauses.

Not this: *I spoke with you on the phone yesterday, and you informed me that the backorder had been placed.*

But this: *When I spoke with you on the phone yesterday, you informed me that the backorder had been placed.*

Bring in the paramedics to revive lethargic sentences. Richard Lanham's paramedic method is a fast and effective way to cut to the essential. This "emergency therapy," as he calls it, also allows you to craft shapelier sentences and reveal the actor.

The steps of Lanham's paramedic method are simple, but they take time to apply. Use this method for your most important pieces of writing until this emergency therapy becomes natural. Here is a slightly modified version of his method:

1. Circle the prepositions.
2. Draw a box around the *to be* verb forms and any passive voice constructions.
3. Ask "Where's the action?" "What's the theme?" "Who or what is kicking whom?" "Is the agent of action or main character clear?"
4. Put this central action into a simple, active verb.
5. Move the doer of the action into the subject.
6. Start fast—no slow wind-ups.
7. Banish any redundancies.
8. Read the passage aloud with feeling and emphasis.

Let's apply this method to this lead sentence in a policy report.

An evaluation of the effects of population growth in Hamilton and the corresponding rise in real estate prices in Hamilton was undertaken and is presented in this report.

Applying the paramedic method, we note the six prepositions (circles) and two passive voice constructions (boxes). If we ask ourselves what the theme is, we realize it's the report itself. In a lead introductory sentence, why would it be the last word in the sentence? Move the main action into the subject, transform the passive voice into active voice, and eliminate a couple of the prepositions, and presto:

This report presents our evaluation of the effects of population growth in Hamilton and the corresponding rise in real estate prices. Or: *In this report, we evaluate how population growth in Hamilton has affected real estate prices.*

Vary your sentence length and type. Sentences that lack variety rapidly become monotonous. Author Gary Provost illustrates this here:

> This sentence has five words. Here are five more words. Five-word sentences are fine. But several together become monotonous. Listen to what is happening. . . . The ear demands some variety. Now listen. I vary the sentence length, and I create music. Music. The writing sings. It has a pleasant rhythm, a lilt, a harmony. . . . And sometimes, when I am certain the reader is rested, I will engage him with a sentence of considerable length, a sentence that burns with energy and builds with all the impetus of a crescendo, the roll of the drums, the crash of the cymbals—sounds that say listen to this, it is important.

Chapter 8 discusses the grammatical types of sentences: simple, compound, complex, and compound-complex. Four types of functional sentences also help the writer introduce more variety: declarative sentences make a statement; interrogative sentences ask a question; imperative sentences issue a command; and exclamatory sentences make an exclamation.

A sentence with the main point at the beginning is referred to as a loose sentence. In English, they are very common, especially in conversation. *We did not agree with the main points of the report, especially the argument that hosting the games would benefit the community.* Periodic sentences reverse the pattern of loose structure by placing the main information at the end. They are useful for making an emphatic point at the end of the sentence or for putting reasons for something before the final clause. *Considering that I am unhappy with my current job and I have always wanted to live in the North, I might take that job offer in Whitehorse.* Periodic sentences are especially useful when you want to conclude with a persuasive flourish.

Business writers can also use other rhetorical devices, such as balanced sentences and antithetical sentences, sparingly for dramatic effect. Balanced sentences emphasize similarity; antithetical sentences emphasize contrast. Here are two examples:

Balanced sentence: *What is written without effort is in general read without pleasure.* ~ Samuel Johnson

Antithetical sentence: *We must learn to live together as brothers or perish together as fools.* ~ Martin Luther King

EXERCISES

A. Revise these sentences by applying the principles reviewed in this chapter.

1. The last decade has seen a growing awareness among regulatory agencies about the need to use plain language.

2. The major framework of her paper involves presenting a discussion of Indigenous land rights.

3. What all regional plans have in common is that they seek to ensure sustainable long-term prosperity throughout an entire region.

4. Moving forward, our plan is to provide fact sheets not only on projects completed within the last 12 months but also on technical updates.

5. The design that is recommended for adoption would accomplish the removal of particulates with the desired degree of efficiency.

6. Through my current employment with Northern Lights College, I have been given the opportunity through a variety of workshops and seminars to enhance my communication skills as well as stress management skills.

7. There were several clues leading to the discovery of the faulty wiring by the electrician.

8. The more than 30-percent elimination of plastics from the disposal stream will be achieved through a market-based system phased in over the next three years.

9. As part of the enhancements to the facility, we built a very spacious training room, and we plan to use it to host classes, workshops, and community events.

10. While a good portion of the changes are well underway with everyone working extremely hard to meet our customers' needs, this proposal will hopefully provide better visibility as to what changes are still to come, including how we communicate with external customers.

B. Try this.

1. Select about 10 pages of your writing, and circle all the words of French or Latin origin you can find. Could you exchange some of them for words of Anglo-Saxon origin? How does that change the style? Does it make the message clearer?

2. Take a sample of your writing, such as a memo or report. Apply Richard Lanham's paramedic method to the piece. After you've circled all the forms of the *to be* verb, what active verbs do you have? If you have several dull verbs, could you replace some of them with livelier, more specific verbs? How many prepositional phrases did you find? Do you have sentences that trail from one prepositional phrase to another? Are your nouns concrete and specific? How clear is the writing?

— CHAPTER THIRTEEN —

Cut It Out:
Concision at Work

Good writing starts with a profound respect for words—
their denotations, their connotations, their force, their
rhythm. Once you learn to respect them, you'll develop a
passion for using them thriftily.

~ JOHN TRIMBLE

Concision: many words have been written about the fine art of fewer words. Concision demands that we detach ourselves from our writing and focus on stripping away the redundancy, the clichéd phrase, the interior chit-chat, the unnecessary detail. But we need to be careful that we don't cut away too much because a style all bone and no flesh will strike our readers as brusque and even unfriendly. As in all sophisticated undertakings, the challenge is to find the balance between too little and too much.

The word *concision* comes to us from Latin: *concisus* is the past participle of *concidere* meaning to "cut up, cut down" from *con-* "completely" + *caedere* "to cut." The word *scissors* comes from the same Latin root. Therefore, when you're thinking of concision, remember its affinity to scissors. Keep them sharp and at hand!

That crisp and compact is preferable to sluggish and sprawling will surprise no one; nor is the concept particularly 21st century. The ancient Greeks might not have been hunched in front of computers, but they knew a thing or two about the power of words. In the classic work *On Style*, probably written in the first century BCE, the Greek philosopher Demetrius outlines the four graces of style. The first one is the grace that results from compression: "a thought that would have been spoiled by dwelling on it is made graceful by a light and rapid touch." Thousands of years ago, the virtues of concision were extolled! Obviously, the wordiness virus is nothing new.

Writers everywhere, of every discipline and in every endeavour, need to be vigilant in their efforts to contain their writing to the essential. Otherwise, we run the risk of being unread. As Churchill reminds us, "This report, by its very length, defends itself against the risk of being read."

Fortunately, the battle against bloat can be won.

WORDINESS: A COMMON CURSE

Did you know that a professional editor can prune many documents by about 25 percent—and maybe even more?

Why make it so easy for editors? Why are so many writers more adept at padding content than pruning it? For many of us, inflating our language begins at school with an assignment like this: submit a 10-page essay on how robotics has revolutionized medicine. Problem: you have only seven pages of content. Solution: inflate content to meet page count. A wise teacher—gazing into her crystal ball and seeing you 15 years later as a popular science writer—would have advised you to write what you know and then stop. In the real world, however, we seldom receive such sage advice. Instead, away we go, stuffing more words in, sentence by sentence, intent on word quantity rather than word quality.

But the business writer's audience is not a teacher who *must* read his students' submissions. The audience is a motley crew of the motivated and unmotivated, the curious and incurious, and the sophisticated and unsophisticated. This audience isn't expecting a pre-determined page count. They're expecting a clean and lean message. Unfortunately, by the time we begin our careers and find, sometimes to our surprise, that much of our workday is taken up with writing, we have some deeply ingrained bad habits.

We can't, however, blame it all on our education. We binge on words, our sentences losing their natural shape and rhythm in the process, for many reasons. Interior dialogue, fine in a first draft, doesn't get removed. Simply not knowing any better is also part of the problem. We assume that pompous and inflated language must be the correct way to write because we see it everywhere. And sometimes we don't make the effort because removing what Lanham calls "the lard factor" takes time. One final culprit could be that we don't have much to communicate, and we pad our words in an attempt to hide this from our readers.

Let's play devil's advocate for a moment and consider whether we lose something when we write less. Some writers are afraid that pruning can lead to an excessively sparse tone. But it doesn't have to be so.

Take this simple sentence as an example: *This chemistry book is not only tedious but also costs a lot.* Most writers know instinctively that this sentence needs an overhaul. First, we note a grammatical problem because *tedious* (an adjective) is not parallel with *costs a lot* (a verb phrase). So *costs a lot* becomes *expensive*, and now we have two parallel adjectives. Then we eliminate the *not only ... but also* construction because it's just padding. (Constructions such as *not only ... but also* should be kept for complex thoughts requiring the juxtaposition.) Now we have an admittedly bald sentence: *This chemistry book is tedious and expensive.*

But this shortened version with its original meaning intact allows the writer to pursue other options, like these two:

1. Make the page *look* better: add more white space or even an image, perhaps an image of the book cover. Looking smart is a good thing.

2. Provide some useful detail. Try this: *This chemistry book is tedious and, at $79.99, is also expensive.* Now you have added some useful information to *expensive,* which is otherwise subjective and imprecise.

Economical writing saves trees, time, and tempers. If your manager needs reassuring because he asked for a five-page report and you submitted a three-page report, remind him that you are frugal with words. Wouldn't he rather digest a three-page leanly written report than a five-page one marbled with fat?

— Anecdotal Evidence —

The writer Truman Capote said he believed more in the scissors than the pencil. As a magazine editor, I learned to keep my scissors handy. We were publishing a small magazine and operating on a shoestring budget; we paid our writers by the word—modestly. Occasionally, a writer would submit a few hundred more words than requested, say 1,300 words instead of the assigned 1,000. The extra words would be accompanied by a note saying that it had been impossible to do the story justice in 1,000 words.

As the editor, I had to ask myself: *Do we want to pay for those extra words?* And the answer was almost always *No.* With the help of a skilled editor, I could usually trim the story back to 1,000 words without losing any significant content.

Now as a teacher, I put that same question to writers: *If you had to pay for that word, would you keep it or toss it?* It's surprising how much fluff people would dispense with if they had to pay for it.

In *To the Point: A Dictionary of Concise Writing,* Robert Fiske maintains that wordiness is an obstacle to success, an obstacle to companionship, and an obstacle to self-knowledge. That's quite a burden of guilt for wordiness to carry.

THE VIRTUES OF CONCISION

"A great ox stands upon my tongue," wrote the ancient Greek tragedian Aeschylus. We need more of these oxen, perched on our keyboards!

So much could be—and has been—written about the benefits of writing less. In the interests of modelling brevity, here are just three of the many advantages:

1. Brevity improves readability and comprehension. Your message stands out. Consider the beauty—and brevity—of Abraham Lincoln's Gettysburg Address (271 words) and St. Francis of Assisi's Sermon to the Birds (174 words).

2. Brevity is good manners. By writing less, you save the reader's time. Brevity frees up more time for the reader to respond, hopefully also concisely.

3. Brevity persuades. In *Making Your Case: The Art of Persuading Judges*, former Supreme Court Justice Antonin Scalia and lawyer Bryan Garner note, "A long and flabby brief, far from getting a judge to spend more time with your case, will probably have just the opposite effect."

PRUNING TECHNIQUES

Use the following strategies to cut to the chase. Don't think of it as clear-cutting; think of it as pruning to remove the deadwood (or in this case, the dead words). Let the sun shine in by eliminating the thicket of jargon, clumsy phrasing, and internal dialogue.

Find compact word(s) that carry the most meaning. Give them a leading role. Winston Churchill excelled at this. One of his aides, Denis Kelly, who helped draft war briefs, recalls preparing this sentence: "Germany was isolated and surrounded on all sides." Churchill drew a line through it and responded, "The word you want is 'crushed.'"

Question every word in a sentence. Is it necessary? Does it interfere with or contribute to meaning?

Look for phrases and clauses that can be shortened. The following list illustrates some examples, but there are hundreds more. Get to know the ones that you are fond of using, and start replacing them with single words or shorter phrases.

Avoid	Use
a majority of	most
at the present time	now
both of these are	both are, they are
despite the fact that	despite
get in touch with	phone, write, contact
he is a man who	he
in a lot of cases	frequently
in close proximity	near
in connection with	with, about, concerning
in exchange for	for
in order to	to
in reference to	regarding, about
in regard to	about
in this day and age	now, today
is able to	can
is of concern to	concerns
necessarily have to	have to, must
on condition that	if
on the part of	among, by
no one but	only
over the long run	eventually
point of view	viewpoint

Avoid	Use
prior to	before
take into account	consider
take offence to	resent
the thing to do before anything else	first
the truth of the matter	actually
up to a maximum of	up to
use x instead of y	replace x with y
with the exception of	except

Edit for redundancy. In *Style: Lessons in Clarity and Grace,* Williams and Bizup identify three common types of redundancies: redundant modifiers, redundant categories, and redundant pairings.

- **Redundant modifier** The word does not need a modifier because the modifier is already implied in the word: *in my past experience* (everything I have experienced is in the past) or *unexpected surprise* (a surprise is, by definition, unexpected). Here are a few more examples:

absolutely essential	personal friend
advance planning	plan ahead
basic fundamentals	prove conclusively
completely unanimous	repeat again
consensus of opinion	revolve around
end result	sudden crisis
first started	time period
free gift	true facts
intimately familiar	ultimate outcome
new initiatives	usual custom

- **Redundant category** The category is implied by the word, but the category is named: *of a strange type* (*strange* implies *type*), *teal in colour* (*teal* implies *colour*). More examples:

extreme in degree	often times
few in number	period of time
honest in character	round in shape
in a confused state	shiny in appearance

- **Redundant pair** The second word reiterates the meaning of the first: *one and only, any and all*. More examples:

each and every	hopes and desires
first and foremost	peace and quiet
full and complete	various and sundry

Watch out for an overly formal style. It will make you seem stuffy and old school.

Uptight	Relaxed
as per your letter	as your letter notes
as per your request	as you requested
at an early date	soon
at your earliest convenience	by (with a specific date)
due to the fact that	because
in respect of the matter of	regarding
in the event that	if
we are in receipt of your letter	we've received your letter
we have your order and will transmit same	we'll forward your order promptly
we shall advise you	we'll let you know

Cut jargon and bizspeak ruthlessly. Jargon, jargon everywhere! But not a thought to think! (Apologies to Coleridge for playing with his stanza in "The Rime of the Ancient Mariner": "Water, water, everywhere, Nor any drop to drink.")

The word *jargon* comes from an Old French word meaning "the twittering and chattering of birds." It's important to distinguish between technical jargon—industry-specific words used to speed up communication but often difficult for outsiders to understand— and everyday jargon—long-winded, unnecessarily complex words or trendy buzzwords and phrases. Some people refer to this second type of jargon as bureaucratese, bafflegab, or bizspeak.

Examples of technical jargon that lawyers use include *motion, party, plaintiff, bench, appellant*; doctors use *bilateral periorbital ecchymosis, neoadjuvant therapy, fertility preserving interventions*; and business writers use *b2b solution, monetize, incentivize*. Although members of a profession use technical jargon to communicate with each other, communication breaks down when this technical jargon is used to communicate with people unfamiliar with it. An architect knows what a corbel is, but most of us will need it defined.

Everyday jargon can be acceptable occasionally in informal communications where all parties understand the meaning. For example, the expression 24/7 is an effective shorthand. But often this bafflegab becomes a crutch for the weak writer who subjects the poor readers to sentences like the following:

Which actions on our list are actionable in Q2?

If we operationalize our best practices, we're going to see a real paradigm shift.

So this is just a heads-up to the team that I need buy-in from everyone.

We'll discuss the low-hanging fruit offline; let's focus first on the end goal. So can I task you with some deliverables?

One of the worst offenders is the expression *going forward* and its siblings *moving forward* and *moving ahead*. *Going forward* is usually followed by a future tense verb, so it is almost always redundant. *Going forward* is so worn out that people tune out when they hear it and see it. As Don Watson reminds us in his book *Death Sentence: The Decay of Public Language*: "*Going forward* is . . . what generally happens without anyone needing to say so. (As in: We have a strategy for continuous improvement outcomes going forward.)" More banal expressions that need banishing from the language include *at the end of the day, drill down, it goes without saying* (then don't say it!), *meaningful dialogue, push the envelope, repurpose*, and *window of opportunity*.

Look for wordiness patterns. Author and writing consultant Stephen Wilbers has some excellent advice for cutting the fat: "Do what experienced editors do. Think in terms of categories of wordiness rather than isolated instances." If you pay attention, you'll observe how wordiness follows certain patterns, making it easier to spot and delete. Once you've identified the pattern, you can eliminate the wordiness. Here are some examples of how you can do this.

Remove unnecessary adjectives and adverbs, and **banish** intensifiers.	Not this: *very silly, extremely tired, really bad*
	But this: *ridiculous, exhausted, dreadful*
	Not this: *I was truly impressed with William Strunk's quite apt description of qualifiers as "the leeches that infest the pond of prose."*
	But this: *I was impressed with William Strunk's description of qualifiers as "the leeches that infest the pond of prose."*

Compress clauses into phrases or appositives.

Not this: *Because Jeff is shy with strangers, he didn't respond.*

But this: *Shy of strangers, Jeff didn't respond.*

Not this: *Mia, who is a strong writer, often helps me.*

But this: *Mia, a strong writer, often helps me.*

Convert prepositional phrases into possessive nouns.

Not this: *The most fascinating building in Montreal ...*

But this: *Montreal's most fascinating building ...*

Combine sentences.

Not this: *Our team has five sales people. These people do an excellent job of generating new leads.*

But this: *Our team of five sales people does an excellent job of generating new leads.*

Strengthen sentence openings and **trim** sentence endings.

Not this: *It seems that beginning two years ago ...*

But this: *About two years ago ...*

Not this: *Does this report read well to you?*

But this: *Does this report read well?*

Delete what readers can infer.

Not this: *Imagine trying to learn the rules for flying a helicopter.*

But this: *Imagine learning to fly a helicopter.*

Turn negatives into positives.

Not this: *did not succeed, not the same, do not include*

But this: *failed, different, omit*

Minimize personal remarks.

Not this: *As far as I am concerned, your writing has improved.*

But this: *Your writing has improved.*

EXERCISES

Tighten up these sentences without removing any content. But do introduce new words if necessary.

1. There is no evidence to support the idea that those new mutual funds are any more likely to do much better than those that you already have.

2. Jean-Paul married his wife last year in the month of May and never returned back to Seattle.

3. In our opinion, the optimal course of action would be to maintain continued use of the alkali reactant.

4. Sexist language contributes to the ongoing prevalence of gender stereotypes.

5. In the modern business world, excessive regulation is seriously destroying initiative among individual businesses.

6. There are a number of incidents that my colleagues have reported that indicate that if we don't update our health and safety policies, it will be a problem for the company moving forward.

7. The purpose of this report is to update our research findings.

8. In order to receive a free gift you must complete all of this online registration form.

9. Would you please record this as being an accident and not an emergency situation.

10. For the purposes of this document variances will be explained that are greater than $25,000 which are based on the formula utilized by the external auditors for the ACCC.

11. Sitha tried to make clear how her co-worker's careless writing was a poor reflection of the company.

12. Due to the fact that the program failed two times during testing, we are now considering other options.

CHAPTER FOURTEEN

Focus on Flow:
Cohesion and Coherence

Consider the postage stamp: its usefulness consists in the ability to stick to one thing till it gets there.

~ Josh Billings

When we admire a passage of writing, what we often like—consciously or not—is the cadence and apparently seamless connection of ideas. We might describe the writing as fluent, a word that comes from Latin *fluentem*, meaning "to flow freely." Writing that flows has an internal rhythm that makes it a pleasure for the reader to follow. The reading journey is smooth and connected, rather than bumpy and disjointed.

Flow is achieved through document cohesion and coherence. The glue that binds sentences together is known as cohesion. Cohesive sentences connect readily to each other. If these sentences follow a logical sequence of ideas from one paragraph to the next, the document will have something important, known as coherence.

Authors Williams and Bizup encourage us to think of cohesion as "pairs of sentences fitting together in the way two pieces of a jigsaw puzzle do" and coherence as "seeing what all the sentences in a piece of writing add up to, the way all the pieces in a puzzle add up to the picture on the box."

SENTENCE COHESION

Cohesion between sentences is often created by the connections between the end of one sentence (predicate) and the beginning of the next (subject). The writer uses the subject to state familiar information contained somewhere within the previous sentence. The predicate, in commenting on the subject, adds new information. This information in the predicate then becomes the subject of the next sentence. Here are some ways to create cohesion:

- **Repetition** Repeat a word from Sentence A in Sentence B. *The difficulty with defining **editing** is that there are so many potential definitions. To some people, **editing** means copyediting; to other people, editing means major substantive editing.*

  If direct repetition is too obvious, try a synonym of the word you wish to repeat. ***Contranyms** are words that are their own opposites, e.g., oversight can mean both oversee and overlook. These **words with contradictory meanings** can confuse the reader if you are not careful.*

  The pronouns *this, that, these, those, he, she, it, they,* and *we* can be used to refer to something previously mentioned, but the antecedent must be clear. *Take the time to check for wordiness in your **reports**. Otherwise, **they** will be longer than necessary.*

- **Linking** Connect the end of Sentence A to the beginning of Sentence B. *The program has not been approved because the flow-through mechanism had several **flaws**. **These flaws** became more evident after several months.*

- **Parallelism** Repeat a structure. *Writers need clarity. Editors need charity.*

- **Passive voice** Passive constructions can be useful to establish cohesion if the subject in the passive voice is known information from a previous sentence. *Glenn is usually able to complete his weekly progress report on time. Unfortunately, he was transferred to Yellowknife last month and fell behind.* Or: *Marion is an outstanding editor. She was laid off by the new manager, however.*

- **Conjunctive adverbs** Because the job of conjunctive adverbs is to connect ideas, they can be a useful device for linking Sentence B to Sentence A. Some examples of conjunctive adverbs include *accordingly, certainly, finally, furthermore, however, meanwhile, nevertheless, otherwise, similarly, subsequently,* and *therefore.* Example: *Sam uploaded the changes to the server; subsequently, he notified his team about the changes.*

- **The conjunctions *and* or *but*** As Bryan Garner notes in *Better Business Writing,* the words *and* or *but* make for excellent transition words at the beginning of sentences. He calls them "short, sharp, and fleet." *Bryan Garner is an American lawyer, lexicographer, and teacher. And he's written more than 20 books about English usage and style.*

- **Organization** Consider the organizational structure of the paragraph, e.g., chronological or contrast, and then select an appropriate transitional expression. The following table provides some examples.

Transitional Expressions

Addition	again, also, and then, besides, furthermore, in addition (to), in the first place, moreover, next, too
Chronological	afterward, again, at that time, concurrently, eventually, in the end, in the future, later, shortly, then, until now, while
Comparison	compared with, in comparison with, in the same way, similarly
Contrast	alternatively, although, even though, however, in contrast, in spite of, instead, nevertheless, on the contrary, regardless, yet
Emphasis	definitely, indeed, of course, specifically
Example	for example, for instance, it is true, let us, namely, thus, to illustrate
Result	accordingly, consequently, for that reason, therefore, thus
Summary	basically, finally, in brief, in conclusion, in other words, in short, on the whole, to summarize

DOCUMENT COHERENCE

If your sentences, paragraphs, and sections are focused and ordered in a way that your readers can easily understand, then the document is coherent; in other words, the document makes sense and is logical. It hangs together. It flows.

When a piece of writing is coherent, its parts connect smoothly; everything supports the purpose and moves in the right direction. A reader struggles to follow a rambling, incoherent document; sometimes the reader isn't even sure what the point is. It's like following a conversation with someone who's had one too many glasses of wine.

Coherent writing incorporates several key aspects of the writing process. The writer works from a clear outline so that readers can move comfortably from introduction to conclusion; she identifies any gaps in overall logic or development; she crafts sensible connections between ideas through sentences that control paragraphs; she uses transitions gracefully to link sentences and paragraphs; and she manages the language so the reader can take the most direct route through the document.

Here's the drill we first learned at school: lead with a sentence that introduces a concept, develop the concept—that is, deliver the goods—and then conclude. Hang these sentences on the clothesline

— Ask Maggie —

I appreciate the advice you offer in this part of the book, but it's a little overwhelming. I write about 30 emails a day, at least a couple of reports a month, and memos and letters as needed. Some days I'm a writing machine! How am I going to apply all these recommendations of yours and still find any time to eat and sleep?

Signed,

Tentative Tabatha

Dear Tabatha,

For your regular round of daily emails, don't worry too much about style. Just check them for grammar, punctuation, and clarity. Apply these style recommendations when working on your more important projects, especially the beginnings and endings of reports, executive summaries, and proposals.

And learn your weak suits. Some of the exercises throughout this book encourage you to critically analyze your own work and see what you're particularly guilty of, whether it's too much jargon or clumsy transitions.

The content in this part of the book is rich stuff, and it takes time to digest. Absorb these principles slowly over time, and you'll see some amazing results.

known as a paragraph. Peg them down with transitional expressions so that they don't blow away. Finally, try hard to stick to one single theme per paragraph.

Although this advice works for the most part, it is definitely a formulaic and somewhat monotonous approach to paragraph composition. Perhaps we'd do better to heed author Sheridan Baker's advice to "think of a paragraph as something you use for your readers' convenience, rather than as some granitic form laid down by molten logic." For example, if a sentence contains an exquisite idea that needs to be highlighted all on its own, then what's the problem with a one-sentence paragraph? Short paragraphs are also great choices for highlighting action items and important information and for serving as transitions from one theme to the next.

No matter your sentence length, take the time to get the first sentence right because that's the sweet moment (or second) where you have the reader's interest. This first sentence is often referred to as the topic sentence. Here are some topic sentences that lead with the key information and will be easy to flesh out in subsequent sentences.

- This recommendation provides a solution to the employee turnover that has been a problem for the last two years.

- We are pleased to inform you that we have hired a new faculty chair.

- Jo Galloway has asked me to provide a reference letter, and I am pleased to do so.

- These instructions explain how to turn on the alarm in case of an emergency.

- Does your company understand the true cost of hiring contractors?

- I would appreciate your approval for Keith to attend a three-day training program on change management.

Here are some ways that you might now complete the paragraph:

- **Example** Cite an example or two of the concept being presented, or relate an incident.

- **Amplification** Repeat the idea(s) presented in the topic sentence more fully.

- **Definition** Define the ideas presented in the topic sentence.

However you decide to complete the paragraph, think of the remainder of it as explaining, establishing, or developing the topic sentence.

In the following paragraph, transitional devices have been used effectively. And because every sentence relates to the topic sentence, *Writing-on-Stone Provincial Park has long been revered as a sacred site*, the passage has paragraph unity. Therefore, this passage is both cohesive and coherent.

> Writing-on-Stone Provincial Park has **long** been revered as a sacred site. **For at least 3,000 years,** people such as the Shoshone, the Kutenai, and the Siksika have been coming to the region. **They** come to celebrate the elemental forces that are here in abundance and in extraordinary form. **Not surprisingly, they** have also come here to pursue vision quests and to carve and paint their stories and dreams on the hoodoos. **To this day,** the Siksika visit the park to pay homage to the ancestors and the powers that be. **One of them,** Quenton Heavy Head, compares the park (in Blackfoot known as *Aisinai'Pi*) to St. Peter's Basilica: "You have the same open cathedral, the reverence for spirits, and the burial sites."

Just as you would place your best writing at the beginning or end of a letter or report, lead your paragraph off strongly and end strongly. The concluding sentence may also anticipate the topic sentence of the next paragraph by introducing a new concept that will be picked up in the next paragraph.

Many business and technical writers prefer a method known as chunking, which breaks up long strings of information into chunks. This approach is especially useful for writing online content. For more information on chunking, see Chapter 6.

It takes some heavy lifting to create a document with cohesive sentences and a coherent structure. But flow is one of the hallmarks of good writing and deserves the same attention as clarity, energy, and concision.

EXERCISES

A. Use the following information to create three short paragraphs about the famous architect Ieoh Ming Pei. In your writing, pay attention to using transitional expressions within each paragraph.

- Brings together the modern and traditional in his work

- Calls this the impossible dream

- Born in 1917 in China

- Perhaps best known for the controversial glass pyramids in the courtyard of the Louvre Museum in Paris

- Finished school in Shanghai and went to the United States in the 1930s to study at MIT

- In the 1960s was selected to design the terminal at the John F. Kennedy International Airport

- His designs are influenced by the International Style, made popular by architects like Le Corbusier

- Also known for a style called Brutalism, an offshoot of the International Style

- Brutalism uses bold forms, utilitarian principles, skillful arrangement of geometric shapes

- When he graduated from MIT, he couldn't go back to China because of the outbreak of World War II

- Father was a prominent banker

- Became a US citizen in 1954

- His use of massive concrete blocks (like the ones used in his design for the National Center for Atmospheric Research, which was completed in 1967) is an example of Brutalism

- Has completed some 30 institutional projects, both in the United States and abroad

- In 1974, gained international recognition for the design of the East Building of the National Gallery of Art in Washington

B. Combine these three overlapping sentences into one sentence.

1. Water quality in the Snake River declined in June. This decline occurred because of the heavy rainfall that month. All the extra water overloaded the municipal district's water treatment plant.

2. Bill is a daydreamer. He spends several hours a day staring out the window. He doesn't get much work done.

3. All my colleagues admire the new CEO. I don't like him. Actually, I'm thinking of resigning.

C. Try this.

1. Take a passage of your writing and read it aloud. Your brain will process the words differently. You will hear the flow, the tone, the rhythm. You might stumble when moving from one sentence to another, and you'll realize the bridge between sentences is missing.

2. Read aloud a passage from one of your favourite authors or someone at work who excels as a writer. Again, listen for flow and cadence. What techniques do these writers use? Can you mimic them?

D. In this final exercise, apply all the principles reviewed in Part Four and improve the following passages.

1. Promotional copy for a "Writing for the Web" workshop:

   There can be little doubt that writing for the web is different than writing for print. Understanding the difference between writing for the web versus writing for print begins with figuring out how people read differently. This five-week workshop brings to light how to engage online readers through writing style appropriate for online, web design, and how to structure the site. This involves watching videos, taking quizzes, and getting active in discussion groups. This course requires approximately two to five hours of study per week, but can vary.

2. A paragraph from the cover letter of a proposal:

   Our non-profit organization has very strong experience with regard to working with seniors. Furthermore, our team has a lot of diverse experience, a hands-on attitude, are very good communicators and result-orientated—well-suited for this particular project. We would apply our expertise to help this pilot project be a success. Please let us know if you require details of similar works or require references regarding our work experience. We would be happy to provide this.

3. An email to your team:

Greetings all,

Eight different groups have used the boardroom on the third floor over the last month. Each time the guidelines for using the boardroom as per the employee manual were not followed. Shannon Starr, the facilities manager, has asked me to bring up the following to your attention.

- When using the boardroom, keep the noise level down. There are several offices in close proximity, and we need to be respectful of them.

- Make sure you have obtained visitor badges for all of the external guests

- It is essential to clean up after using the boardroom.

- In the event of a circumstance requiring changes to be made to a booking, booking changes must be made in the Outlook calendar at least one day prior to the booking.

PART FIVE

The Writer and Editor Toolbox

The expectations of life depend upon diligence; the mechanic who would perfect his work must first sharpen his tools.

~ Confucius

The beautiful part of writing is that you don't have to get it right the first time, unlike, say, a brain surgeon.

~ Robert Cormier

You write to communicate to the hearts and minds of others what's burning inside you. And we edit to let the fire show through the smoke.

~ Arthur Plotnik

The more tools you have, the more choices available. The more choices available, the better the writing can be.

~ Elizabeth George

What is it we like so much about toolboxes? In part, it's because they speak to our sense of craft and pride in our work. If we just fool around with a hobby occasionally on the weekends, we might have only a few random tools. We might not even know where our paintbrushes are because we use them so infrequently. But if we have a well-organized and well-used toolbox with practical tools, we're practising a craft. And our toolbox reminds us that we are committed to that craft.

Every profession requires tools, yet many business writers have remarkably few—to their detriment. Any competent editor knows, however, that tools are a non-negotiable job requirement. Without them, the job slows down and the errors speed up. Knowing this, editors assemble and use an array of tools. These editorial tools include style guides and style sheets, and a healthy supply of print and online resources.

Writers need these tools too because they often write in isolation, without the benefit of an editor. Even if you do have an editor, as a successful writer you'll still do plenty of self-editing. Therefore, it makes good sense to develop some skills working the other side of the desk—the editor's side.

This final part of the book reviews some editing fundamentals and explores some resources and tools that you can select from when filling your own toolbox. Over the years, you'll continue to refine your tools and add new ones. You'll come to appreciate your toolbox as a trusty aide in all your writing projects.

— CHAPTER FIFTEEN —

Become Familiar with Editing Fundamentals

Editing is not a cosmetic process.
It's a thinking process.

~ RICHARD RHODES

Few writers have the luxury of having a professional editor by their side. A more useful approach is to consider yourself both writer and editor—and to do so early in the process. Put on an editor's cap as you move through the structuring, the revisions, the final edits, and the proofreading. This will help you to grasp that a document requires different levels of editing and that the term *edit* can be used at many stages of the writing and rewriting process. By applying the tools and techniques of an editor to streamline this process, you'll work more efficiently and be happier with the results.

Don't think of writers and editors as wildly different species of the writing kingdom. Both work with words toward the same goal: to generate lean and lucid prose that achieves its goals efficiently and elegantly. Writers who think and work more like editors will discover that they manage their writing tasks with more competence and ease.

Let's start with a few definitions.

EDITING TERMS

Rewriting. Revising. Editing. You'll hear these terms bandied about, and like other issues we've explored in this book, you won't find agreement about the meanings of these terms or the differences between them. Some writers use *rewriting* to mean a drastic rework of a document and *revising* to mean more minor surgery. And these same writers use *editing* to mean—incorrectly, by the way—a final polish, a quick dust and tidy. Some writers see *revising* as what they do and *editing* as something carried out by someone else. Other writers ask for a proofread when they mean—and need—a copyedit. Others undervalue the importance of editing, and so the edit is left to the last minute when it is usually too late to make more than superficial corrections.

The confusion about terms and the blurring of tasks that should take place at different times can easily lead a writer astray. It also means that writers often miss certain things when "revising" or "editing." This chaotic state of affairs leads to an unsatisfactory outcome for the writer—and the reader. Let's clear up this confusion by using the following terms:

Copyediting Carolyn Rude, author of *Technical Editing*, defines this level of editing as editing for correctness (spelling, grammar, punctuation, missing words); consistency (spelling, terms, numbers, visual design, etc.); accuracy (dates, model numbers, quotations, etc.); and completion (all parts are present, all hypertext links work correctly, etc.). This is a useful definition. For Canadians, this could also include making sure the language fits Canadian standards, e.g., spelling and metrification. Wherever you live, you will need to tailor your language to the standards of your country.

Stylistic editing Editors Canada, an association for professional editors, defines this level of editing, in part, as "clarifying meaning, eliminating jargon, smoothing language and other non-mechanical line-by-line editing. May include checking or correcting reading level." Your focus here is on clarity, concision, and ease of reading.

Structural editing This level of editing, also referred to as substantive editing, focuses on structure and overall content; a structural edit could include reorganizing a document. Structural editing makes a document more logical and reader-centred. When doing a structural edit, you may decide, for example, that a certain section of a report is in the wrong place or needs more detail.

Proofreading This term is often used incorrectly. Proofreading means to read final proofs of a document after it has been edited and laid out to verify that no errors remain or were introduced at the design stage, e.g., too many end-of-line hyphens. Proofreading is done toward the end of the production process.

THE EDITORIAL PROCESS

With these terms in mind, let's briefly look at how most editors work. Ideally, an editor carries out two reviews of a document: a macro-edit and a micro-edit.

1. In the first review, the macro-edit, the editor focuses on the structural editing (content and organization) and asks how well the document addresses the subject, the audience, and the purpose. The editor keeps the reader foremost in his mind and asks himself if the document meets the needs of the reader. At this stage, the editor does not carry out any copyediting or stylistic editing (e.g., correcting grammar or improving style).

2. In the second review, the micro-edit, the editor focuses on a stylistic edit and a copyedit. Remember the madman, architect,

carpenter, and judge roles discussed in Part One? The micro-edit is where the judge takes over. Time permitting, the editor might break the micro-edit into two reviews: one for a stylistic edit and one for a copyedit.

3. The document is returned to the writer, and the writer and editor work through any changes.

4. The document is sent for design and layout.

5. The document is proofread to ensure that no errors remain and that no new issues were introduced at the production or design stage.

How can you apply this process to your own writing? For informal emails, do at least a quick copyedit (e.g., grammar, spelling, missing words) before you hit send. For more formal emails, do a more thorough edit. The time you spend editing will be determined by the audience and the importance of the email. Those of us who write dozens of emails a day will want to edit briskly and efficiently.

But business writing involves more than emails. You might work for weeks—or even longer—on a major report. Every time you work on the report, you could warm up to the task at hand by thinking like a structural editor. As you're scrolling through the document and gearing up to start writing again, ask yourself questions such as the following:

■ Is this content appropriate in Section 3? Or should I move it?

■ Will my readers understand my definitions in Chapter 2? Or do I need a glossary?

■ Was there a better way to present the information on page 18?

■ To the best of my knowledge, are my facts accurate?

■ Did I answer all the questions the reader might have about the new software?

- Is the tone appropriate for an audience of salespeople?

- Should I ask a colleague to review the instructions on page 41?

The beauty of asking these questions as you write is that they will help you keep your purpose and audience clearly in mind. The more attention you pay to structural editing early on and throughout the process, the better. It's difficult, even for an experienced editor, to carry out major structural edits at the 11th hour—which is when many editors begin their work, unfortunately.

During the macro-edit, you might write several drafts before you are satisfied that you have answered all the questions. You might also have reviewers step in at various stages to provide feedback. The macro-edit includes incorporating changes and suggestions and reconciling different opinions. Along the way, you may have done some micro-edits, but they won't be your primary focus.

After you are satisfied with the final draft, it's time to put on your jaunty micro-editor's cap and work through the document again, now focusing on style and correctness. At this stage, you ask questions such as the following:

- Is every sentence clear on first reading?

- Have I pruned the dead words?

- Have I used active verbs and guarded against excessive nominalization?

- Is the document consistent, e.g., have I applied the in-house style guide?

- Is the document free of grammatical and punctuation errors?

- Are all the parts in place?

AN EDITOR'S PERSPECTIVE

What's going on inside an editor's brain as she's editing? And what recommendations would she make to a junior editor? Here are a few things she would want to share:

- Before you begin editing the work of others, agree on what level of edit you are going to do so there are no surprises or unrealistic expectations.

- Editors work primarily "top down." They consider the overall document (the structural edit or macro-edit) first because this level of edit affects all the others. It's a waste of time to fix the style of a sentence if you realize later that the sentence needs deleting.

- It's easier to edit someone else's work than your own. And it's more fun! As H.G. Wells put it, "No passion in the world is equal to the passion to alter someone else's draft." When it's your own work, there's less passion for the project. It's trickier to see your own lack of clarity or thoroughness. If possible, ask a colleague to review any challenging sections.

- Thinking like an editor also allows you to detach from your work and see it more impersonally. Editing requires us to think less like a writer, caught up in the tensions of writing, and more like an advocate for the reader.

- It takes time to develop a complex multi-layered understanding of your own work. Be patient with yourself, especially if you've never done much self-editing. But do start to ask the questions that a structural editor would pose as you work through your document. Don't wait until the end to start asking the questions that should have been asked early on.

- When you're absorbed in the stylistic edit and the copyedit, make sure you have a good chunk of quiet, focused time to work through the many details.

- Let time be your editorial assistant. Try to leave time between writing and editing. When working on a complex project, step away between drafts so you can regain some objectivity. If you're stuck in a particular place, take a break, ideally a day or more. If nothing else, at least go for a walk. A change of place can give you a new perspective.

- Build up the necessary editing resources: e.g., an in-house style guide, grammar book, style manuals, a dictionary.

- Even if you or your organization has an editor, the more self-editing you do, the cleaner the document will be when it's sent to the editor. This will allow the editor to work more efficiently and perhaps help you with more complex issues.

GRACE UNDER PRESSURE: TRIAGE EDITING

Perhaps you are the *de facto* editor in your organization because you have the strongest writing skills. Again, you can apply the process outlined above and do two separate reviews of a document, the macro-edit and the micro-edit.

That's certainly a wonderful ideal, but the reality might be much different. What do you focus on when you have an hour to review and improve a 12-page proposal? Answer: Perform the editorial equivalent of triage. In her book *Technical Editing: A Guide for Editors and Writers*, Judith Tarutz advises us to "bridge the gap between the writer's or client's expectations and what you actually have time to do by performing triage."

Here are the key emergency editing steps that Tarutz recommends we perform:

1. Take a few minutes to evaluate the content. How good or bad is the document overall? Determine the most critical needs.

2. Run any technical tools you have (see Chapter 18 for some suggestions).

3. Prioritize. What is most important to fix, and what can you easily fix in the available time? Not all errors are critically important. Keep your eye on the big picture, not the details.

— Anecdotal Evidence —

When I first started editing other people's work, I found that I enjoyed the work but found it stressful. Turnaround times were usually tight. It was hard to know what to focus on when I only had two hours to edit a 10-page report.

One day a friend told me about a designer she knew who had a business card with this inscription: *Good Fast Cheap: Pick Two*. Those words struck home. I realized that I couldn't achieve perfection, especially if the clock was ticking loudly, but I could attend to the priorities.

Whenever I start to worry about a rapidly approaching deadline, I remind myself of that business card. I do the best I can in the time I have and let the rest go.

What is critical?

- Accuracy: Always fix factual errors to the best of your knowledge and time. As Mark Twain cautions us, "Be careful reading health books. You may die of a misprint."

- Clarity: Once again, make everything clear on first reading.

- Display copy (e.g., titles, headings, and captions): Mistakes here will jump out at the reader.

- First and last paragraphs: These are the paragraphs readers will remember.

- Profanity, trademark use, copyright: Check for anything that might get you in legal hot water.

- Hyperlinks: Do they work?

- Grammar and punctuation basics: Watch for errors that will distract the reader: e.g., mixing up *its* and *it's* and run-on sentences or sentence fragments.

- Names: Spelling someone's name wrong is never a good thing.

- Completeness: Be sure that all the document's parts are in place: e.g., if the table of contents states that there are three appendices, make sure three are included.

— Ask Maggie —

I'm the go-to person at work when anyone has a question about language. And I enjoy helping people although I tend to correct instinctively, which I know isn't the best approach. Management doesn't share my passion for good writing, and sometimes we send out reports that need more polishing. I wish I could convince them that sloppy writing makes us all look bad!

Signed,

Eager Elsbeth

Dear Elsbeth,

Your company is fortunate to have someone who cares about language. Keep strengthening your language skills by reading books like this and style manuals. And think about taking an editing course; if you look around, you'll find some fantastic courses. A deeper understanding of how words work will help you edit with more confidence. And consider writing an in-house style guide for the organization (see Chapter 16) so that your colleagues start to write more efficiently and more consistently.

It takes time to motivate others to care about language the way we do. But these suggestions should win over your managers once they see the improvements that you've helped implement.

What is less critical?

- Awkward constructions, wordiness, and tangled prose: If you have time, untangle and cut the fat. But if you start to slow down, move on.

- Grammatical refinements: Do what you can, but worry less about fixing things such as *who* versus *whom* and style choices such as Oxford commas. Try to reduce excessive passive voice.

- Flow: Again, do what you can, but if the writing is choppy and poorly organized, you won't be able to improve it much without significant effort.

Keep your eye on the clock. You don't want to rewrite the first page and limit yourself to fixing minor mistakes in the rest of the document.

EDITING IN THE WORKPLACE

Do you find yourself in the sometimes uncomfortable position of having to edit other people's work—maybe even that of your manager? This is a task that requires diplomacy and the ability to refrain from imposing your own style on someone else's work. As author and editing guru Carol Fisher Saller reminds us, "Restraint is a virtue in copyediting. And the less experienced you are, the better it is to hold back."

When editing other people's work, be constructive in your criticism. Pointing out weaknesses isn't sufficient; you must also offer solutions. And don't change a word just because you'd prefer a synonym; you must be able to justify your changes. An explanation such as "The comma feels right because that's where I would pause if reading this sentence" isn't helpful. A clearer and more credible justification would sound something like this: "You need a comma before a coordinating conjunction that is followed by an independent clause."

The first time you edit someone else's work, let her know beforehand that there could be several tracked changes or red ink. Otherwise, she could be surprised by the number of suggested changes. If you're applying a policy or following an in-house style guide, let her know. You might add a comment like this: "We follow Canadian Press style, so please write out numbers below 10."

Tactful language

Explaining your edits without offending or irritating the writer can be challenging. Here are some examples of using tactful language to get the point across.

Write: *This chapter didn't explain—although it needs to—what the instructions for updating the online policies are.* This makes the chapter wrong, not the writer.

Write: *How about* or *consider.* These words will sound more collaborative than writing *You've already said this* or *Use clearer language.*

Write: *This interrupts the flow. I think readers would prefer to read this description in Chapter 3.* Focus on being an advocate for the reader.

Write: *This sentence confused me. I think we need to find a better definition. How about using the definition in the glossary?* Don't just comment on what's wrong. Suggest a solution.

Write: *This analogy really strengthened the report; I'm sure the reader will also enjoy the comparison and find it helpful.* Use a collaborative tone.

Editing your boss's work

Ideally, your boss will respect your edits and see the value of them. Follow these guidelines when editing your boss's work:

- Find something positive to say: *generally well written, persuasive content, well-articulated arguments.*

- Phrase your stylistic edits as suggestions only. Let him know that he is free to accept or reject any changes. Try prefacing your comments with *think about* or *perhaps.*

- Let him know that you would be happy to discuss your edits.

A work culture that cares about language

Be patient if colleagues or managers don't see the value of professionally written documents. Change takes time, and it helps if you are in the right position in the organization to influence the decision makers. Here are some suggestions to help others appreciate the value of good writing:

- Encourage open and constructive discussions about how the group can improve. If your team has recently completed a major writing project, meet to evaluate it and to discuss how the process could be improved next time.

- Start to acquire some in-house reference materials, and ask staff to use them.

- Draft a simple style sheet, and share it with staff. Once you have agreement on the style sheet, you can follow up by creating an in-house style guide. (See Chapter 16 for more information on style sheets, manuals, and guides.)

- Suggest occasional informal lunch-and-learns where staff take turns giving brief presentations on issues of process, style, or usage, followed by a discussion. For example, Sonny might give a 10-minute presentation on the correct use of the colon and the semicolon and lead a discussion with the help of a reference book or two. Three months later, Renata could give a presentation on guidelines for team writing projects.

EDITING AND PROOFREADING CHECKLISTS

Below is a sample checklist to use as you work your way through a macro- or micro-edit. Tailor this checklist for things you specifically need to guard against. For example, the grammar section of this checklist does not include subject–verb agreement, but if that's something that can trip you up, make sure to add it.

Macro-Edit: Structural Edit

Organization and content

- Is the structure immediately apparent?
- Have I used sufficient transitions and connections between sentences and paragraphs?
- Did I answer all anticipated reader questions?
- Does the document meet the purpose I originally set?

Design

- Have I used appropriate visuals?
- Are the headings clear and informative?
- Does the design help the reader move from one concept to the next?
- Does the document have an inviting and accessible format?

Micro-Edit: Stylistic Edit and Copyedit

Style

- Is each sentence understandable on first reading?

- Have I varied the length of sentences?

- Are the sentences free of wordiness, jargon, and ambiguity?

- Is the tone appropriate to the audience and consistent?

Grammar

- Are there any problems with pronoun usage?

- Are there any sentence fragments and run-on sentences?

- Is there any faulty parallelism?

- Have I corrected all dangling, misplaced, or squinting modifiers?

Punctuation and mechanics

- Are thoughts within sentences broken up correctly by commas?

- Have I used colons and semicolons correctly?

- Have I used dashes and hyphens correctly?

- Have I spelled out all abbreviations on first use?

Proofreading

- Are all pages numbered and in order?

- Have all the edits been handled, e.g., accepted, rejected?

- Does the document design meet our specifications?

- Have I done a final spell check?

Proofreading: take nothing for granted!

Watch out for the following issues that can easily trip you up:

- double words: especially *the the* and *and and*
- missing words: especially the articles *the*, *a*, and *an*
- spelling nightmares: e.g., *ei* and *ie* words, e.g., *receive, weird, believe*; words that add *–ing* and *–ed*; and words with one or more sets of double letters, e.g., *accommodate, embarrass*
- commonly misspelled words: e.g., *occur/occurred, complimentary/complementary*
- skinny letters: *l, t,* and *i*: e.g., *travelling, belittle*
- endings such as *–ability* and *–ibility*: e.g., *dependability, reliability*
- words with possible but incorrect endings: e.g., *editing* for *edition*
- homophones: e.g., *they're/their, it's/its, who's/whose, you're/your*
- hyphenated words at the end of lines: confirm that the break is okay
- widows and orphans: a widow is a short last line of a paragraph stranded at the top of the page or column; an orphan is the first line of a paragraph left behind at the foot of a page or column

Also watch out for the places where errors like to lurk:

- first and last lines of a page
- headings, chapter titles, captions, headers, and footers
- text in figures
- in clusters—if you see an error in one line, review the line and the lines nearby for other errors
- text in the largest type size on the page—sad but true

Tips for proofreaders

Here are some suggestions to help you proofread like a pro:

- If ever there is a time not to multitask, this is it.

- It's extremely difficult to catch your own mistakes. If possible, have someone else proofread anything you've worked on extensively. If it's an important document, enlist more than one proofreader.

- Start with a fresh eye and mind. Give yourself at least a 10-minute break between reading or writing and proofreading.

- S l o w   d o w n. Read aloud. Or read with a ruler, which forces you to proofread line by line.

- Read backward and then forward and maybe even upside down.

- Look at every individual character, one line at a time. Don't read for meaning; your brain will deceive you. Look at the physical characters themselves. To prevent reading on autopilot, read the text out of order.

- If you are proofreading your own work, double check for the kinds of errors you know you tend to make.

- Take advantage of word processing functions such as "find and replace," but don't depend on them completely.

- Proofread in several small chunks of time, if possible. And know which medium you proofread best in—print or computer.

- Always do one proofreading pass to check solely for visual errors—spacing, type style, alignment, margins, etc.

— CHAPTER SIXTEEN —

Discover Style Manuals, In-House Style Guides, and Style Sheets

*The point is, your style guide—or any given "rule"
you learned in school—was created so you would do
something the same way every time for the sake of
consistency, for the reader's sake.*

~ CAROL FISHER SALLER

Editors rely extensively on style manuals, in-house style guides, and style sheets to ensure that their work is consistent and correct. Writers who use these tools will soon appreciate what a superb resource they are.

A **style manual** (sometimes referred to as a style guide) lays out rules for language use, such as for spelling, italics, citation of references, and punctuation. A major purpose of these style manuals is to ensure consistency.

Many writers and editors in North America use *The Chicago Manual of Style* as their primary reference tool. Most Canadian journalists follow *The Canadian Press Stylebook*; most American journalists follow *The Associated Press Stylebook*. Canadian editors also refer to *Editing Canadian English* and *The Canadian Style*. For a list of online style manuals, visit http://www.onlinestylebooks.com.

An **in-house style guide** is a style document specific to the organization. It specifies which option to use when several exist, e.g., *percent* versus *%*; serial comma versus no serial comma; *21st century* versus *twenty-first century*. It can also set style for topics too technical for general style and usage manuals, e.g., how to display computer commands in text. An in-house style guide allows the organization to bend standard style rules to fit its specific needs.

An in-house style guide ensures a consistent style for the organization. It also makes the job of editors and writers easier: they don't have to reinvent the wheel for every new project. It also contains rules that are non-negotiable and suggestions that are negotiable.

Make sure to discuss and update your in-house style guide regularly. Items can be added as questions arise and changed as new decisions are made. Do not include process information or grammar tutorials. Ideally, an in-house style guide should be only a few pages.

If your organization doesn't have an in-house style guide, suggest creating one!

A **style sheet** is a document that an editor uses to record choices about punctuation, abbreviations, spelling, capitalization, hyphenation, and other items specific to the document being edited. Take, for example, a book editor. She will use the style manual the publisher provides and create a style sheet specific to the book she's editing. For example, if she's editing a book about First Nations, it might include the spelling of *Mi'kmaq* to ensure that it's spelled the same throughout the book because there are other possible spellings of the word.

A style sheet is also a valuable tool for a writer because it helps streamline the revision and proofreading stages. To create your own personalized style sheet, take your in-house style guide—or a style manual if you don't have an in-house style guide—and place the items essential to you on the style sheet. See the style sheet as a "cheat sheet" to record things you tend to forget. If Spanish is your first language, for example, you may need to remind yourself that it's *the people are*, not *the people is*. Or the style sheet might just be a reference guide to common spelling or punctuation choices that you want to refer to quickly.

You can list topics alphabetically or break them down into sections, such as punctuation, numbers, or abbreviations. Make your style sheet a quick reference document that contains all the important things in one place. And keep it handy on your desktop.

Sample Style Sheet

A	B	C	D	E
a.m.	backward before (not "prior to") build up (v.) buildup (n.) businessperson	centre centred cooperative coordinate counsellor co-worker	decision makers decision-making body	ebook e-business e-commerce email e-reader
F fine-tune fulfill	**G** grey	**H** hard-working home page hypermedia	**I** Indigenous instalment Internet intranet	**J** judgment
K kilowatt hours (kWh)	**L** licence (n.) license (v.) log in lowercase	**M** medallist meter (device) metre (measurement)	**N** non-profit	**O** off-line online on-site on-time (adj.)
P percent p.m. PowerPoint province-wide	**Q/R** questionnaire round table (n.) round-table (adj.)	**S** skill set start up (v.) start-up (n.)	**T** toward travelling turnaround (n. and adj.)	**U** Prefer United States and United Kingdom to U.S. and U.K.
V/W/X web web page web server website well-being (n.) worldwide	**Y/Z** year-end (n., adv., adj.)	**Other** No serial comma Write out numbers one to nine; figures for 10 and up Acts: put in italics	**Dates** On June 26, 2018, we . . . Em dash (—) no space before and after En dash (–) to join inclusive names and compound numbers	**References** *Canadian Oxford Dictionary* *The Canadian Press Caps and Spelling* *The Canadian Press Stylebook*

CHAPTER SEVENTEEN

Cultivate Lifelong Writing Habits

All excellent things are as
difficult as they are rare.

~ Spinoza

Writing well is an arduous and challenging workout. At times, you will sweat and curse. Bad writing days will happen just like bad hair days. But like any decent workout, it's worth it. A well-crafted and articulate document reflects something deeply meaningful. It demonstrates that you take pride in your work and that you care about your audience. In a world often overshadowed by haste, bad manners, and sloppiness, your efforts speak to your commitment to dispelling everything that clouds your writing.

This commitment requires dedication. Dedication to order and coherence. Dedication to clarity and concision. Dedication to cordial relations with your readers. Initially, this may require extra effort and time, but with practice, you will expend less time and energy organizing your thoughts, your writing, and your editing.

Yes, this dedication means you need to attend regularly to your writing skills. In fact, it's a lifelong journey—a stimulating adventure, full of discoveries and inspiration. And on this journey, you'll meet some charming characters, such as fellow writers, editors, and language enthusiasts.

Rules (or conventions) and their mechanical applications will take us only so far. Rules provide guidance for fixing punctuation and grammar mistakes. But to write engaging and reader-centred documents, you need a finely tuned ear, a nose for nonsense, a taste for natural language, an eye for detail, and a feel for the right turn of phrase. In other words, your senses need to be in working order.

The following suggestions will help you cultivate lifelong writing habits:

- Read and learn from the best writers. Read writers who specialize in your field, other technical and business writers, and accomplished writers in your preferred literary genres. Read attentively and analytically. How well is a particular section organized? Are there some particularly well-written passages? Is there an especially satisfying conclusion? Through reading and identifying styles that inspire you, you will develop your own unique voice and style.

- Select some passages from a few of your favourite writers and read them aloud. Pay attention to the rhythm and the pace. What can you learn from how they write?

- If you don't have much time for reading, check out sites like https://www.aldaily.com, a web portal that links to a diverse array of news stories, features, and reviews from across the humanities written by some of the world's finest journalists. Also consider subscribing to one or two business publications.

- Build up your resources. Buy a grammar reference, a couple of books on how to write well, and a dictionary. And wear them out.

- Find opportunities to practise writing. Consider writing something for publication in your field. Expand your horizons beyond business writing. Write a story for children. Pen a love poem. Start a blog and share a passion. Join the ranks of the twitterati.

- Use technology. Readability tools, for example, can help you determine how difficult your content is to read by providing information such as words per sentence, percentage of passive sentences, reading ease, and grade level. For more information on readability tools that can be found on your computer or online, see Chapter 18.

- Lift some vocabulary weights! A muscular vocabulary will help you choose the right word for the occasion. Here are a few of the many ways to strengthen these muscles:

  - Learn the common roots of words.

  - Sign up online to have a word a day delivered to your inbox.

  - Keep a journal with a list of the new words you have found. This can be especially helpful if you're writing in a specific field or need some dynamic new words for your resumé.

  - Keep a dictionary and thesaurus handy.

  - Play word games—board games such as Scrabble or online vocabulary games.

  - Read, read, and read to see words in context.

- Deepen your knowledge of the vocabulary of writing. Hone your command of grammar and usage terms. Know the terms so that you can use a range of reference materials and help others.

- Find a business writing blog you like and subscribe to it.

- Take classes at a local college, university, community centre, or online. The more you learn about the English language, the more you will appreciate its richness and versatility.

Always remember that your readers will appreciate your efforts.

— CHAPTER EIGHTEEN —

Rely on Resources: Books, Websites, and Online Tools

Learning is not attained by chance. It must be sought for with ardor and attended to with diligence.

~ Abigail Adams

It's time to get some great resources into your toolbox. You need to own a couple of the best reference guides and style books and have a few equally good websites within easy reach. Learning from others, especially those who have spent their careers exploring the writing craft and sharing their knowledge, will inspire you to become the best writer you can be.

Here are some of my favourite books, websites, and online tools. Many of these outstanding resources have been instrumental in the writing of this book, although this list is by no means a complete record of all the works and sources I have consulted. Most of the authors noted below have written extensively on various aspects of language intricacies; once you find the writers who resonate the most with your writing aspirations and voice, you can seek out more of their works.

These resources have helped me immensely as a writer, editor, and teacher, and I'm confident they will serve you just as well.

BOOKS

Grammar and reference books

Casagrande, June. *The Best Punctuation Book, Period: A Comprehensive Guide for Every Writer, Editor, Student, and Businessperson*. New York: Random House, 2014.

Clark, Roy Peter. *The Glamour of Grammar: A Guide to the Magic and Mystery of Practical English*. New York: Little, Brown and Company, 2011.

Crystal, David. *Making Sense of Grammar*. Harlow: Pearson Education, 2004.

Garner, Bryan A. *Garner's Modern English Usage*. 4th ed. New York: Oxford University Press, 2016.

Hacker, Diana, and Nancy Sommers. *A Canadian Writer's Reference*. 6th ed. Boston: Bedford/St. Martin's, 2016.

Lester, Mark, and Larry Beason. *The McGraw-Hill Handbook of English Grammar and Usage*. 2nd ed. New York: McGraw-Hill Education, 2012.

McCarten, James, ed. *The Canadian Press Caps and Spelling*. 21st ed. Toronto: The Canadian Press, 2015. Also available in a web-based searchable edition at http://stylebooks.thecanadianpress.com.

McCarten, James, ed. *The Canadian Press Stylebook: A Guide for Writers and Editors*. 17th ed. Toronto: The Canadian Press, 2013. Also available in a web-based searchable edition at http://stylebooks.thecanadianpress.com.

Ruvinsky, Maxine. *Practical Grammar: A Canadian Writer's Resource*. 3rd ed. Don Mills: Oxford University Press, 2014.

Style books

Baker, Sheridan. *The Longman Practical Stylist: The Comprehensive Guide to Solid, Eloquent, and Persuasive Writing*. New York: Pearson Education, 2006.

Fiske, Robert Hartwell. *To the Point: A Dictionary of Concise Writing*. New York: W.W. Norton & Company, 2014.

Handley, Ann. *Everybody Writes: Your Go-To Guide to Creating Ridiculously Good Content*. Hoboken: John Wiley & Sons, 2014.

Lanham, Richard. *Revising Business Prose*. 4th ed. Needham Heights: Pearson Education, 2000.

Pinker, Steven. *The Sense of Style: The Thinking Person's Guide to Writing in the 21st Century*. New York: Viking Penguin, 2014.

Plotnik, Arthur. *Spunk & Bite: A Writer's Guide to Bold, Contemporary Style*. New York: Random House, 2007.

Tredinnick, Mark, and Geoff Whyte. *The Little Black Book of Business Writing*. Sydney: University of New South Wales Press, 2010.

Trimble, John. *Writing with Style: Conversations on the Art of Writing*. 3rd ed. New Jersey: Pearson Education, 2011.

Watson, Don. *Death Sentence: The Decay of Public Language*. New York: Alfred A. Knopf, 2006.

Wilbers, Stephen. *Keys to Great Writing: Mastering the Elements of Composition and Revision*. 2nd ed. Fort Collins: Writer's Digest Books, 2016.

Williams, Joseph M., and Joseph Bizup. *Style: Lessons in Clarity and Grace*. 11th ed. New Jersey: Pearson Education, 2013.

Zinsser, William. *On Writing Well: The Classic Guide to Writing Nonfiction*. 30th anniversary ed. New York: Harper Collins, 2006.

Business, science, and technical writing books

Alley, Michael. *The Craft of Scientific Writing*. 3rd ed. New York: Springer, 1996.

Gaertner-Johnston, Lynn. *Business Writing with Heart: How to Build Great Work Relationships One Message at a Time*. Seattle: Syntax Training LLC, 2013.

Garner, Bryan A. *HBR Guide to Better Business Writing*. Boston: Harvard Business Review Press, 2012.

Lamb, Sandra E. *Writing Well for Business Success: A Complete Guide to Style, Grammar, and Usage at Work*. New York: St. Martin's Griffin, 2015.

Lannon, John M., and Don Klepp. *Technical Communication*. 5th Canadian ed. Toronto: Pearson Education, 2011.

McMurrey, David A., Wendy Wilson, and George A. Tripp. *Power Tools for Technical Communication*. 1st Canadian ed. Toronto: Thomson Nelson, 2006.

Editing books

Einsohn, Amy. *The Copyeditor's Handbook: A Guide for Book Publishing and Corporate Communication*. 3rd ed. Berkeley: University of California Press, 2011.

Rude, Carolyn D. *Technical Editing*. 5th ed. New York: Pearson Education, 2010.

Saller, Carol Fisher. *The Subversive Copy Editor: Advice from Chicago*. Chicago: University of Chicago Press, 2009.

Tarutz, Judith A. *Technical Editing: The Practical Guide for Editors and Writers*. Reading: Hewlett-Packard, 1992.

Virag, Karen, ed. *Editing Canadian English: A Guide for Editors, Writers, and Everyone Who Works with Words*. 3rd ed. Toronto: Editors' Association of Canada, 2015. Also available online at https://editingcanadianenglish.ca.

Design books

Knaflic, Cole Nussbaumer. *Storytelling with Data: A Data Visualization Guide for Business Professionals*. Hoboken: John Wiley & Sons, 2015.

Williams, Robin. *The Non-Designer's Design Book*. 4th ed. San Francisco: Peachpit Press, 2015.

Dictionaries and thesauruses

Every writer needs a good dictionary. Canadians will probably want the *Canadian Oxford Dictionary*, and Americans often use *The Merriam-Webster Dictionary*. The latter is also available online and includes both a dictionary and a thesaurus https://www.merriam-webster.com/. Several other thesauruses—and who doesn't need help finding the right word—are available online, including http://www.thesaurus.com.

WEBSITES

It would be impossible to do more than touch lightly on the immense offerings of the online universe. The following are a few of the websites that I use regularly and that I recommend all writers visit at least once. I have also included a few sites at the end for language aficionados.

Daily Writing Tips discusses a great range of topics and publishes a new article every day. https://www.dailywritingtips.com

Editors Canada has some resources that all editors and writers will find useful. http://www.editors.ca

Grammar Girl is a well-known face in the online grammar world. In her own words, she is "your friendly guide to the world of grammar, punctuation, usage, and fun developments in the English language." http://www.quickanddirtytips.com/grammar-girl

Information is Beautiful will give you some great ideas about how information can be represented visually in ways everyone can understand. http://www.informationisbeautiful.net

Purdue University Online Writing Lab is a superb site with hundreds of resources. It contains clear explanations and some exercises with answer keys. https://owl.english.purdue.edu

Termium Plus is the Government of Canada's terminology and linguistic data bank and gateway to many fantastic resources. If you link to "The Language Portal of Canada," you'll find some quizzes. If you link to "Writing Tools," you'll find The Canadian Style, which covers topics such as capitalization, punctuation, plain language, and spelling. http://www.btb.termiumplus.gc.ca

The Chicago Manual of Style Online is a subscription-based and searchable guide to grammar, documentation, style, and much more. http://www.chicagomanualofstyle.org/

Wise Old Sayings hosts "The Ultimate Grammar Resource Guide," which has some excellent links to other grammar resources. http://www.wiseoldsayings.com/ultimate-grammar-resource-guide.php

A few sites for language aficionados

Online Etymology Dictionary describes the history and evolution of more than 30,000 words. http://www.etymonline.com

Phrontistery compiles word lists and language resources "to spread the joy of the English language in all its variety through time and space." http://phrontistery.info

Word Spy is for those who want to keep up with the latest words. Not all the words featured on the site will endure, but it's a fun read, nevertheless. http://www.wordspy.com

ONLINE TOOLS

Grammarly is an app that scans text for many common writing mistakes. It won't catch all the issues, and it doesn't provide the context or feedback you'd get from an editor. But some people find it helpful. https://www.grammarly.com

The Hemingway Editor app is another app popular with writers keen to eliminate adverbs and the passive voice. It's not perfect, but it will highlight hard-to-read sentences, complex words or phrases, and passive voice. http://www.hemingwayapp.com

The PerfectIt app is a great consistency checker. If you want to ensure that your abbreviations, capitalizations, in-house style, punctuation, and spelling are consistent throughout a document, consider purchasing this tool. http://www.intelligentediting.com

A readability test can help you determine how difficult your content is to read by providing information such as words per sentence, percentage of passive sentences, reading ease, and grade level. A readability test is available in both Microsoft Outlook and Microsoft Word. For general business writing, aim for the following: words per sentence: fewer than 30; percentage of passive sentences: less than 5 percent; Flesch Reading Ease: greater than 50; and Flesch-Kincaid Grade Level: between 8 and 10.

The WritersDiet Test, developed by Helen Sword, is a tool that will tell you whether your writing is flabby or fit. You can enter a sample of 100 to 1,000 words and run the test to identify some of the sentence-level issues that bog writing down. http://writersdiet.com

— APPENDIX A —

English Not Your First Language?

If English is not your first language, you will have different language challenges than someone whose first language is English. Much depends on your first language. Is your first language an Indo-European language (e.g., Greek or Hindi) like English is? If yes, then you will find mastering the complexities of English less challenging than someone who does not speak an Indo-European language. Other factors that will influence your ability to write English fluently include how long you have studied English, how comfortable you are with languages in general, and how long you have used English as a working professional.

I'm not going to sugar-coat some of the difficulties that English will present you with: the articles, the prepositions, and the verbs, in particular. Occasionally, you will probably wonder if you will ever master all the idiosyncrasies of the language. But never forget that you have a few significant advantages over many native speakers of English. First, you speak more than one language, perhaps several. And as someone who is bilingual or multilingual, you will be far more linguistically adept and aware than a unilingual speaker. Second, your understanding of grammar and its fundamental role in how we speak and write is far more advanced than someone who speaks one language and perhaps has had minimal grammar instruction at school. Finally, you are obviously a disciplined person because it takes a lot of persistence and resolve to learn a language.

Articles and prepositions are particularly challenging. The following summary provides a brief overview. For a comprehensive explanation, consult reference materials, such as the ones suggested at the end of this appendix.

ARTICLES

Using the definite article *the* and the indefinite articles *a* and *an* correctly is a challenge for all non-native writers of English. Space does not permit a full discussion of using articles correctly, so what follows is a brief overview of the basic rules of article usage.

To select the appropriate article, decide first whether the noun is count or noncount, common or proper, singular or plural, and specific or general. Count nouns have both a singular and plural form and can be preceded by an indefinite article: *a banana*. Noncount nouns have only a singular form and should not have an indefinite article: *money*.

Use the definite article *the* in front of singular and plural nouns and adjectives when referring to something that both the writer and reader are familiar with. Example: *She came to work with a package in her arms. **The package** contained a gift for Ben.* In the first sentence, the package is introduced to the reader for the first time. The second mention of the package refers to an entity familiar to the reader from the previous sentence.

When using the indefinite article, use *a* before words that begin with a consonant sound and *an* before words that begin with a vowel sound. Exceptions: Words that begin with a silent *h* are preceded by *an*: *an honour*. Words that begin with a *yoo* sound are preceded by *a*, even though the first letter may be a vowel: *a union*. Words that also begin with *eu* and *ew* also take an *a*: *a European, a ewe*. And the word *one* takes an *a*: *a one-stop print shop*.

There are no shortcuts to learning proper article usage. Study the rules and keep practising. Pay attention to how your colleagues who are native English speakers use articles.

PREPOSITIONS AND MULTI-WORD VERBS

Not only does English have more prepositions than many other languages, but the prepositions are also maddeningly inconsistent. The differences are often subtle and idiomatic. Why do we write *I'm in the car* but *I'm on the* bus? If you write *I'm on the car*, the reader assumes you were on the roof of the car, and if you write *I'm in the bus*, the reader knows that you aren't a native English speaker. There's nothing wrong with not being a native English speaker, but there are better ways to share that information with the reader than by writing incorrectly.

In addition to familiarizing yourself with prepositions that indicate time and place, you will need to learn common adjective + preposition combinations: *anxious about, responsible for, terrified of*. Pay particular attention to the combinations that are different from the combinations in your native language.

Many verbs combine with other words to create multi-word verbs that are often idiomatic. These are discussed in Chapter 11. These multi-word verbs can be problematic because the word(s) that follows the verb changes the meaning. Think of the difference between *break into, break up, break down* and *break out in*. For better or worse, these constructions abound.

LANGUAGE-SPECIFIC ISSUES

- Some languages, such as Japanese and Spanish, do not require a subject in every sentence. Every English sentence does, except for imperative sentences: *Be quiet!*

- In English, verbs can be followed by gerunds or infinitives. *He started swimming again* (verb + gerund). *I went to see a movie* (verb + infinitive). Certain verbs can be followed only by either a gerund or an infinitive. And some verbs can be followed by either, but sometimes the choice will change the meaning. For example, *I stopped to talk to Ghazan* has a completely different meaning than *I stopped talking to Ghazan*.

- English does not use a noun and a pronoun to perform the same grammatical function. Not this: *The lawyer he advised me not to sign it*. But this: *The lawyer advised me not to sign it*.

- In English, adjectives do not agree grammatically with the nouns they qualify; instead, they occupy a certain position within the sentence. Example: *I've lost my new blue coat*.

- Adverbs also occupy certain positions. For example, do not place an adverb between a verb and its direct object. Not this: *He often prepares quickly dinner*. But this: *He often prepares dinner quickly*.

- In English, unlike some languages, the pronoun must agree in gender and number with its antecedent. In the sentence *All the managers have submitted their reports*, the pronoun *their* must agree with its antecedent *managers*.

- The basic word order in English is subject–verb–object. Word order in other languages may follow other patterns.

- Double and triple negatives are not used in Standard English. Not this: *The pilot can't find no place to land*. But this: *The pilot can't find any place to land*.

The errors you are likely to make in English depend on your first language, as the following list illustrates. It is by no means a comprehensive list, and not all the languages grouped into the families or into the East Asian geographic region will display all the characteristics noted. Furthermore, the list highlights only a handful of the more than 6,000 world languages. The Indo-European language family alone has about 445 living languages according to *Ethnologue*, a publication devoted to the study of world languages. But I hope it will provide a sense of the differences between English and a few other languages to show how this might influence your writing.

1. First, the Indo-European languages: These are the English language's relatives. But like all relatives, some of them seem very different to us, and there are many mutual misunderstandings.

The Romance Branch: French, Spanish, Italian, Portuguese, Romanian, and so on

- All nouns have gender (e.g., masculine and feminine).
- The word order is similar to English, but the position of adverbs can be very different.
- Reflexive verbs (e.g., *I wash myself*) are more common than in English.
- Relative pronouns (*who*, *which*, *that*, and *what*) are used differently than in English.
- The possessive apostrophe (e.g., *the boss's laptop*) is not used.
- Double negatives are permitted (e.g., *I cannot find my keys nowhere*).

The Slavic Branch: Russian, Ukrainian, Polish, Czech, Slovak, Bosnian/Croatian/Serbian, Bulgarian, and so on

- The definite and indefinite articles are seldom expressed.
- The number of verb tenses tends to be quite limited; the linking verb *be* either is not used or is not used the same way as in English.
- A loose word order is permitted, but the neutral word order is subject–verb–object.

- Speakers often have difficulties positioning adverbs, verbs, and adjectives in English.

- Double negatives are permitted (e.g., *I cannot find my keys nowhere*).

- These are highly inflected languages (that is, words are modified to express different categories such as tense, gender, and case).

- Speakers do not distinguish between the relative pronouns *who* and *which*.

The Indo-Aryan Branch: Hindi, Bengali, Urdu, Marathi, Panjabi, Gujarati, and so on

- These languages are rich in honorifics (titles that display respect) that cover formal and informal relationships.

- The verb tenses are similar to English, but the difference in their use leads to mistakes in English: *I am not knowing the answer* should be *I don't know the answer*.

- Subjunctives are often used for polite requests, which do not translate well into English: *You may lend me your dictionary* sounds like a command in English.

- No definite article (*the*) exists.

- Standard word order is subject–object–verb: *I the dog love*.

- The preposition often comes after the noun or pronoun.

2. Now for a different family altogether.

Afro-Asiatic Family, Semitic Branch: Arabic, Amharic, Tigrinya, Hebrew, Aramaic, and so on

- The indefinite articles do not exist.

- Unlike English, adjectives follow the noun they qualify, and they change form to indicate gender and number.

- The pronoun needs to be included in relative clauses (e.g., *the book that I read it*) unlike in English (e.g., *the book that I read*).

- In most, if not all, of these languages, there is no present perfect tense. This leads to mistakes such as *I finished my report. Can you edit it?* A native English speaker would write *I have finished my report. Can you edit it?*

- The word order in most languages is verb–subject–object: *Love I the dog.*

- Possessives present problems: *the man's coat* in English would be *coat the man* in Arabic.

- There is no linking verb *be* in the present tense, leading to mistakes such as *She good manager* instead of *She is a good manager.*

3. And finally, a group of languages that do not belong to one family, but rather to a geographical region.

East Asian: Mandarin, Cantonese, Japanese, Vietnamese, and Korean

The term East Asian does not refer to a language family but to a geographical region; these languages have similarities but belong to different families. The following list highlights some of the common features of these languages while respecting that they are very different languages:

- The definite or indefinite articles do not exist.

- Speakers have difficulties positioning adverbs, verbs, and adjectives in English.

- Often no plural forms of nouns exist (e.g., *one pen*, *two pen*), or plural forms are used at the writer's discretion.

- Verb tenses in Mandarin and Cantonese do not exist. These languages also do not have relative pronouns (*who*, *which*, and *that*).

- In Korean and Japanese, the verb is placed after the subject and object: *The woman the book wrote.* In these languages, the subject and verb are often quite separate from each other, unlike English where readers expect to see them together early in the sentence.

- A Vietnamese writer will usually place a transitional word between the introductory clause and the main clause, which sounds awkward in English: *Because I like to dance, therefore I took lessons.*

TIPS FOR STRENGTHENING YOUR ENGLISH

In Chapter 17, you will find some suggestions for developing some good lifelong writing habits. The following advice is specific to the needs of non-native writers of English:

- Read, read, read. Reading helps with understanding grammar, sentence structure, and technical jargon. Create a personalized dictionary, and as you're reading, write down idiomatic expressions, niche jargon, irregular verbs, and multi-word verbs.

- Listen with care to native speakers. This will help you especially with idiomatic expressions—and those troublesome multi-word verbs.

- Collect resources—both print and online—specific to the genres you write in to help you improve your command of English.

- Use templates for reports, letters, and emails. Learn and model the standard openings and closings in emails and letters used by native speakers who are also good writers.

- Finally, if you get discouraged, remember that some outstanding writers learned English at a relatively late age. Here are three examples that I hope will inspire you:

  - At the age of 21, Joseph Conrad was fluent in Polish but could speak only a few words of English. Eleven years later, he published his first novel in English and went on to become one of the greatest novelists to write in English.

  - Ha Jim was born in China and received only a brief education before the schools in China closed in 1966 at the beginning of the Cultural Revolution. He began to study English at the age of 20. He eventually moved to the United States and earned a PhD in English. He has written several award-winning novels and books of poetry.

  - Russian-born Ayn Rand did not start learning English until after she graduated from university. She published her first novel in English 11 years later and continued to write novels and philosophical works.

RESOURCES
Books

Al-Maskari, Khaled. *A Practical Guide to Business Writing: Writing in English for Non-Native Speakers*. Chichester: John Wiley and Sons, 2013. Business writers will appreciate this informative guide to writing clean and concise emails, reports, and letters.

Boyne, Martin, and Don LePan. *The Broadview Book of Common Errors in English: ESL Edition*. Peterborough: Broadview Press, 1993. This book is an excellent resource and includes many exercises and an answer key.

Emmerson, Paul. *Email English*. Oxford: Macmillan Education, 2004. This book is for intermediate or upper-intermediate learners of English. It provides strategies for writing better emails and a phrase bank of useful expressions.

Swan, Michael. *Practical English Usage*. 3rd ed. Oxford: Oxford University Press, 2005. This is a great reference book covering a range of issues, including vocabulary, grammar, style, and spelling.

Websites

Dave's ESL Cafe provides an online forum for both students and teachers, along with some excellent resources, including lists of phrasal verbs and idioms. http://www.eslcafe.com

The University of Victoria's English Language Centre's Study Zone has topics, lessons, and exercises for five different language levels so you can choose your level and progress at your own pace. http://web2.uvcs.uvic.ca/elc/studyzone/

Using English has an excellent collection of tools and resources, including quizzes, polls, and articles. www.usingenglish.com

Mixed-Up, Tumbled-Up, Shook-Up Words

The abundance of words in the English language makes it difficult, at times, to decide on the right word. And that right word is essential! As Mark Twain reminds us, "The difference between the almost right word and the right word is really a large matter—'tis the difference between the lightning-bug and the lightning."

The following is a list of a few common words that might challenge you. Although this list does not detail every possible definition, it does illustrate some of the ways that these words can give writers grief.

Affect = to influence or have an effect on; it's used primarily as a verb. *His tears affected me.*

Effect = to have an influence or impact; it's used primarily as a noun. *What effect did it have on you?* It can also be used as a verb meaning "to bring about." *Tariq effected a major change.*

A lot is always two words.

Alternate = in turns, first one and then the other: *a day of alternate snow and rain.* It can also mean "substitute." *Please send your alternate to the meeting.*

Alternative = offering or expressing a choice. *We have several alternative ideas.*

All together = collectively or in a group. *We went to the workshop all together.*

Altogether = completely or entirely. *The workshop was altogether useless.*

Ambiguous = having two or more meanings. *That's definitely an ambiguous answer!*

Ambivalent = having mixed feelings. *Dragan is ambivalent about grammar.*

Among = a connection among three or more things. *Among the candidates, he was the best.*

Between = a connection between two persons or things; it is also appropriate when drawing a connection. *I can't decide between salad or fries.* And it can be used to express that three or more persons or things are interacting with one another on a one-to-one basis. *The negotiations between the lawyers, the buyers, and the sellers were faltering.*

Amount = how much? *There's only a small amount of rice left.*

Number = how many? (individual items that can be counted) *Can you count the number of sharks in the water?*

Anxious = worry or unease. *Mingus is anxious about driving in the blizzard.*

Eager = anticipation. *Serena was eager to ride her new bike.*

Assure = to guarantee (a thing to a person). *I assure you I will come.*

Ensure = to make certain. *Lindell registered the letter to ensure it reached its destination.*

Insure = related to insurance. *Please insure your car within 24 hours.*

Beside = at the side of. *Marjan sat beside me at the meeting.*
Besides = in addition to. *What do you need besides the agenda?*

Complement = a supplement or a completion. *Your pink blouse complements your skin tone.*
Compliment = praise or flattery. *Thank you for the compliment.*

Composed of = made up of. *This book is composed of five parts.*
Comprise = contains all the parts. *Canada comprises ten provinces and three territories.*
Include = contains some of the parts. *This appendix includes some commonly confused words.* (This means it is not an exhaustive list.)

Continual = renewed frequently and regularly. *We had continual discussions about the appropriate course of action.*
Continuous = uninterrupted. *The brain needs a continuous supply of oxygen.*

Definite = clear, positive. *Businesspeople who write well have a definite advantage over those who don't.*
Definitive = most reliable. *His book is the definitive guide to the geology of the Rocky Mountains.*

Dilemma = a difficult choice between two or more bad alternatives. *What a dilemma—should we cancel the trip or cancel the party?*

Discreet = tactful, prudent, circumspect. *I can always confide in Rémi. He is discreet.*
Discrete = distinct or separate. *There are five discrete pieces to this table.*

Disinterested = unbiased, impartial. *The mediator must be a disinterested person.*

Uninterested = not interested, bored. *I am uninterested in your excuses.*

Due to = caused by, attributable to, resulting from. *My fitness is due to my daily exercise regime.* Starting a sentence with *due to* is usually incorrect. Not this: *Due to insufficient data, we could not complete our study.* But this: *Because of insufficient data, we could not complete our study.*

Each other = use for two. *Sebastian and Galen respect each other.*

One another = use for three or more. *Eva and her pet snakes respect one another.*

If = expresses a single condition. *If it rains, we'll cancel the luncheon.*

Whether = expresses two possibilities. You can usually omit the *or not*. *Whether the report will be done on time depends on Sheri.* But if you want to convey "regardless of whether" or give equal emphasis to both possibilities, use *or not*. *Whether it rains next week or not, the luncheon will still go ahead.*

Lay = to lay something down; it's a transitive verb. *I laid the book down yesterday.*

Lie = to recline; it's an intransitive verb. *I lay in bed yesterday.*

May = expresses what is possible, factual, or could be factual. It's also a request for permission. *I may be able to help you later today.*

Might = suggests something that is uncertain, hypothetical, or contrary to fact. *Arianna said that she might come.*

Personal = private, individual. *Colette didn't want to discuss her personal affairs at work.*

Personnel = a group of people employed in an organization. *The change in personnel has affected us.*

Principal = primary, main person, original sum of money lent or invested. *Her principal problem in writing is the overuse of passive voice.*

Principle = basic truth, tenet, or law. *Those are my principles, and if you don't like them . . . well, I have others.*~ Groucho Marx

Stationary = unmoving. *I have a stationary bike that I never use.*

Stationery = writing paper. *My mother bought me some beautiful stationery in Italy.*

Than = connects two parts of a comparison. *Hungarian grammar is harder than English grammar.*

Then = denotes a point in time. *Felix wrote the report, and then he edited it.*

Unique = the only one of its kind. There are no degrees of uniqueness. *Please consider this unique business opportunity.*

Answer Key to Exercises

Note: This answer key is not an exhaustive list of all possible answers. In the answers to Part Four especially, you will probably have some different answers. The intent of the exercises and the answers is to illustrate the principles of the chapter and to show you some potential fixes. Please also note that the answers are based on the style conventions used in this book (e.g., single-digit numbers written out, percent not % or per cent). These conventions may differ from the ones you use.

Chapter 1 Plan First: Purpose, Audience, Context, and Tone

A.

1. Please return the enclosed card by May 31, 2018, so we can keep your records up to date.

2. Your warranty will become effective once you send in your registration.

3. You will receive your refund by registered mail early next week.

4. We want to activate your account by September 15, so please submit the information by June 30.

5. We'd like to finalize our agreement with you as soon as possible, so please send us your audited financial statements by December 1.

B.

What are you trying to achieve here? You obviously want the agenda and minutes to be sent out earlier, maybe a week before the board meeting. Try the following:

Hi Mike,

I know we're all volunteers on the GAC board, and it's hard to keep up with everything. But it's difficult to have productive meetings when we don't get the minutes from the last meeting and the agenda for the upcoming meeting in good time. Ideally, we'd get them a week before the upcoming meeting.

Is there something one of us could do to make this easier for you? I have a great template that we use at work for taking minutes and setting agendas. If you want, I could email it to you.

Look forward to seeing you shortly, and maybe we can talk about this after the meeting tonight.

Cheers,
Tazmin

Chapter 2   Hold Fast to the Four Writing Stages
A.

Prewriting strategy using a list: welcome, time management, my experience, patience, manage stress, and start slow.

Completed email

Hi Doug,

Welcome to PawsPooch! I'm confident you're going to enjoy working with us. I wanted to review one of your responsibilities that you may find a bit challenging—the issue of time management.

When I was a dog walker, I learned to manage my time through trial and error. Some days are intense, and you must manage many things within three busy hours. Your job will be demanding, and you need to be able to think creatively and solve problems in a hurry.

I would like to share with you what I did; I hope you find it helpful.

- Be patient. You might have difficulty with a house key. Or you might go into a house and find a sick dog. The job is unpredictable, so don't be hard on yourself. Get to know your dogs and their specific issues.

- Use your time in the office to keep your daily schedule current and to keep track of specific client requests and any medications your dogs need.

- Meet with your supervisor once a week to discuss route planning and scheduling.

I'm here to help you in any way I can. We won't have you take on more than four dogs until you're ready.

Regards,
G. Bernard

B.

1. b, d, g
2. c, f
3. b, e, g
4. a, d

5. c, e, f
6. h
7. b, e, g

Chapter 3   Look Good Too: Visual Smarts
A.

There are several design issues that need fixing. Here are some that you may have noticed:

1. The first line reads *Join us in Support of Mental Illness*, making it sound like the request is to support mental illness. The first two lines need to be adjusted to make it read better.

2. The capitalization in the title is inconsistent. Capitalize *us*.

3. There are too many different fonts and text treatments (e.g., bold and italics).

4. Line spacing is inconsistent.

5. There are no visuals. A picture of Mr. Edwards or some other image would be helpful.

6. The underlining on "what," "when," and "where" needs removing.

7. Remove the parentheses from (403) in the phone number, and use a hyphen instead.

Here are some questions that the reader may have:

1. What does "U of C" stand for?

2. What is the address of the event? Is there parking?

3. Is there any cost to attend?

B.

Hi Luis,

I wanted to share some thoughts with you if we're going to proceed with writing an in-house style guide.

Benefits

We'll need to convince senior management that a style guide will pay for itself quickly. Here are some things we could point out:

- It is going to improve our image.
- It will clarify some language and design issues (e.g., logo use and colours).
- It is going to ensure better consistency.
- People will spend less time correcting their work and debating usage choices.

People

How about the following people for the style guide committee?

- Nawara in marketing
- Charlie in finance
- Yuri, the new designer
- Ruth, the CEO's EA

Cost and Timelines

- $1,500 estimated, but I'll draft a budget.
- Start in July and finish by September 1.

I look forward to hearing from you.
Sylvia

C.

The bar chart represents the information better than the pie chart. The bar chart allows the reader to grasp all the necessary information with one glance. When reading the pie chart, the reader must keep looking back at the legend. Furthermore, when the slices of the pie are similar, they become hard to distinguish. The only thing better in the pie chart is that you can more easily see that the values add up to 100 percent.

Chapter 4 Write Reader-Centred Emails and Letters Quickly and Efficiently

A.

1. Hi Crystal, We've talked many times about the importance of good business communications. So I hope that you'll see the value of my request for the company to pay for three business communications courses (details attached). I'm confident that I'll be more productive after taking these courses and better able to support you in your role.

2. Hi everyone, Imagine arriving at work next Monday and not being able to grab a coffee and put your lunch in the fridge! Well, if we don't get serious about keeping the kitchen clean, that could easily happen.

3. Hi Jack, I know that sending in an electrician during the daytime is inconvenient for you. But it's going to be a great upgrade— you'll be able to install new devices and appliances without any risk of blowing a fuse.

Chapter 6   Navigate the Online Universe: Websites and Social Media

A.

Staff Party To-Do List

Date and Venue

- Check with the assistant to the president to confirm availability
- Finalize the date
- Secure a good venue that will seat 250 people for dinner

Logistics

- Liaise with the venue on the logistical details
- Meet once a week with the event committee to discuss entertainment
- Send the staff a "hold the date" email three months before the party
- Send a formal invite to staff four weeks before the party
- Ask Helen to manage the RSVPs
- Ask Murray to confirm the president has a speech for the event

Financials

- Update the event financials from Q1 to see how much money is available
- Contact the finance manager to discuss potential extra funds
- Meet with the event committee to determine if this party is a free or ticketed event

Chapter 8   Appreciate Grammar: The Language of Language

A.

If you want to practise writing, it's handy to have a short list of things you could easily write about. It's much easier to write about something you like, such as Mexican food, than something you don't know much about, such as nuclear physics. Use the list you created to write short stories, blogs, poems, letters—whatever strikes your fancy. The more you practise writing, the easier it will become.

B.

Did you have trouble coming up with five descriptive and unusual adjectives? If so, this is a cue that you need to read more and strengthen your vocabulary.

C.

1. I (PRO) drove (V) slowly (ADV) to (PRP) the (ADJ) workshop (N) although (CON) I (PRO) was (V) late (ADJ).

2. The (ADJ) closest (ADJ) languages (N) to (PRP) English (N) are (V) Frisian (N) and (CON) Dutch (N).

3. She (PRO) gave (V) us (PRO) a (ADJ) remarkably (ADV) difficult (ADJ) exercise (N).

4. Some (ADJ) critics (N) scorned (V) Webster (N) because (CON) he (PRO) allowed (V) slang (N) and (CON) jargon (N) in (PRP) his (PRO) dictionary (N).

5. The (ADJ) shortest (ADJ) and (CON) most (ADV) commonly (ADV) used (ADJ) word (N) in (PRP) English (N) is (V) the (ADJ) word (N) I (PRO). Amazing! (I)

D.

1. no

2. reluctantly

3. the, French, the, pugnacious, northern

4. active (If you answered passive, don't be fooled by the past perfect tense *had given*. The time that something happens [the verb's tense] has nothing to do with whether it is active or passive [the verb's voice]. Here's this sentence written in the passive voice: *The pugnacious Vikings had been given land in northern France in 911.* You might add *by the French ruler Charles the Simple* at the end, but you don't have to.)

5. the French ruler Charles the Simple

6. land in northern France

7. in (used twice)

E.

1. <u>They met</u>. <u>They fell</u> (in love). <u>She abandoned</u> him. Three simple sentences

2. <u>William the Conqueror, who was</u> the first Norman king (of England), never <u>learned</u> English. Complex (There are two clauses: the independent one is *William the Conqueror never learned English.* The dependent one is *who was the first Norman king of England.*)

3. <u>Meiling went</u> (to the bank), and <u>she met</u> the manager. Compound

4. The <u>pen is</u> the tongue (of the mind). ~ *Cervantes* Simple

5. When <u>the people</u> <u>arrived</u> (at the ski hut), <u>some</u> (of them) <u>built</u> (a fire,) and <u>others</u> <u>cooked</u> (dinner) (on the gas stove). Compound-complex

6. Since <u>he</u> <u>was</u> always late (for meetings), <u>they</u> <u>demanded</u> his (resignation.) Complex

7. (In South Africa), there <u>are</u> <u>11 official languages</u>. Simple

F.

1. (When everyone was in the living room) is an adverb clause telling us *when* they brought in the birthday cake.

2. (which was supposed to be on the previous Saturday) is an adjective clause giving us more information about the party.

3. (What had caused the party to be rescheduled) is a noun clause functioning as the subject of the sentence.

4. (Because the party was now on Tuesday evening) is an adverb clause telling us *why* the guests were reluctant to stay long.

5. (after the presents were opened) is an adverb clause telling us *when* the guests went home.

G.

1. There are many opportunities in Western Canada for someone eager to live here. (Subject–verb agreement: *many opportunities* is the subject, and it's plural.)

2. I dislike dishonesty. (Faulty predication: a characteristic is not a person.)

3. After reading several books, I still find cybersecurity as puzzling as ever. (Dangling modifier: cybersecurity wasn't reading the books, but that's what this sentence targets as the subject because the true subject is missing.)

4. Let Dmitri and me help you with that heavy box. (Pronoun case error: take away *Dmitri*—he doesn't change the case—and you'll see the mistake. It's not *Let I help you.*)

5. Magda respects me more than Fay does. (Faulty comparison: another potential fix is *Magda respects me more than she respects Fay.*)

6. Neither of your suggested solutions is going to get your boss's approval. (Subject–verb agreement: *neither* is the subject and takes the singular verb *is.*)

7. The winners of the tournament, Jamila and I, will now receive our awards. (Pronoun case error: *Jamila and I* is an appositive and renames the subject *the winners of the tournament.*)

8. Esmahan is smart, creative, and hard working. (Faulty parallelism: *smart* and *creative* are both adjectives; *works hard* is a verb phrase. The fix has three adjectives in a row.)

9. I love grammar because it is so fascinating. (Faulty predication: *the reason* does not equal *because.* Never write *the reason is because.*)

10. If Cornelia were sensible, she would never take that job. (Subjunctive mood error)

11. The analysts stopped working on the nearly completed report to talk to Jill and me. (Misplaced modifier: it's not the analysts who are nearly completed, it's the report. And there's a pronoun error: it's *Jill and me*, not *myself.*)

12. Here come the winners. Please tell them I feel bad about being such a poor loser. (Subject–verb agreement in the first sentence, and a mix-up between the adjective *bad* and the adverb *badly* in the second sentence)

13. As I was running down the path, my wig flew off. (Dangling modifier: the wig wasn't running, I was.)

14. She did really well on her exam. (The adverb *really* is needed, not the adjective *real*.)

15. To find our office, you can either go right on Broadway Avenue or go left on Rosewood Street. (Faulty parallelism: *either go right . . . or go left*)

16. Gareth removed the brush from the pot and washed the brush carefully. (Ambiguous pronoun reference: the sentence would also be correct as *washed the pot carefully*.)

17. Please contact either Peng or me if you have any questions. (Pronoun error)

18. Freight costs for the second quarter were 15 percent higher than for the first quarter. (Faulty comparison—15 percent higher than what?)

19. Only the landlord was allowed to store anything in the attic. (Misplaced modifier: This sentence makes it sound like you can't store anything in the attic, except the landlord. You could write *No one except the landlord*, but why not save words and write *only?*)

20. Of the group, only she and I attended the seminar. (Pronoun case error: *She* and *I* are the subjects of this sentence.)

21. The reviewer's online comments aggravated me and embarrassed all of us. (Faulty parallelism)

22. Molly told Helen, "I hate my new haircut!" (Ambiguous pronoun reference: There are other potential fixes to this situation. But it needs to be clarified whose haircut Molly hates.)

23. The executive assistant scheduled a meeting with a software company that is using a newly released web platform. (Unclear modifier: did the executive assistant use a newly released web platform to schedule a meeting or was the software company using a newly released web platform?)

24. If Jabari had attended the meeting, he would have met the new manager. (Sentences with *if* clauses can be challenging. In this example, *If* + past perfect [*had attended*] + past conditional [*would have met*] is the correct formula.)

25. Chess is harder than any other game. (Faulty comparison)

26. Craig likes playing banjo, collecting antiques, and skiing because he likes to keep busy. (Faulty parallelism; and although *due to the fact that* is technically correct, it's stylistically awful, so let's change it to *because*.)

27. A dictionary is a book that lists the definitions of words. (Faulty predication: a dictionary is not *where*; it's a book.)

28. If you check the questionnaire again, you will find fewer mistakes. (Incorrect verb tense and *fewer* not *less*)

29. I insist that he attend the workshop tomorrow. (Subjunctive mood error)

30. The manager and the engineering team examined the test results carefully because they wanted to focus on cost savings and efficiency. (Ambiguous pronoun reference: the fix clarifies that it's the manager and the engineering team that want to focus on costs savings and efficiency.)

Chapter 9   Make Peace with Punctuation: Marks and Remarks

A.

1. There are several boys' skates in the locker room, but the men's are by the rink.
2. Alex's car, a '92 Mustang, is actually his father's.
3. Whose laptop is this?
4. John and Jared's car needs a new transmission.
5. Kiera lived in Iqaluit in the '90s and managed her brothers-in-law's company.

B.

elephant's foot	six years' experience	bachelor's degree
policy's cash value	the Joneses' condo	a week's vacation

The other examples do not require any changes.

C.

Numbers 1, 3, 5, 6, and 8 are run-on sentences.

D.

1. Each week's menu featured a different African country's cuisine.
2. We visited Europe last year and went to Madrid, Spain; Venice, Italy; and York, England.
3. The company held a one-day retreat on November 24, 2017.
4. The wholly owned subsidiary is in Chicago, which is one of the largest cities in the United States.

5. The reduction in expenditures was due to several factors: a reduced number of project teams, fewer employees in Q1, and the delayed recruitment of a new executive director.

6. "Can you believe," Neville asked me, "that it has been almost a year since we've seen each other?"

7. But we still need to revise the budget and preliminary estimates of additional work required.

8. After eating, the baby always slept soundly.

9. Sally, the new editor, is really helpful; therefore, you should ask her what she would do.

10. The suspect in the lineup who has red hair committed the crime.

11. The two Harrys had breakfast with the Joneses and the Alvarezes.

12. Who's writing down the pros and cons of hiring a full-time assistant?

Chapter 10 Explore Mechanics: Conventions of Print

A.

1. The year 2013 was a good year for me. I won first place in three spelling bees.

2. I want to travel east this summer.

3. Kelley holds a PhD in biology.

4. Did you finish the layout and design of the document yet?

5. From 2012 to 2016, the crime rate decreased by 10 percent.

6. I travelled to St. John's, Newfoundland, in the fall of 2017 to give step-by-step instructions to three board chairs.

B.

1. Hi Dean,

   Thank you for your email of January 19. I discussed your long-term plans to cut costs with Dr. Beckett, and he wants to meet with you to discuss further. I need at least two weeks' notice to set up a meeting with him. Are you available on February 2 at 3 p.m.?

   Regards,
   Jane

2. Hi Nguyen,

   I have not been able to process your claim for $27,532.50 because there are still several line items missing. Do you remember that I asked you to fill in three line items before submitting it? Once I have received the completed claim, I can process it right away. If you need additional information, please contact me at 416-123-4567.

   Best regards,
   Ruth

Chapter 11 Express Yourself with Clarity and Sparkle

A.

Numbers 1, 3, and 7 are passive. The rest are active.

B.

1. It is our understanding that Kasem recruited her. (The lead of the sentence *It is our understanding* is a weak lead, but it is not an example of passive voice.)

2. To save time, we sent the agreement by courier.

3. Please record any changes to these balance sheets by fiscal year-end. (Write instructions using the imperative mood of the verb, not the passive voice.)

4. Staff will need to take extensive training in the new procedures.

5. The cleaners vacuum and dust our offices every evening.

C.

1. Maurice seems ready for a holiday. (Some people change *seems to be* to *is*, but doing so changes the meaning.)

2. Please decide by November 30. (The nominalization *decision* is better expressed as the verb *decide*. Then, anticipate the reader's questions: *November* is too vague. The reader will want to know *when* in November.)

3. The committee chair, an outstanding citizen, made these recommendations. (Removing *these are* and *who is* and the sexist language [*chairman*] improves the sentence.)

4. An editor corrects grammar and improves style. (In the original sentence, the subject is *the role of an editor*; now the subject is *an editor*; once that's in place, the verbs become *corrects* and *improves*, rather than *is*.)

5. I wish my boss would explain the new benefits package. (The nominalization *explanation* is better expressed as the verb *explain*.)

6. I am submitting this request for a project scope amendment because of changes to cost and timing. (The original sentence is clumsy, but introducing an agent of action at the beginning of the sentence helps.)

7. This is an instruction manual. (Watch out for *end users*; it's IT jargon; it's better to simply state what this manual is.)

8. Our field operations conform with the association's standards. (The nominalization *conformity* is better expressed as the verb *conform*.)

9. Did Patrick finish editing the updates to the orientation manual for employees? (Watch out for the noun stack.)

10. Junior editors often ask me how I quote an editing job. (Now it's one sentence instead of a question and a sentence, and it's in the active voice.)

Chapter 12 Energize Your Writing with Dynamic Words and Sentences

A.

1. Over the last decade, regulatory agencies have become increasingly aware of the need to use plain language. (The original sentence begins with faulty predication; *the decade* doesn't *see* anything. The sentence also needs a better character as a subject.)

2. In her paper, she examines Indigenous land rights. (You don't need to weigh the sentence lead down with *the major framework of her paper*; also, the word *involves* is unnecessary.)

3. All regional plans seek to ensure long-term prosperity. (Rework the subject, remove the word *sustainable* [it has too many meanings], and remove the phrase at the end *throughout an entire region* because it's redundant.)

4. Future fact sheets will focus on projects completed within the last 12 months and on technical updates. (Don't lead with *moving forward*, which is just filler; place *future fact sheets* into the topic position, and the rest of the sentence falls into place easily. There's also no need for the *not only . . . but also* construction.)

5. We recommend adopting the design that would remove particulates with the desired degree of efficiency. (Lead with a person in the topic position.)

6. During my employment with Northern Lights College, I have taken various training to improve my communications and stress management skills. (Take a walk through the original sentence and tighten the language.)

7. Several clues led to the discovery of the electrician's faulty wiring. (There are two problems with this sentence: first, the dummy lead *There were,* and second, the potential of two different interpretations because the sentence could also mean *Several clues helped the electrician discover the faulty wiring.*)

8. Plastics will be eliminated from the disposal stream by more than 30 percent through a market-based system phased in over the next three years. (*The more than 30-percent elimination of plastics* is a weak subject; make *plastics* the subject [another potential subject is *a market-based system*] and change the nominalization *elimination* to the verb *eliminated.*)

9. As part of the facility upgrades, we built a spacious training room to host classes, workshops, and community events. (Again, tighten the language throughout the sentence, and let the sentence breathe a little more freely.)

10. While many of the changes are well underway, I hope this proposal will provide a better understanding of upcoming changes, including how we will communicate with customers. (At 43 words, the original sentence is too long. What is the writer trying to express? If he needs to express that everyone is working hard, he should write a new sentence. The original sentence has too many ideas packed into it.)

Chapter 13 Cut It Out: Concision at Work

1. There is no evidence those new mutual funds will perform any better than your existing ones. (Cut *to support the idea* because that's what evidence does, and use the verb *perform* not *do*.)

2. Jean-Paul married in May xxx and never returned to Seattle. (You should state the year because *last year* will soon become meaningless.)

3. We think the best course of action would be to continue using the alkali reactant.

4. Sexist language contributes to gender stereotypes.

5. Excessive regulation is destroying business initiative. (You don't need the weak lead *In the modern business world.*)

6. My colleagues have reported several incidents that indicate we need to update our health and safety policies. (Do you really need anything else? If you do, state it in a new sentence.)

7. This report updates our research findings. (Try not to lead with *The purpose of this report, the purpose of this email,* etc.)

8. Complete this registration form to receive your gift. (All gifts are free, supposedly.)

9. Please record this as an accident and not an emergency.

10. For the purposes of this document, variances greater than $25,000 will be explained. These variances are based on the formula used by the ACCC's external auditors. (This is better as two sentences. Also note that the missing comma after the word *document* in the original sentence causes confusion.)

11. Sitha tried to explain how her co-worker's careless writing reflected poorly on the company.

12. Because the program failed twice during testing, we are considering other options. (Don't lead with *due to the fact that.*)

Chapter 14 Focus on Flow: Cohesion and Coherence

A.

The transitional words are bolded.

Ieoh Ming Pei was born in China in 1917, the son of a prominent banker. **After** completing his schooling in Shanghai, he moved to the United States in the 1930s to study architecture at MIT. When he graduated, **however**, he was unable to return to China because of the outbreak of World War II. **Instead**, he remained in the United States, eventually becoming a citizen in 1954.

In his work, Pei brings together the modern and traditional, which he calls the impossible dream. His designs are influenced by the International Style popularized by architects like Le Corbusier. **However**, he's also known for Brutalism, an offshoot of the **International Style** that emphasizes bold forms, utilitarian principles, and a skillful arrangement of geometric shapes. **For instance**, his use of massive concrete blocks for the design of the National Center for Atmospheric Research, completed in 1967, is a brilliant example of Brutalism.

Pei has completed some 30 institutional projects, both in the United States and abroad. In the 1960s, Pei was selected to design the terminal at the John F. Kennedy International Airport, and he gained international recognition in 1974 when he designed the East Building of the National Gallery of Art in Washington. **Although** he designed many other impressive buildings **in the United States**, he is probably best known for the controversial glass pyramids that he designed in the courtyard of the Louvre Museum in Paris.

B.

1. Water quality in the Snake River declined in June because of the heavy rainfall, which overloaded the municipal district's water treatment plant.

2. Bill is a daydreamer who spends several hours a day staring out the window and not working much.

3. All my colleagues admire the new CEO, but I don't, and I'm thinking of resigning.

D.

1. Learn how to write effectively for the web and how to engage your online readers in this five-week workshop. Highlights of this workshop include web design, appropriate writing style, and website structure. You'll learn through videos, quizzes, and online discussion groups and will need from two to five hours each week to complete the course.

2. Our non-profit organization has extensive experience working with seniors. The team has diverse experience, excellent communication skills, and a results-oriented approach. We are confident that we have the expertise to carry out this project successfully. Please let us know if you would like details of other projects we have worked on or references.

3. Greetings all,

    Eight different groups have used the boardroom on the third floor over the last month. Unfortunately, the guidelines for using the boardroom as outlined in the employee manual were not followed. Shannon Starr, the facilities manager, has asked me to bring the following to your attention:

    - Please keep the noise level down. People have offices close to the boardroom.

    - Make sure you have visitor badges for all guests.

    - Clean up the boardroom when your meeting is finished.

    - If you need to change a booking, update the Outlook calendar at least 24 hours before the booking.

— INDEX —